OPERA MULIEBRIA
Women and Work in Medieval Europe

McGraw-Hill Series

New Perspectives on European History

CONSULTING EDITOR

RAYMOND GREW
University of Michigan

Gutmann: *Toward the Modern Economy: Early Industry in Europe, 1500–1800*
Herlihy: *Opera Muliebria: Women and Work in Medieval Europe*
Jacobs: *The Cultural Meaning of the Scientific Revolution*

OPERA MULIEBRIA

Women and Work in Medieval Europe

David Herlihy
Brown University

McGRAW-HILL PUBLISHING COMPANY

New York St. Louis San Francisco Auckland Bogotá Caracas
Hamburg Lisbon London Madrid Mexico Milan Montreal New Delhi
Oklahoma City Paris San Juan São Paulo Singapore Sydney
Tokyo Toronto

This book was set in Baskerville by the College Composition Unit
in cooperation with Ruttle, Shaw & Wetherill, Inc.
The editors were Christopher J. Rogers and Jeannine Ciliotta.
The cover was designed by Karen Quigley.
R. R. Donnelley & Sons Company was printer and binder.

Cover art credit: Women shearing sheep, spinning, and weaving.
(Cambridge University, Trinity College, M.R. 17.)

OPERA MULIEBRIA
Women and Work in Medieval Europe

3 4 5 6 7 8 9 0   DOH DOH   9 4 3 2 1 0

ISBN 0-07-557744-5

Library of Congress Cataloging-in-Publication Data

Herlihy, David.
  Opera muliebria: women and work in medieval Europe / David
Herlihy.
      p.   cm.—(New perspectives on European history.)
  Includes bibliographical references.
  ISBN 0-07-557744-5
  1. Women—Employment—Europe—History.   I. Title.   II. Series.
HD6134.H47   1990   89-13191
331.4′094′0902—dc20

CONTENTS

FOREWORD

New knowledge and fresh understanding, the goals of all research, demand constant change in the way that research is conducted. At the same time, research in any field is the expression of a cultural tradition that largely shapes the questions asked, the methods used, and the results presented. This tension between new perceptions and established standards is the heartbeat of academic disciplines, and modern universities are organized to keep that tension high. Although no longer confident that this process guarantees the progress of civilization, we sustain it because in a more limited sense it works. Year by year we command more information and learn to organize and analyze it in ever more elaborate and sophisticated ways. Specialization is the serious price paid for such gains. New information can be acquired and its validity carefully tested within a narrow focus. It is more difficult to determine how bits of new knowledge should be integrated with what was known before.

The benefits of specialization and the problems it brings have been particularly significant for the discipline of history. Over the last generation, the study of history has expanded and changed as much as any discipline in the social sciences or humanities. It has done so in large part by borrowing heavily from them, while maintaining most of its traditional concerns. The interests, theories, and methods of sociology, demography, economics, anthropology, semiotics, and literary analysis, which are readily apparent in current historical writing, have also directly affected historical research.

Thus a score of specialties have been added to the familiar ones of period and place by which historical expertise is identified. In addition, the present continues, as it always has, to stimulate new perspectives on the past. Contemporary concerns—about social order, the family, welfare, racism, women's roles, and inequality; the experience of mass culture, political oppression, and demands for democracy; the fact that European power does not dominate the world as it once did; and increased knowledge of non-Western societies—have led historians to pose fresh questions about European history. The historical study of Europe is also now more international in the double sense that historians of many nations study the same problems and that they are less inclined to confine those topics within national boundaries.

So the discoveries and successes of one historical field quickly influence work in others. The emphasis in this generation upon social history has enabled us to learn more than ever before about all eras of European history and in particular about the attitudes and lives of ordinary people with little power. By definition, this type of social history explores detailed knowledge. Its larger significance requires that the disparate facts about daily life, local behavior, or the activities of unorganized groups be related to some general view of social relations and patterns of change. Theory is essential to analysis.

As historians mine old archives for new information, the meaning of which may only be revealed through complicated techniques of cultural or quantitative analysis, they do so because they have posed fresh questions. Minute research and (at least implicit) theory must be combined to create a history that integrates new knowledge of ordinary life with the larger fabric of historical interpretation. Discovering the significant patterns and establishing a coherent perspective that can encompass both new findings and what was known before remain the great challenges of historical study. The search for such a synthesis is the very essence of historical writing. That is not new, but in the past this quest was expressed primarily through a powerful rhetoric redolent of larger purpose and was organized in sweeping narratives that gave to chronological sequence the aura of cause and effect. Newer methods and more specialized knowledge have made those established devices more difficult and less satisfactory.

The modern synthesis is likely to move on several levels at once. It must define an important problem or set of problems, using evidence both to define them and to establish their significance. These problems must then be carefully placed in historical context. The modern synthesis, which must relate the latest findings to the relevant theories, is also expected to address the scholarly debates from which central questions derive. Thus coherence is less likely to result from narrative flow or rhetorical values than from a consistent interpretative argument. When well written, as of course it should be, the carefully elaborated historical synthesis can nevertheless join with the best of older historical writing in conveying the color and fascination of a way of life now passed and the intellectual challenge of seeking to understand a particular society.

The books in this series present that sort of modern synthesis. The excitement of recent research, with its diverse topics and methods, makes this an excellent moment for such a publishing venture. And historical synthesis, which must operate on several levels at once, offers the advantage that it can speak to many kinds of serious readers—to freshmen discovering the patterns that make sense of the panorama of Western history, to advanced students interested in the meaning of historical context and important scholarly debates, to scholars ready to wrestle with a new perspective offered by a distinguished colleague, and to anyone who enjoys thinking about how to understand significant historical developments. The authors of these books have accepted the challenge of attempting in a single volume to accomplish so much. Active scholars building upon their own research, these authors set forth arguments that specialists will need to consider. Their assessment of recent findings and of the general scholarly literature will be especially helpful to graduate students and advanced undergraduates. Their perspectives on important aspects of European history should prove useful and stimulating to beginning students in introductory courses and to their teachers who wish to integrate current research into an established framework. In short, different readers can all appreciate the same well-written and intelligent book whether initially drawn to its broad picture of an important epoch, the scholarly debate of which it is part, or the new findings it presents—and that remains one of the glories of historical study even in an age of specialization.

Of all the topics and methods that in the last twenty years have given life to historical studies, none has been more exciting or fundamental than the history of women. Historians, like unobservant husbands, had tended to assume that social circumstance or historical change affected the two sexes similarly; they are being corrected. New research has brought to the fore the contributions made (and battles fought) by individual women. More important, increased attention to the lives of ordinary women has enriched (and often altered) familiar accounts of notable events and periods. Most important of all, when scholars systematically inquire about women's roles and gender relations, fresh perspectives emerge that can expose some overlooked facets of almost any topic—not just family, childhood, and education but also theology, law, and politics, culture, exchange, and work. This study builds upon and contributes to this growing body of literature.

In looking at women's work, David Herlihy makes use of and modifies another body of literature as well, the history of work. That too is a field that has attracted much new research for reasons that go beyond the obvious importance of economic history. Many of the most influential social theories, including those most indebted to Marx and Weber, tend to make analysis of the structure of work a critical test of the theories themselves. Anthropological and quantitative methods not only point to evidence overlooked before, but raise new questions about how the nature of work is affected by culture, population, and wealth. Social history, vigorously explored in the seventies and eighties, has highlighted the importance of work in daily life and all social relations. Women's work is thus a topic that brings together many of the most exciting developments within the historical discipline, making this a good time to reassess what we know and to reconsider how the topic should be conceived.

It is most readily studied and most often written about, however, in modern rather than medieval history. More investigated and debated in the nineteenth century than before, women's work so concerned contemporaries that they left vast amounts of evidence, much of it still to be assimilated by historians. In the preceding centuries, from the Renaissance on, the growing European state collected statistics and published reports that remain a mine of information. For the Middle Ages, the record is skimpier and most of the evidence indirect; yet we need to know whether a characteristic pattern was established then. Did European civilization at its founding and in its first millennium assign a special place to working women, encouraging certain tasks and prohibiting others? It takes great knowledge and special skills even to sketch an answer, for women at work rarely held power, wrote laws, or challenged the existing order.

In this book Professor Herlihy provides the best answer we have. A distinguished scholar of medieval Europe, he is able to arrange shards of information into a mosaic that presents a coherent and sometimes surprising picture. The process itself proves fascinating. With unusual clarity, he lets us see the historian at work—listening to the stories that people told, probing tax records and lists of occupations for hints encoded in their sober purpose, examining paintings the way a jeweler looks at diamonds, finding the revealing phrases hidden in fables and formal documents alike. Evidence so closely probed can reveal much of the world that produced it, and Herlihy lets the reader share the discovery of ordinary life. Women mixed medicines and cosmetics, cooked, and wove for wages as well as love. We learn about noble women, poor women, and prostitutes, about different trades, about the towns in which people worked, and about the attitudes they shared. Values that marked a civilization shaped the work that women did. The richly colored fragments of evidence serve the historian's larger purpose, for this study makes important arguments about differences between northern and Mediterranean societies and about changes from the early to the late Middle Ages. A growing economy and more elaborate social structures, Professor Herlihy argues, shifted the boundaries of exclusion, redefining the places where women should labor and the kind of work they were allowed to do. The argument is compelling. His picture of toiling women, gathered together at Europe's beginnings and dispersed centuries later, is unforgettable.

RAYMOND GREW

PREFACE

...strenuos non sexus, sed virtus facit....

...not sex, but character, makes the strong....

—Ambrose (d. 397),
Liber de viduis, I. 24.

In the societies of both classical and barbarian antiquity and in the early Middle Ages, until as late as the twelfth and thirteenth centuries, women were prominent participants in many forms of productive activity. The presence of women was highly visible not only in agricultural work but also in the making of cloth, in the brewing of beer, in high administration, and, among other skills, in the arts of healing and in the interpretation and dissemination of sacred knowledge. In the society of the late Middle Ages, clearly by the fifteenth century, women's participation in economic life had become circumscribed. Most dramatically, they lost the central role they had once played in the manufacture of quality woolens. Their importance (or at least their visibility) diminished in many other fields too, such as medicine and administration. The virtual confinement of women's labor to work within the home, which historians found at the start of the modern age, was not an ancient arrangement. Rather, the extreme domestication of women's labor was specifically the heritage of the closing Middle Ages.

In this book, I examine and try to understand this long and complex evolution. It must be conceded that the sources are notoriously few and difficult. For example, a central institution in our story is the women's fabric shop, called most commonly the *gynaeceum.* From the times of early Hellas to the thirteenth century in Europe, references to this gathering of women appear sporadically but continuously in the sources. Although most allusions to it are words said in passing, in tracts devoted to other subjects, they are also numerous enough to yield, I believe, a coherent picture. The survival of this institution over two millennia, amid vastly different material and social surroundings, seems unmatched in the Western experience.

The dearth of medieval records regarding many aspects of women's lives reflects the distinctive way these documents were generated. As we shall see, literacy was viewed as a skill appropriate for noble women in the Middle Ages, even for those outside convents. But their mastery of letters was usually confined to the vernacular, and they had no role in the redaction of the formal and official records and the learned treatises, written in Latin, which were most likely to survive. In the social world of the central Middle Ages, the clerics or clerks read Latin, noble women read the vernacular, and noble men read nothing at all. It is therefore not surprising that one of the longest descriptions of a gynaeceum we possess appears in a vernacular document, a chivalric romance, by Chrétien de Troyes. But it is also true and regrettable that, particularly in the early medieval period, we can read about women's activities only in fragments.

From the late thirteenth century, medieval sources explode in numbers and variety, and they even include comprehensive and statistical examinations of the work force. The city which offers perhaps the earliest and best records is Paris. It possesses an extraordinary compilation of guild statutes done about 1270 by the prévôt of merchants, Etienne Boileau. And it can boast of a series of seven *tailles,* or tax assessments, dating between 1292 and 1313 during the reign of Philip IV the Fair. Four of them have been published. Two of them, the earliest and latest, from 1292 and 1313, respectively, I have edited into machine-readable form. The taille of 1292, with more than 14,000 entries, or hearths, is also the largest of the set. The Parisian tailles are exceptional in their enumeration of a large number of women bearing occupational titles. They will give us our principal view of women and work in a great political and cultural capital of the medieval world. They also invite comparison with three later tailles of Paris, unfortunately much smaller in size, dated, respectively, 1421, 1423, and 1438. Here too, I have enlisted the aid of the computer in their analysis.

In these sources, we shall seek descriptions of what well could be called the public labor of women. By "public labor" I mean work that serves a function beyond a woman's personal needs or those of her immediate family. Public work includes the production of goods and the performance of services for which compensation is received. It also embraces uncompensated activities, such as giving religious counsel, for which the reward might be only gratitude and enhanced reputation.

From these sources we must also attempt to judge the social value, the honor or prestige, accorded to working women and to the labors they performed. These is a delicate task, particularly for the early period, when we must work with literary texts exclusively. Our tactic here is primarily to look for associations of feminine skills with high moral attributes or with honored figures—goddesses in the ancient world, saints in Christian times, queens and princesses, mythological or literary heroines. For example, in numerous Roman grave inscriptions commemorating women, skill at working wool is mentioned along with the moral attributes of fidelity, chastity, charity, or cheerfulness. Roman women, it seems safe to conclude, not only were expected to work wool, but were honored for it, in death and surely too in life. Similarly, the association of the Virgin Mary with both literacy (she is surprised while reading a book in countless depictions of the Annunciation) and sewing shows that these skills were honorable in all women. In other words, we judge the social value accorded feminine skills and women workers by the context in which they are described, by the literary company they keep. By the late Middle Ages, we can utilize harder data. The wealth that women workers accumulated, evident in the late medieval fiscal assessments, gives some measure of the moral value of the work they performed.

This book will, I hope, make a contribution to the history of women and of labor. But the value of women's history is not restricted to what it may report about women; a knowledge of their participation in work offers a new perspective on medieval civilization in the broadest sense. It was a civilization only partially and imperfectly reflected in the surviving literary records, for much of medieval culture was molded and transmitted orally. Women played a much larger role in the oral transmission of skills and values than they did in the redaction of written documents. Historians must be aware of the skewed images their documents present; they must be careful not to mistake records for realities. A better appreciation of women and work, of the skills they exercised and passed on to their daughters, of the values they nurtured, will eventually yield a more balanced and a more accurate view of European civilization in its formative age.

In finding my way across millennia and across a continent, I have depended on the help and counsel of many experts. Barbara Lesko gave me leads concerning women and weaving in ancient Egypt; Geoffrey Russom elucidated Anglo-Saxon terminology; and Michel-André Bossy offered guidance in medieval French literature. All are my colleagues at Brown University. I learned much from a conversation with John Baldwin of Johns Hopkins University on noble women in France in the thirteenth century. Maria-Jesus Fuente directed me to Spanish records that refer to women workers. Judith M. Bennett, University of North Carolina; Barbara Hanawalt, University of Minnesota; and Martha Howell, Rutgers University, reviewed the manuscript and provided valuable comments. My son Gregory P. Herlihy accomplished the computer-assisted analysis of the statistical surveys. My wife Patricia Herlihy, a historian in her own right, gave me the benefit of her critical judgment concerning words, phrases, themes, and interpretations. I thank them all and hope that I have not here misused or misinterpreted the information they have so generously supplied.

DAVID HERLIHY

CHAPTER 1

The Ancient Mediterranean World

...[Deus] mulieribus dedit texturae sapientiam....

...[God] gave the wisdom of weaving to women....

> —Ambrose of Milan,
> *Exameron, v.9.11*

Medieval society inherited from classical and barbarian antiquity both traditions of skill and a cultural sense of the appropriate division of labor between the sexes. And for a millennium, people remained faithful in thought and practice to these ancient notions of what was suitable work for men and for women. Given the durability of this heritage, we must inquire into the division of labor in the two parent societies of the Middle Ages, the classical and the barbarian. Of the two, the classical Mediterranean world, with its abundant surviving sources and monuments, is by far the better seen.

Women participated in many productive activities in the classical world, but in none quite so prominently as in the manufacture of textiles. The long centuries of ancient history show many civilizations that were quite diverse in their fundamental characteristics; it is remarkable that seemingly in all of them, women played a central role in the making of cloth.

TEXTILES

The Ancient Middle East

Since the origins of civilization in the ancient Middle East, women were intimately associated with cloth making. In Egypt

1

during the Old Kingdom, women alone seem to have done the weaving. Tomb art portrays them delivering cloth and receiving payments, usually in jewelry. We hear further of "houses" of weavers, supervised by female overseers—perhaps an early anticipation of the Greek gynaeceum.[1] The Hebrew Bible sings the praises of the worthy wife, and among her virtues is skill at making cloth:

> When one finds a worthy wife,
> her value is far beyond pearls.
> Her husband, entrusting his heart to her,
> has an unfailing prize.
> She brings him good, and not evil,
> all the days of her life.
> She obtains wool and flax,
> and makes cloth with skillful hands.
> She puts her hands to the distaff,
> and her fingers ply the spindle.
> —*Proverbs 31:10–13*

Hellas

According to the mythology shared by both Greeks and Romans, the goddess Athena (Latin, Minerva) first demonstrated "the processes of wool making, how to weave the cloth and how to dye the wools."[2] In Homer's *Odyssey*, Penelope, wife of the long absent Odysseus, uses her work as a weaver to put off importunate suitors. She spends three years pretending to weave a winding cloth for her father-in-law Laertes, promising to choose a new husband when the cloth is finished. Her impatient suitors clearly believe that this task is appropriate for, even required of, a woman.

Hesiod, the Boetian didactic poet writing in the eighth century B.C., composes for his brother a list of agricultural activities and names the days when they could be most propitiously performed. "On that day," he says of one of his recommended dates, "a woman should set up her loom and get forward with her work."[3] Herodotus, honored as the father of history, writing in the fifth century B.C., tells a story about the Amazons, the nation of women warriors thought to be living north of the Black Sea. A band of young Greek men encounter them and, attracted by them, propose marriage. The Amazons refuse, affirming that "we do not learn women's work."[4] The Amazons would not abandon the masculine role of warriors in favor of the work that Greek women performed, importantly the making of cloth. In Aristophanes' comedies (late fifth century B.C.), Athenian women, anxious to abandon Lysistrata's sex strike and return to their husbands' embraces, give as their excuse that they must go home to clean wool and strip flax. One of his heroines, Praxagora, proposes to create a communist regime; to win support among the men, she must assure them that even under communism women will make their clothing.[5]

Presumably, Greek women set up their looms and got on with their work within the confines of their homes. Among affluent Greeks, the part of the house reserved for women is called the *gynaikeion* or *gynaikonitis* (from *gyni*, "woman"). The Latin borrowing I utilize here is *gynaeceum*. The Latin author Cornelius Nepos, writing about 40 B.C., explained: "In Greece the mother of the family sits only in the interior part of buildings, which is called the *gynaeconitis*, where no male goes unless a close relative."[6]

In Hellenistic times, women remained active participants in all phases of cloth making, in both linen and wool. From Ptolomaic Egypt in the second century B.C., surviving papyri illuminate a cloth making enterprise; its owner was a man named Apollonius, and it was located on his estate near Memphis.[7] There, women slaves and, apparently, also hired free girls labored at making cloth. They are called *paidiskai*, a name associated with the Greek word for "child." The implication is that the girls working for Apollonius were very young.

Later, in Roman Egypt, papyri from the second century A.D. show us another estate owned by another Apollonius, called "the general" or Strategos.[8] On his estate too, *paidiskai*, working under the supervision of his mother Eudaimonis, made cloth. These and other papyri show us women, both slave and free, spinning, weaving, dyeing, and finishing both linen and wool. They learned these arts through formal apprenticeship. Women even appear as owners of fulling mills and dye works.[9] The papyri do not give a count of the relative numbers of Egyptian men and women working in the cloth industry, but they leave no doubt that women were present and important in all its phases.

For Greece itself, about A.D. 173, Pausanias, author of the one complete description of Hellas to reach us from antiquity, describes free women employed in cloth making. In describing the town of Patrae in Elis, Pausanias observes that the women of the town outnumbered the men by two to one and that they "are the most charming in the world."[10] Most of them gained their livelihood, he reports, "from the fine flax that grows in Elis, weaving from it nets for the head as well as dresses." Their very numbers indicate that they did not work as members of family units. Probably they worked at home alone or in small shops for wages.

The Greek Christian writers also make several allusions to women and fabric production. Writing in about A.D. 200, Clement of Alexandria denounces the swollen number of slaves who crowd the palaces of the wealthy. Tall Celts carry their debauched mistresses about on litters; other slaves amuse the women with erotic stories. "But as for wool workers occupied in spinning and weaving, women's work or household supervision, there are none."[11] In Clement's Greek, the names for the woolworkers, spinners and weavers, are given in the feminine gender, and he clearly equates these tasks with "women's work." They were, he implies, honorable skills, though allegedly no longer cultivated. A later Greek patristic writer, St. John Chrysostom (d. 407), says this of the women's work carried on in the big households: "…domestic science depends upon the woman, and in this she as much surpasses the male as an artisan does a layman, in the things of his trade."[12] And "domestic science" surely included the making of cloth.

Later in the third century, another Christian writer from Alexandria, Origen, also associates women and cloth production, though not in a traditional gynaeceum. In his great work of apologetics, the *Contra Celsum*, Origen has the pagan Celsus denounce the Christians as "woolworkers in houses, laundry workers and the most obtuse yokels." Unable to argue with the learned pagan masters and schoolteachers, they entice the youths to "leave father and their schoolmasters and go along with miserable women and little children who are their playmates to the wooldressers' shop (*gynaeconitis*), or to the cobbler's or to the washerwoman's shop, so that they may learn perfection."[13]

Modern translators have had difficulty with the word *gynaeconitis,* rendered in the passage above as "wooldressers' shop." Its usual meaning of "women's quarters" is impossible here. A mixed group of boys and girls could not have trooped into this restricted part of the household. This woolworking establishment had to be outside the house, as it provides an escape from the master's authority. The word most likely signifies a separate establishment, analogous to the cobbler's shop and the washerwoman's shop, where small groups freely gather. Unlike the classical women's quarters, Origen's shops are independent and open. But they continue to represent a predominantly feminine domain. They are crowded with "miserable women" (Celsus uses for purposes of disparagement a diminutive form of the Greek word for women). And they are centers of religious proselytizing as well as fabric production. Even as the women spin and weave, they entice naive youths, Celsus complains, into the Christian superstition.

The Christian saint Piamun of Egypt provides an example of a woman supporting herself by her own labors, though she seems to have worked at home and not in a shop: "There was a virgin named Piamun, who lived the years of her life with her own mother, taking the evening meal alone with her, and sewing linen."[14]

Rome

Textiles and women were joined no less intimately in Roman society. In the tale of Philomela that Ovid retells in his *Metamorphoses,* the poet makes of fabric a mode of communication between women. Philomela is raped by her brother-in-law Tereus; he cuts out her tongue and confines her in an isolated prison. But she weaves a cloth, and relates in the weave the *indicium sceleris,* the story of the crime. A servant takes the cloth to her sister Procne, who reads it and rescues her. The sisters extract from the wicked Tereus a horrible vengeance (they feed him his own murdered son for dinner).

Roman women moved much more freely in society than did their Greek counterparts, and Roman houses did not contain restricted quarters. But Roman women were no less committed to working cloth, the quintessential *opus muliebre.*[15] In seeking to set an example for Roman society, Emperor Augustus insisted that his daughter and granddaughters learn to work wool.[16] (He had his grandsons instructed in reading and swimming.)

Roman grave inscriptions of antiquity sometimes include a *laudatio funebris*, praise of the deceased. The feminine virtues most frequently cited are piety, modesty, chastity, amiability, and dedication to working wool. "She gave weight to her duties and to the working of wool," reads a grave inscription from the Republican era.[17] The so-called *Laudatio Turiae*, an inscription raised sometime between 8 and 2 B.C., honors an unknown Roman patrician woman possibly named Turia. Her husband expresses his gratitude: "Should I recall her modesty, obedience, companionship, grace and assiduity in her working of wool?"[18] A young Roman woman named Claudia, married with two children, who died about A.D. 100, was "of clear speech, kept the house comfortable, and made wool."[19] One of the most eloquent characterizations of womanly virtues dates from the Flavian period (A.D. 69–96) and honors a freedwoman named Allia Potestas, the apparent mistress of the man who commemorates her. Allia is strong, pious, dedicated, blameless, well-groomed (*munda*) at home and "sufficiently well-groomed outside." She was the first to rise in the morning and the last to retire at night, "after all things had been put in order." "And wool never left her hands without reason."[20] Some gravestones even carry representations of the cloth tools the women used so conscientiously in life.[21]

Women who worked in wool did not do so simply to clothe their own families. The elegiac poet Tibullus (first century B.C.) warns a faithless young woman that in old age she will be poor (*inops*); she will spin and work with trembling hands at a rented loom.[22] The poor old woman, alone, is not producing for her household, and the allusion to a rented loom suggests some sort of "putting-out" system, in which an entrepreneur provides the tools (for a fee) and also what Tibullus calls the "snowy fleece."

In the countryside, the great Roman villas seem commonly to have included fabric works; cloth was needed to clothe the slave laborers, and some cloth, as we shall see, may have been produced for sale. According to the Spanish writer Columella (first century A.D.), the well-equipped estate should keep tools "which are used in the making of wool."[23] *Servuli* (little slaves) would be using them daily, and the text implies that the little slaves are female. The wife of the steward, the *villica*, supervises this work. She is enjoined to employ women slaves in wool-working, especially on rainy and frosty days, when they could not work in the fields. She is to keep them supplied with wool; she even watches over the shearing of the sheep. The women could thus make the cloths which they and the other favored slaves (those held *in honore*) need. She also inspects the looms, giving instructions when she knows how to do better but also learning from those more skilled than she. She is at all events the chief repository of this technical knowledge, and the villa's staff of cloth workers are chiefly women.[24]

Archeology confirms the frequent presence of cloth works within a villa's complex of buildings. A "big woolen factory" (the characterization is M. I. Rostovtzeff's) was found at a villa (Chiragan) near Toulouse and at another in Britain.[25] Rostovtzeff further believed that Batavian and Frisian cloths, made in the Belgic provinces and widely distributed throughout the empire, were produced on the region's estates. This probably means that they were made by women who, as Columella unmistakably shows, principally staffed these rural workshops.

The Edict on Prices (301) of Emperor Diocletian, preserved in both Greek and Latin versions, sets maximum wages for a long list of textile workers. Most of them do not receive maintenance—that is, they do not live in the homes of their employers. Either they work in a shop or, like Piamun, under a putting-out system. The edict uses either plural or masculine forms to describe most workers, and the generic references could also have covered women. One type of weaver, that "of soft finished cloth," is specifically identified as feminine.[26] The edict also sets maximum prices for a variety of raw materials and finished garments. All this supposes that the system of cloth production was commercialized in the late empire and that women participated in it as salaried workers.

The reverse side of this close association of cloth work with women's work is that the ancients regarded woolworking as demeaning, even shameful, for the free male. In one of his edicts liberating the Christians from punishments incurred during the period of persecutions, Constantine expresses compassion for those who were sentenced to forced service in the imperial fabric shops (presently to be discussed). This, he attests, caused them "shame and indignity."[27] The Greek text says explicitly that they were condemned to perform "women's works." The ancient legend of St. Hesychius of Antioch, martyr under Emperor Maximian, presents the saint as prefect of the imperial palace. When he refuses to renounce Christianity, he is dressed in a slave's tunic and delivered "to the wool workers in a fabric mill to be cruelly ridiculed."[28] For Hesychius, doing the work of women was the culminating disgrace.

In the fourth century, the Christian writer Lactantius summarizes the late ancient and now Christian notions concerning the division of labor. He criticizes Plato, who makes proposals in his *Republic* that are "against human custom and against nature."

> Because he saw that among other animals the functions of males and females are not distinguished, [Plato] thought it necessary that even women serve in the army and in government councils and hold magistracies and receive commands. Thus he assigned to them arms and horses; in consequence, he gave wool and cloth and the carrying of infants to men.[29]

For Lactantius, cloth work is as natural to women as the bearing of children.

The Late Empire

The organization of cloth production under the empire acquires a new clarity from the middle of the third century. Apparently beset by labor shortages, the imperial government strove to ensure that all essential services would be performed and essential commodities supplied. In the closing years of the third century, Emperor Diocletian (284–305), the great "restorer of the world," put in place (or is thought to have put in place) a system of state manufactures, of which fabric works were the capstone.[30] The abundant imperial legislation of the fourth and fifth centuries contains no direct mention, but there are several allusions to them.[31]

Christian writers also mention the imperial cloth works as places of punishment. Numerous Christians, especially women, paid for their beliefs by serving time as cloth workers. I have already cited the legend of St. Hesychius of Antioch, prefect of the imperial palace, whom Emperor Maximian stripped of his office and sent off to work in a gynaeceum.[32] Writing on the miserable and merited deaths of the persecuting emperors, Lactantius relates how the cruel Galerius deprived noble men of their offices and honors, while "free and noble mothers of families were carried off into gynaecea."[33] Constantine, as already mentioned, freed the noble men and women from the fabric shops even as he liberated them from other forms of forced service.[34] The fifth-century Church historian Sozomen sums up his gracious acts:

> [Constantine] commanded that all should be free, all those who for confessing Christ had been sentenced to exile; forced to live on islands or elsewhere against their wills; condemned to work in mines or in public works; required to labor in gynaecea or textile shops; or made to serve in courts when before they were not liable.[35]

But even under the Christian emperors, the fabric shops continued to be used as penitentiaries, especially for women. St. John Chrysostom, the eloquent patriarch of Constantinople, commiserates with the widow of Theodorus of Sicily, who for political reasons had been "suddenly deprived of her property and freedom and numbered among the State women cloth workers."[36]

The system of state cloth works flourished under the Christian empire. By 423, the government no longer needed to requisition military clothing from its subjects. The former contributions in clothing were commuted into money payments, with one-sixth of the sums given to the state weavers.[37] Their output was apparently meeting the government's pressing needs.

The *Notitia Dignitatum* (List of Offices) is the only surviving ancient record that mentions the imperial cloth works other than indirectly. It identifies those found in the western provinces by type, number, and location; it does not include those in the eastern provinces, which, from the many allusions to them, were probably even more numerous.[38] The fabric shops in the West consisted of seventeen gynaecea, two *lynifia,* or linen works, and upward of nine dye works. The distinction made between gynaecea and the linen works implies that the former were primarily, if not exclusively, engaged in working wool.[39] The shops were each under a procurator, who answered to the Count of Sacred Largesses and of the Privy Purse, the chief fiscal officer in the imperial bureau-cracy.

In Italy, gynaecea were found at Rome, Canusium, Venusia, Milan, and Aquila; in Dalmatia, at Jovia; in Pannonia, at Bassania (later moved to Salone) and at Sirmium. Gaul had works at Arles, Lyon, Rheims, Tournai, Treves, and Autun (later moved to Metz). The concentration of cloth works in the northern Belgic provinces is especially noteworthy; the same regions would be a principal center of cloth manufacture in the Middle Ages.

The two linen works were at Vienne in Gaul and Ravenna in Italy, suggesting that linen production was a southern specialty. The dye works were also concentrated around the Medi-terranean shores, doubtless reflecting the availability of the pur-ple fish dye that was the principal tincture.

To judge from the imperial edicts mentioning them, the im-perial fabric shops supplied three sets of patrons. First, the em-peror himself and members of his immediate family demanded brocades and other silk fabrics dyed in purple and embroidered with gold thread. Fine silks displayed their exalted status. The imperial government prohibited private persons from wearing purple silk, and it equated the private sale of purple dye or of the silk itself with high treason.[40] Second, the imperial shops produced the cloth and clothing that the emperors distributed every year to high officials and courtiers, and that was a major part of their salaries. The making of luxury clothing seems to have been the special function of the linen shops.[41] Finally, the shops supplied the army. Soldiers doubtless were their chief customers. The making of military cloaks seems to have been the principal function of the gynaecea and helps explain their location close to the northern frontiers and to the legions that watched over them.

The texts say nothing about the output of the shops or about the number of workers who labored within them. They do, however, permit partial answers to two fundamental questions: Who worked in these shops? And did private enterprises mak-ing cloth continue to exist alongside the state factories?

The laws most commonly refer to the workers as *gynaeceiarii* and always use the word in the masculine gender. Nonetheless, much evidence indicates that women were counted among the *gynaeceiarii* and may even have been more numerous. An edict of Emperor Constantius, dated 339, orders that women "who were formerly employed in Our imperial weaving establishments and who had been led by the Jews into the association of their turpitude" should be returned to their former place of work.[42] In 371, Emperors Valentinian I, Valens, and Gratian decreed that if any person should accept a wife from among the purple-dye workers, "he should know that he must be bound to her ignoble status."[43] The provision seems designed to keep the woman, and her children after her, active in the art. Similarly, Emperors Theodosius II and Valentinian III in 427 determined that if the daughter of a purple-dye fish collector should marry a man also of ignoble status, they must "assume the bond of their mother's assignment to State service."[44] Women were evidently occupied in the art of concocting dyes and probably were passing along the skill to their daughters.

Vegetius, a fourth-century writer on military affairs, advises that fabric workers be excluded from the army: "Linen workers, and all those who have anything to do with fabric shops, in my opinion should be kept far from military encampments."[45] He does not say so, but the passage implies that male fabric workers, because of the work they performed, were effeminate.

The laws reveal little about the legal status of the workers. Their ranks certainly included some slaves.[46] But the imperial edicts also regulate the marriages of workers, which they seem to have freely contracted; presumably, the workers were free, even if "of ignoble status." It is not clear how the fabric shops guarded and employed conscripts and those sentenced to forced labor. Chrysostom's characterization of the young widow as numbered among "the State cloth workers" makes it appear that the convicts worked alongside slaves and hired persons. Like late ancient society itself, the work force was probably a mixture of slaves, freedmen, and the free.

The imperial legislation shows that cloth making was not entirely a state monopoly: The emperors condemn the solicitation of state workers by others or the harboring of workers who had fled the public establishments.[47] Private shops were apparently in keen and unlawful competition with the state enterprises for skilled and scarce labor.

The obscurity surrounding the private production of textiles under the late empire is almost impenetrable. One version, possibly late, of the legend of St. Agatha (martyred under Emperor Decius) first presents her as a pagan girl who wants to keep busy at home. Her mother allows an old woman, a *vetula*, to enter their house in order to teach Agatha how to weave.[48] The old woman also secretly professes Christianity, and she converts as well as instructs the young girl. Again, the weaving room functions as a cultural as well as an economic center. Agatha, incidentally, becomes a Christian Penelope. She promises her parents that she will marry once she has finished weaving a veil, but what she weaves by day she unravels by night.

Arnobius Afer, a Christian apologist writing about 300, offers a surer glimpse into Roman homes. He mentions *textriculas puellas* (little girl weavers). Working alongside one another, they make up stories to pass the boring hours—stories which, Arnobius claims, were more credible than the pagan myths.[49] Who were the little girls, busily working at their looms? Presumably, they were young female slaves or employees working in a domestic gynaeceum or an independent shop. They clearly formed a group, and they worked (and talked) together. We shall see, later in our inquiry, other examples of weavers escaping the tedium of their work through songs and stories.[50]

Unmistakably, the ancient Mediterranean world looked on women as the principal suppliers of cloth and clothing; women, as Ambrose affirmed, possessed the wisdom of weaving. Many of these women worked in groups, serving great houses, serving a market, serving the state. We do not know how many were slaves or how many were free. We cannot judge the relative participation of men and of women in cloth making, except to note that women loom larger in the sources. The ancient economy and society, and the ancient style of life, would have been inconceivable without the woman cloth worker.

LIBERAL PROFESSIONS

The pedagogues of the ancient world distinguished the liberal arts from the mechanical or manual arts. A "liberal" art was appropriate for the free man (*liber*), but seemingly not for the free woman. The Roman patrician lady is not congratulated for assiduous reading or study. Rather, she works wool alongside her slave girls and is honored for it.

Ancient women were all but excluded from two of the professions based on liberal learning: those of philosopher and lawyer. The Christian writer Lactantius in his discussion of the sexual division of labor claims to know of only one woman who had been taught to philosophize, a lady named Themiste. "[Women] cannot learn everything," he explains, "because in childhood they must master the duties that will eventually meet domestic needs."[51] A crucial factor is the young age of Greek and Roman girls at marriage. The women of the classical world would usually be married before their twentieth year; they were afforded little time to gain a formal education.

Legal expertise was closely related to government service, and that in turn to military command. Lactantius condemns Plato, in whose republic women would hold public office and assume the command of armies.[52] In spite of Plato's novel proposals, the common ancient opinion was that camp and court, and derivatively military and legal training, were unsuitable for women. Crucial here, for both late antiquity and the Middle Ages, is an imperial edict of 393, preserved in the Theodosian Code. It prohibits women from appearing in court as lawyers or advocates, except in their own cases.[53]

Medicine

Ancient women were much more visible in the healing arts. They served exclusively as midwives, for classical Latin has no masculine form corresponding to the feminine *obstetrix*. Midwives are commonly mentioned in ancient literature.[54] Some women bear the title on their gravestones—sure evidence that midwifery was a recognized and honorable profession. The fifth-century life of Melany the younger tells of a woman in childbed. She is attended by midwives, but the baby dies before it can be delivered. Then male doctors (*medici*) replace the midwives when surgery is necessary; they try to save the mother by cutting into the womb and removing the dead fetus.[55]

Women occasionally bear the proud titles of *medica* and *physica*. The Roman satirist Martial tells of a young wife married to an aged and impotent husband; she convinces him that her good health requires sex. "At once the male doctors arrive, the lady doctors leave…O serious medicine!"[56] An Iberian inscription commemorates a woman named Julia Saturnia, dead at forty-five years: "incomparable wife, the best of doctors."[57] A young Christian woman named Scantia Redempta, who died at the age of twenty-two, was also skilled in medicine.[58] A woman named Aemilia Hilaria, the aunt of the fourth-century Gallo-Roman poet Ausonius, worked as a physician all her adult life and never married.[59]

Ancient religions were often closely associated with the healing arts, and Christianity was no exception. In an early Christian legend, St. Philip the Apostle had four daughters, virgins, who, according to Luke the Evangelist, "had the gift of prophecy." One of them, Hermione, was also an expert in curing the sick. A great crowd of the ill and infirm flocked to her, and these she healed, while invoking the name of Christ. She opened a public hospice in Asia, in which she aided and helped all who came, "both in spirit and in body."[60] According to the legend of the triplet martyrs Speusippus, Eleusippus, and Meleusippus (they trained horses—hence the *-ippus* in their names), their Christian grandmother Leomilla knew medicine and was "incomparable" in the art.[61] The probably mythical and certainly misty Catherine of Alexandria knew medicine along with every other science, as we shall shortly see.

Religion

Women served as priestesses in several pagan religious cults; this was appropriate, since the pagan pantheon included female deities, though women served in the cults of male gods too.[62] Women appear as deaconesses and prophetesses in the early Christian Church, but they did not apparently exercise sacerdotal functions. The crucial texts defining the position of women within the Church are two famous passages of St. Paul:

> Let women keep silence in the churches, for it is not permitted them to speak, but let them be submissive as the Law also says. But if they wish to learn anything, let them ask their husbands at home, for it is unseemly for a woman to speak in Church. (1 Corinthians 14:34–35)

Let a woman learn in silence with all submission. For I do not allow a woman to teach, or to exercise authority over men; but she is to keep quiet. For Adam was formed first, then Eve. And Adam was not deceived, but the woman was deceived and was in sin. Yet women will be saved by childbearing, if they continue in faith and love. (1 Timothy 2:11–15)

Women corresponded with such great Fathers of the Church as Jerome and Augustine, but significantly, their letters have not been preserved, only the responses from their male mentors. Within Jerome's circle of Roman matrons, the lady Marcella was actually called upon to settle theological disputes. But, as Jerome reports:

...when she answered questions she gave her own opinion not as her own but as from me or someone else, thus admitting that what she taught she had learned from others. For she knew that the apostle said, "I suffer not a woman to teach" and she would not seem to inflict a wrong on the male sex.[63]

We have many direct quotes from women of the early Church, particularly in narratives of saints' lives. The life of the Carthaginian martyr Perpetua contains a first-person account of her passion and of the visions that accompanied it.[64] Though this and other texts seem to carry authentic feminine voices, women did not contribute any surviving tract on formal doctrine to the vast body of late ancient Christian literature. Paul's admonition carried weight—yet it may also be misleading. The pagan Celsus attributes chiefly to women and to the small groups they dominated the successful dissemination of the Christian message.

Christianity was, after all, a "book religion," and literacy for women as well as men aided in its practice. Emperor Augustus, in setting a model for the Romans, had had his daughter and granddaughters instructed in woolworking but not in reading. A Christian family with sufficient means was expected to instruct daughters as well as sons in letters. "Divine reading," Jerome writes to one of his many female friends, "should always be in your hand."[65]

The life of Melany the younger, a woman from a Roman senatorial family who married but became an abbess in later life, exemplifies the levels of erudition that rich Christian women might attain. (Melany lived until 437, and her life was written by a contemporary.) She read both Latin and Greek with such fluency that she hardly noted whether she was reading the one language or the other. She read the Old and New Testaments in their entirety four times every year, as well as canonical writings and exegetical works.[66] All week long she wrote "on parchments" while listening to one of her nuns read, apparently, a different text.[67] Melany attentively corrected her reader if she slipped in pronouncing a single letter. And she enjoyed "like treats of honey" conversations with learned bishops and monks on theological subjects. Her dedication to reading seems to echo Jerome's advice: "a book never left her hands."[68] Perhaps too this quotation from her life parodies the conventional praise bestowed upon the matrons of pagan Rome, from whose hands wool was never absent.

The learning of a Christian woman is celebrated in the legend of Catherine of Alexandria, supposedly martyred under Emperor Maxentius (her legend does not appear in writing until the ninth century). According to the *Synaxarium Constantinopolitanum,* a Greek martyrology of that century, Catherine had learned "all Greek and Roman science, was familiar with the writings on medicine, and knew all the foreign languages of all peoples."[69] The pagan emperor Maximian, frustrated in argument by the girl's learning, summons from the provinces fifty pagan philosophers, all males of course, who knew all the sciences plus the secrets of the Egyptians. Catherine, eighteen years old, debates them in a public disputation before the people of Alexandria. She confounds the fifty and converts them. Her legend wins extraordinary popularity in the West as well as the East, and she is honored in the Middle Ages as the patron saint of scholars. However fabulous her story, surely there is significance in the fact that the medieval patron of learning was a woman.

Mastery of letters and acquaintance with the Scriptures gave Christian women a real, even if still obscure, role in the transmission of Christian beliefs. Paul admonished women to keep silent in the churches—not in homes or workshops (or in disputations before the people of Alexandria). And their role in childbearing—their salvation, according to the apostle—extended into the domain of child rearing and the early education of the young. Jerome himself gives a salient example of the transference of religious knowledge in the feminine line:

Saint Catherine with the doctors of Alexandria.
(Historical Pictures Service, Chicago)

...The sister of Celerinus, the father of Ageruchia, who nourished the little girl as a baby and received her when born in her lap, for twenty years without the solace of a husband educated her niece, teaching what she had learned from her mother.[70]

Mothers, and sometimes older sisters, influenced the spiritual formation of many late ancient male saints. Macrina, sister of the Cappadocians Basil the Great and Gregory of Nyssa, adopted a religious life from her early teens, without entering a cloister. At home she took chief responsibility for rearing her younger brother Peter, then an orphan; according to her life, she was for him "father, teacher, pedagogue and counselor."[71] The Iberian woman Florentina was the older sister of Isidore of Seville. She recognized that her baby brother was destined to be a great saint and scholar. "And since she knew," her life relates, "that blessed Isidore would be so admirable, she was zealous in nourishing him, not by the milk of the body but by the milk of the spirit, with all diligence; she guarded him from every defilement of vice."[72]

The formal texts of theology surviving from this epoch make little mention of women. Yet women seem to have played a crucial role in the elaboration and dissemination of Christian faith and piety.

SURVIVALS

The Roman empire, with its new capital at Constantinople (after 324), survived until 1453. The imperial fabric shops also persisted into this, the Byzantine period of the empire's history. We shall not follow their history, except to make a single observation.[73] About 570, a pilgrim named Antoninus from Piacenza in Italy traveled east to visit the holy places. He encountered women's workshops at Tyre in Palestine. His cryptic description points to a new turn in their long evolution:

> At Tyre, powerful men, their life most wicked with so much licentiousness that cannot be described; public *genicia* in silk and different types of cloth. From thence we came to Ptolomaida, a righteous city, good monasteries.[74]

Antoninus links sexual license and the gynaecea; Tyre's cloth works were apparently doubling as brothels, and the women cloth workers as prostitutes. In the early medieval West, as we shall see, rulers were also complaining about the sexual license of the women's workshops and of the women working within them.[75]

The link between the women's workshops and sexual license invites attention, but our terse sources allow little beyond speculation. Slave girls were of necessity subject to the sexual wants of their masters, but the sources do not suggest that these were simply private harems. Antoninus knew them well at Tyre. Would he have known in his brief stay private and secluded harems? The profession of prostitute required that the woman wear fine and attractive clothing. The Egyptian courtesan Thais, later a saint, wore glittering garb before her conversion. Could she also have made the garments? Skill in cloth making could serve many purposes; perhaps not all of them were reputable, but all were supportive of women.

The collapse of imperial authority in the western provinces was cataclysmic, and with it disappeared many of the characteristic social and political institutions of the classical Mediterranean world. Towns shrank, magistracies vanished, and the Roman colleges and guilds did not survive. But the gynaeceum shows an amazing resilience. Sporadic allusions to it continue from the fifth to the thirteenth centuries, right across the "dark ages" of western European history. It is one of very few bridges that incontrovertibly span the gulf between the classical world and the Middle Ages.

Minerva's Maidens

Sidonius Apollonaris (ca. 430 to 486 or 487) from Lyons in Gaul, who died as a Christian bishop, included in one of his poems a depiction of a gynaeceum, full of fantasies but also full of instruction. The poem is an *epithalamium*, a celebration of a marriage.[76] The genre required that he laud the virtues of both groom and bride. In the poem, the goddess Minerva presides over two establishments: in the one, males, including the groom, philosophize; in the other, women make cloth and clothing. The women's weaving establishment, called the *textrinum*, claims the poet's chief attention. In it, "virginal hands" produce clothing worthy of the gods, or "whatever might surpass it." Among the virgins, said to be from Athens or from Corinth, the bride-to-be, Araneola, surpasses them all. She even excels the goddess in her cloth making talents. She clothes her grandfather and father in their official robes of consular office; she recounts in embroidery the love stories of ancient myth. And she quite literally needles Minerva's other establishment, the school of philosophers where her future husband is training, by tracing in her embroidery caricatures of the male philosophers, specifically the Cynics. In the end, Minerva calls a halt to the cloth making and directs Araneola to turn her work over to an older woman (a *mater*) and to marry her philosopher groom.

Minerva's weaving shop has several notable features. It is staffed largely by young girls; presumably, they learn the skilled arts of weaving and embroidery and practice them until, like Araneola, they marry and depart. But there are also some senior women present, the *mater* who takes up Araneola's work and Minerva herself, the shop's director. There is no mention of slaves. Moreover, the shop is a lively center of cultural communications, where Araneola produces ceremonial garments, recounts in thread the pagan myths, and tweaks the male philosophers.

Is Minerva's textile shop pure poetic fancy? Poets of course build imaginery worlds, but to be effective they must do so out of familiar elements. Consider Sidonius' depiction of virginal hands clothing the gods and the highest officials of Rome—does it not suggest that the making of quality cloth remained in the hands of women, even in this disturbed Gaul of the fifth century? And the division of labor Sidonius describes merits reflection. Philosophy belongs to men; the making of quality cloth to women. But the wisdom of philosophy and the wisdom of weaving, both under Minerva's patronage, are presented as coordinate achievements. Their unification in the marriage of male philosopher and female weaver, Sidonius implies, is the foundation of civilized life.

Traces

In Spain in the early seventh century, that great collector of ancient lore, Isidore, bishop of Seville, knows the word *gynaeceum* and defines it thus: "a Greek term [meaning] gatherings of women [who] come together to engage in working wool."[77] The tutelage of the Roman state by now has vanished, but the women remain together at their looms.

The legend of St. Theodoric of Rheims presents an example of the possible survival of an imperial workshop. Rheims in Gaul was the site of an imperial gynaeccum, according to the *Notitia Dignitatum*. Theodoric was a disciple of St. Remi who, sometime about 496, converted the Frankish king Clovis to the orthodox Christian faith. One day, as the two men strolled in the suburbs of the town singing psalms, they chanced upon a community of forty women.[78] As at Tyre, this community was a brothel, and the women were prostitutes.

Is it possible that this feminine community in the suburbs of Rheims had some connection with the imperial factory found there a century earlier? At Theodoric's urging, St. Remi replaced the women with forty Christian widows. Like many Merovingian nuns, they doubtless supported themselves by their spindles, looms, and needles. From women's quarters in the houses of ancient Hellas to Egyptian shops to Roman villas to imperial fabric works to brothels to medieval convents, the link tying these gatherings of women together was their continuing engagement in producing cloth.

Theodoric's legend also depicts a woman as a religious mentor. There was in the city of Rheims a famous abbess named Susanna. "To her most gentle bosom, like that of the kindest mother, St. Theodoric betook himself. Then he opened the secrets of his heart known only to God alone."[79] She gave him "salubrious counsel." She even climbed "to the top of a forested mountain" with him, in order to select the site of his monastery.

Theodoric's legend takes us to the kingdom of the Merovingian Franks under the first of its historic kings, Clovis. We have entered the Middle Ages.

NOTES

1. This information comes from H. G. Fischer, from a paper delivered at a conference on the topic "Women in the Ancient Middle East," held at Brown University, November 1987. See Lesko (ed.), 1989, p. 25. See *ibid.*, p. 63, for women as weavers in ancient Sumer.
2. The citation comes from the late ancient encyclopedist Isidore of Seville, 1911, 1985, xix.20, "De inventione lanificii." He writes: "Minervam quamdam gentiles multis ingeniis praedicant. hanc enim primam lanificii usum mostrasse, hanc etiam telam ordisse et colorasse lanas perhibent." Minerva was also credited with the invention of many other manual arts, was the patroness of all artisans, and was honored by her votaries with the title *ergane* (the worker).
3. Hesiod, 1982, epigrammata no. 753.
4. Herodotus, 1971–82, 4.114.
5. *Lysistrata*, lines 735 ff. *The Ecclesazusae*, lines 1031 ff. Both are in *Greek Drama*, 1938, I.
6. Nepos, 1984, praf. 7: "In Graecia mater familias non sedet nisi in interiore parte aedium, quae gynaeconitis appellatur, quo nemo accedit nisi propinqua cognatione coniunctus."
7. Rostovtzeff, 1922, 1979, p. 115, who reconstructs Apollonius' economic activities.
8. See Wipszycka, 1965, for the Egyptian textile industry under Roman rule, including Apollonius' enterprise.
9. *Ibid.*, p. 58, for apprentices; p. 148, for a dye works owned (and sold) by two women, Sarapias and Aunichis, daughters of

Harthomios, in a papyrus of the third century A.D.; and p. 136 for a woman owner of a fulling mill.

10. Pausanias, 1954, 7.21.14.
11. *Paedagogus,* 3.4 *PG,* VIII (1891), col. 593.
12. Ad viduam juniorem. *PG, XLVIII* (1862), col. 616.
13. *Contra Celsum,* iii.55. Origen, 1953, 1980, p. 166. The translation is by Henry Chadwick. "Fuller" might be a better translation than "washerwoman."
14. *ASS,* I Martii, p. 240: "Fuit enim Virgo Piamun, quae annos vitae suae vixit cum matre propria, sola cum sola vespere comedens, et lineum nens."
15. On Roman women and work, see Maurin, 1983.
16. *De Vita Caesarum,* 64. Suetonius, 1914, I, 220.
17. "...gravitatem officio et lanificio praestitei," cited in Lattimore, 1962, p. 297.
18. *Laudatio Turiae,* 1950, cap. 30 (p. 9): "...pudicitiae, opsequi, comitatis, facilitatis, lanificiis suis adcuitatis, ...cur memorem?"
19. "sermone lepido, tum autem commode domum servavit, lanam fecit." *CIL,* 1862, I, p. 218, n. 28.
20. Lattimore, 1962, p. 297: "lana cui e manibus nuncquam sine causa recessit."
21. *ILCV,* 1961, no. 645, woman dead at age 32, reign of Claudius.
22. Tibullus, 1982, I.6.77: "at quae fida fuit nulli, post victa senecta / ducit inops tremula stamina torta manu / firmaque conductis adnectebit licia telis, / tractaque de niueo uellere ducta putat."
23. Columella, 1956, XII.iii.1 (III, p. 188): "...in altera parte, quibus ad lanificia utuntur...deinde quibus quotidie servuli utuntur, quae ad lanificia...pertinent."
24. *Ibid.,* XII.iii.6 (III, p. 190).
25. Rostovtzeff, 1957, II, 617–18, with abundant bibliography.
26. Edictum Diocletiani, in Frank, 1940, p. 378.
27. *De Vita Constantini,* ii.34. Eusebius, 1890, p. 508.
28. The legend of St. Hesychius survives as an appendage to the passion of another saint of Antioch, Romanus. For the text as preserved in Latin form, see Passio S. Romani, 1932, pp. 269–70. The Latin version reads: "expoliavit vestimentis et induit eum colobio laneo et tradidit eum in geneceo lanariis ad inludendum in injuriam."
29. Divinae institutiones, iii.22. Lactantius, 1890–97, I, 252: "...consequens est ut lanam et telam viris et infantium gestationes."
30. On the obscure origins of the state manufactures, see Persson, 1923, p. 131.
31. See note 41.
32. See note 27.
33. *De mortibus persecutorum,* 21. Lactantius, 1890–97, II, 196–97: "Matres familias ingenuae ac nobiles in gynaeceum rapiebantur."

34. See note 28.
35. *Historia ecclesiastica*, i.8. *PG*, LXVII (1864), col. 878.
36. Ad viduam juniorem. *PG*, XLVIII (1862), col. 604.
37. Edict of Honorius and Theodosius, dated 423. *CT*, 1955, 7.6.5 (pp. 164–65).
38. Wipszycka, 1965, however, finds no reference to them in the Egyptian papyri of the late imperial period.
39. *Notitia*, 1876, pp. 150–52. The dye works of Africa are not separately enumerated.
40. *CT*, 1952, 10.20.18 (p. 287), edict of Theodosius and Valentinian, dated March 8, 436, mentioning that "innumerable constitutions" had prohibited such sales in the past.
41. *CT*, 1952, 10.20.6 (p. 286), edict of Valentinian, Valens, and Gratian, dated June 27, 372, mentioning "workmen who devote their labor to weaving linen garments to be used for Our issuance of supplies."
42. *CT*, 1952, 16.8.6 (p. 467).
43. *CT*, 1952, 10.20.5 (p. 286).
44. *CT*, 1952, 10.20.17 (p. 287).
45. De re militari, 1.7. Vegetius, 1885, p. 11.
46. *CT*, 1952, 10.20.1 (p. 285).
47. *CT*, 1952, 10.20.6–9 (p. 286).
48. *ASS*, I Februarii, p. 609.
49. Arnobius Afer, 1934, p. 187: "cum historias, quaeso perlegitis tales, nonne vobis videmini aut textriculas puellas audire taediosi operis circumscribentes mores...exprimere?"
50. See page 58.
51. Lactantius, 1890–97, I, p. 258: "quibus intra puberes annos officia mox usibus domesticis profutura discenda sunt."
52. See note 29.
53. *CT*, 1952, 2.12.5 (p. 48), dated September 28, 393.
54. See *TLL*, 1900–, under the word *obstetrix*.
55. Vita Melaniae, 1889, p. 55. There is a recent English translation of this remarkable life; see *Melania*, 1985.
56. Martial, 1903, 1929, 11.71.
57. *CIL*, 1862–, II, no. 497.
58. *ILCV*, 1961, no. 615: "antistis disciplinae in medicina fuit."
59. Herlihy, 1985a, p. 20, n. 93.
60. Her life, translated from the Greek, is in *ASS*, II Septembris, p. 185. There is evident confusion between Philip the Apostle and the Philip of Caesarea mentioned in Acts 21:9. "Hermione autem medicinae operam dedit, ad quam magna hominum copia confluxit, quos illa invocato Christi nomine omnes curavit....Tunc Sancta publicum aperuit in Asia hospitium, in quo omnes tam spiritu quam corpore, consolabatur et juvabat."
61. *ASS*, II Januarii, p. 437: "Quorum avia, Leomilla nomine, medicinam instructe cognoverat, et notis diligenter instructa, ut incomparabilis haberetur."

62. On women as priestesses, see MacMullen, 1980.
63. Jerome, Epistle 127, in *PL*, XXII (1877), col. 1091, cited by Ruether in Ruether and McLaughlin, 1979, pp. 75–76.
64. Passio Perpetuae, 1972. This remarkable life may betray the influence of the Montanists, a heretical sect from Asia Minor who maintained that prophecy continued within the Church and that women could speak in its voice.
65. Ad Salvinam. *PL*, XXII (1877), col. 730: "Semper in manibus tuis sit divina lectio."
66. Vita Melaniae, 1889, p. 38: "Legebat autem novum et vetus testamentum per annos singulos quater."
67. *Ibid.*, p. 36: "Scribebat etiam per totam septimanam in membranis. Cum autem scribebat ipsa, una de sororibus legebat...."
68. *Ibid.*, p. 35: "...cujus etiam numquam liber de manibus recedebat."
69. The Synaxarium is edited in *ASS, Novembris, Propylaeum.* See pp. 253–54 for the entry of 24 November concerning Catherine.
70. Ad Ageruchiam. *PL*, XXII (1877), col. 1047: "Soror Celerini, patris Ageruchiae, qui parvulam nutrivit infantem et in suo natam suscepit gremio, per annos viginti mariti solatio destituta, erudit neptem, docens quod a matre didicit."
71. Cited by Ruether in Ruether and McLaughlin, 1979, p. 74.
72. *ASS*, V Junii, p. 17: "Et quia B. Isidorum tam admirabilem fore sciebat: ipsum nutrire, non lacte carnis, sed lacte spiritus, cum omni diligentia studebat; ipsa sese custodiens ab omni inquinamento vitiorum."
73. On fabrics, especially silk, in the Byzantine empire, see the classic study by Lopez, 1945.
74. Antoninus, 1898, p. 160: "Tyro homines potentes, uita pessima tantae luxuriae, quae dici non potest; genicia publica oloserico uel diversis generibus telarum. Et inde venimus Ptolomeida Ciuitas honesta, monasteria bona."
75. See pages 20, 36.
76. See Sidonius, 1980, no. XV, lines 126 ff.
77. Isidore, 1911, 15.6.3: "...graece dictum, eo quod ibi conventus feminarum ad opus lanificii exercendum conveniat."
78. *ASS*, I Julii, p. 60: "...transiens secus locum, qui Cedrius vulgo dicitur, ubi prostibula meretricum erant...."
79. *ASS*, I Julii, p. 56.

CHAPTER 2

The Early Middle Ages (ca. 500–800)

...Non licet christianas mulieres vanitatem in suis lanificiis observare, sed Deum invocent adjutorem, qui eis sapientiam texendi donavit. ...It is not allowed to Christian women to observe superstitious practices in their workings of wool; rather, let them call upon God the Helper, who bestowed on them the wisdom of weaving.

—Council of Braga, *cap. 75 (*A.D.* 579)*

A double interpenetration marks the history of late antiquity and the early Middle Ages. Northern peoples, whom the Romans called barbarians, passed within the ever more porous frontiers of the western empire. They came first as captives and slaves; then as mercenaries, colonists, and federated allies; and finally as high administrators and conquerors. From even earlier times, Mediterranean culture, most aggressively though not exclusively in the form of Christianity, was penetrating into the north. Christianity itself would prevail in regions that were never part of the Roman empire. Out of this double displacement, of peoples and of cultures, the civilization of the early Middle Ages was formed. Medieval conceptions of the appropriate division of labor between the sexes also emerged out of this mixture. We look first at labor assignments among the barbarians (insofar as we can know them) and then at women's work in the early medieval world.

THE IRISH

To illuminate the division of labor within a tribal society, we focus on early medieval Ireland. Several considerations explain

25

this choice. Ireland, set on the northern margins of Europe, was never part of the Roman empire and was never reduced to a province within a strong and centralized state. For a long time it knew no cities, the characteristic social formation of classical civilization. Deep into the Middle Ages, kindreds, tribes, and shifting petty kingdoms dominated its society.

But the intense social conservatism of the Irish did not preclude the growth of a rich literary tradition. It attracted Christian missionaries, the bearers of literacy, very early, probably from the fourth century. Its great missionary, Patrick, preached the gospel there in the mid-fifth century.

The exceptional society of early Christian Ireland has provided exceptional sources for social history. Its vernacular literature is justly regarded as the oldest in Europe; it preserves numerous traces of late iron age Celtic (La Tène) culture.[1] Its Latin sources, particularly its large collections of saints' lives, also manifest a pronounced archaism. To be sure, the tradition by which these texts has reached us is very obscure. The saints of early Christian Ireland number nearly a hundred, and they flourished principally in the sixth through eighth centuries. But the surviving manuscripts date only from the fourteenth century, and the lives themselves, in the versions that have reached us, were probably composed in the twelfth.[2] But incontrovertibly they preserve elements of a much older tradition. The Latin lives I principally use here, written in a correct but unadorned style, abound in homely allusions to the labors of field and home and to the work of women.

Agriculture

A society without cities, the people of early Christian Ireland lived primarily by agriculture and by pastoralism. Women helped in the work of planting and harvesting. One of the chores which her malevolent stepmother imposed upon the little St. Brigid was "the work of the harvester."[3] This, however, seems unusual. When later in her life Brigid wished to harvest a field, "she called together for collecting the fruits some working men, whom she found ready to work for pay."[4] St. Daveca "digging the earth by her own labor sowed it with seed."[5] But her biographer makes clear that this was an act of heroic asceticism; her efforts further showed that "she carried a manly soul in her feminine body." Planting, hoeing, and harvesting seem not to have been the principal responsibility of women.

Women's special domain was the raising of animals—pigs, sheep, cows, and perhaps chickens. Brigid as a little girl watched over her father's pigs.[6] St. Lugidus of Molua once warned his disciples: "Where there is a sheep, there will be a woman; and where women, there sin...."[7] Whenever he heard the bleat of a sheep, the saint fled to another place, lest he encounter women and sin. Women nonetheless pursued the handsome saint. One day, some women, "wishing to see Lugidus," deliberately let the calves have access to the heifers. As this meant less milk for human use, the women began to raise an alarm "in loud voices, as if they wished to separate [calves from heifers]." They hoped that the commotion would bring the handsome saint forth from his seclusion.[8] The ruse did not work, but the account clearly indicates that women were managing the herd and that they showed considerable assertiveness. The culture did not insist women be demure and retiring.

Women owned sheep. One day, little St. Aedan was "playing in the field with the shepherds of the sheep of his maternal aunt."[9] The boy was approached by eight hungry wolves, and Aedan, having pity upon them, let them eat eight sheep; he thus enraged his aunt. Owning her own flocks and employing her own shepherds, she was clearly a wealthy woman.

Besides watching animals, women performed many household chores. They churned butter and made cheese, prepared and cooked meat, and brewed beer. Brigid's cruel stepmother made the young girl perform all these tasks, though the life implies that they were unworthy of her.[10] In later life, Brigid became an abbess to whom the poor would flock, "one seeking bread, another drink, some milk, others cheese or butter, still others either flour or cereal, and also linen or wool or any kind of clothing."[11] Almost certainly, Brigid and her community of women were producing all these commodities. Once Patrick, in blessing a lineage, wished for its future women "prosperity of storehouse."[12] Thus, women not only played crucial roles in producing and processing food but also seem to have played major roles in storing it and distributing it to the community.

Textiles

Among the Irish, as elsewhere, the making, mending, and washing of cloth were among the most important of the "offices of the household." There are many references to Irish washerwomen. St. Aedan forbade women to wash their cloths in a spring he had miraculously called forth from dry earth. But a young girl, "the daughter of a rich man," defied him. She was trampling her cloths underfoot in the water to clean them when her foot stuck to the cloths and the cloths stuck to the rocks.[13] Her rich father had to make a special appeal to Aedan to loosen her limb.

Brigid was forced to assume at her stepmother's command the *textricis officium* [the duties of a (female) weaver]. The word *officium* indicates a specialized skill, and the use of the feminine form of "weaver" suggests that this was work done chiefly by women.[14]

One day, on a journey, Brigid finds hospitality in the house of a poor woman:

> The old woman, hiding her extreme poverty with a happy and courteous face, at once cut down the woods suitable for the making of cloth (for she was accustomed to do the work of a weaver). She made of them a fire for her guests, so much the more pleasing as it was less smokey [than peat?].[15]

The old woman must have had in her house a simple vertical loom, made of valuable wood but easily dismantled. Brigid of course noted her generosity, prayed to God, and the next morning "...there was found in the same house a cloth loom, which replicated the magnitude and shape of the old one and astonished the viewers."[16]

St. Columba's mother, when pregnant with the saint, dreamt that "she was doing the work of weaving and made a *pallium* with a great variety of colors."[17] An angel took it from her; it symbolized the coat of beautiful virtues that the future abbot would wear.

The life of St. Boecius associates a woman with one of the most skilled of the textile arts: the dyeing of cloth. A married woman named Mend complains one day to the saint that "the color, with which she was accustomed to dye the mantle of the king was lacking that year."[18] "For the ancients," the life informs us, "had a certain garden herb by the name of *glassen* [woad], from the juice of which they made the dye for their clothing." St. Boecius directs the woman to gather the herbs that grew beneath his chariot, add green seed, and mix the compost in the name of the Lord, "adding nothing dirty." Mend does this, and produces enough dye "to color all the cloths of all the country." Even the petty Irish kings wanted special garments, skillfully dyed, that would identify their status and enhance their dignity. They depended on women to supply them.

The ninth-century vernacular *Cáin Adamnáin* [The Law of (St.) Adamnan], purports to be "the first law made in heaven and on earth for women."[19] Adamnan claims that he is changing the traditional division of labor between the sexes. Women are exonerated from waging battle. No longer may their husbands flog them and drive them into the fray, to kill and be killed, while the men remain safely in the rear. Freed from fighting, the woman still "holds the spindle and...clothes everyone."

In a big household (such as that of Brigid's father), the slaves and serving girls (such as Brigid herself) probably worked together in a workshop, as did the virgins and widows in religious communities. But I have not found in the Irish lives explicit reference to a gynaeceum.

Nurturing and Learning

Women in early Christian Ireland also served as nurses, a function that extended their services into the realms of healing and of education. The fostering of children—their transfer into different and sometimes even distant households—created a permanent bond between the child and its *nutrix* and *nutritor,* its foster parents.

Brigid served as a nurse within her father's household. When her own nurse fell sick, "she stayed by her bed continuously days and nights and sought to warm her with both food and salutary words and to show her humanity with all her strength."[20] She ultimately cured her nurse by drafts of beer, which she had miraculously produced from water. Though she worked many cures, Brigid was not learned in the medical arts. When she herself developed a severe headache, she went to see a bishop, "for he both by learning and by practice understood both the types of diseases and their cures."[21] Some women were medical experts. St. Daveca ran a hospital—an institution not often encountered in early Ireland. "For the Most High gave to her the grace of conferring health upon the sick and of driving out demons."[22]

A favored practice closely related to medical treatment among the Irish was the bath. "For then and now the use of baths is very frequent among both the Irish and the Scots."[23] Women frequently, perhaps even usually, prepared the baths. St. Ite seems always to have welcomed her frequent visitors, many of them bishops, with a meal and a bath. Brigid cures a leper by washing his deformed body.[24] Once, she changed bath water into beer, for distribution to the thirsty poor.[25] The ability to draw a good bath was another of the arts appropriate for women.

At least for those women who entered the religious life, and perhaps for others, literacy was an indispensable skill. An angel spirits away a young girl named Lasra from her father's home, thus rescuing her from an unwanted marriage. Espousing the religious life, Lasra "learned the letters suitable for her under the direction of St. Finnian."[26] Another young nun, named Brignat, was sent by St. Daveca to study in Britain. She stayed in a cell outside a monastery, "where she read the psalms and the other books necessary for her."[27]

Literacy in turn made it possible for women to pass on to their wards sacred knowledge. St. Columban was the student of a woman named Rychena, with whom he maintained a warm relationship in later life.[28] Among Ireland's great religious pedagogues was St. Ite. She reared, for example, her nephew Mochoemog, the son of her sister, from infancy. "And for twenty years the most blessed abbess Ite instructed him in honest morals and a knowledge of letters...so that he could become a priest and build a place for God."[29] Ite is credited with rearing "many of the saints of Ireland from their infancy."[30] St. Aedan's maternal aunt was also his *nutrix,* his foster mother, responsible for his upbringing. Both examples are interesting variants of the "avunculate," the special relationship thought to link a brother and his sister's son.[31]

The role which women played in the transmission of religious knowledge seems to have prepared them for important roles in Church administration. A curious text out of early Irish hagiography describes "the three orders of the saints of Ireland."[32] The first and holiest of the orders included some 350 bishops, founders of churches, the immediate followers of St. Patrick. Unlike those in the later second and third orders, these bishops "did not spurn the administration of women and their company, because, founded upon Christ the rock, they did not fear the wind of temptation." It is not clear what the women administered or how they served the chaste bishops. According to the legend of St. Patrick, the great apostle to the Irish was aided in his work by five nieces, daughters of a sister.[33] And the most renowned of these early Irish saints, ranking only after Patrick himself, is a woman, Brigid.

The culture of early medieval Ireland resembles that of the classical Mediterranean world in the prominent role it assigned to women in skills such as cloth making or nursing. But there are subtle differences too, which may be broadly characteristic of northern societies. Women had sole or chief responsibility for certain essential services: the care of animals; the making of butter, cheese, or beer; the gathering and use of herbs; domestic *officia* generally. Professions learned in school and dominated by males did not, as in Mediterranean lands, overshadow in prestige these examples of *opera muliebria*. Adamnan's law, in stating that the woman "holds the spindle and…clothes everyone," holds her in respect. Irish women seem to have worked quite independently, without close male supervision or even much male participation in their particular labors. How did Lugidus know that the bleat of a sheep necessarily meant the presence of a woman? The vital economic roles of northern women may have protected them from falling under the perpetual male tutelage to which women were subject in some southern traditions. This experience of independence they carried over into other cultural activities shared with men, such as the transmission of religious values.

Special skills, independently exercised, earned for the women of early Christian Ireland, and perhaps of tribal societies generally, a special dignity. The Law of Adamnan gives a quaint but firm assurance to women: "one-half of your [husband's] house is yours, and there is a place for your chair in the other half."[34] Women earned chairs in many rooms within the house of early Irish culture.

GERMANS AND ROMANS

Between 300 and 900, the great migration of peoples, followed by the establishment of the Frankish empire and the work of Christian missionaries, brought the Germans fully into the mainstream of western civilization. The writers of the classical world frequently mention these northern peoples. The description of *Germania*, written by the Roman historian Tacitus in A.D. 98, is especially renowned.[35] But it is hard to know how accurately these ancient authors (or their informants) observed and how objectively they reported. The Germans themselves did not have writing until they were converted to Christianity (from the fourth century), by which time they were already subject to strong Christian and Roman influences. The gynaeceum, for example, appears in three of the Germanic national laws, but it is not known whether this is an indigenous institution or a classical borrowing.[36]

At all events, the national laws of the Germanic peoples, put in writing between about 500 and 800, are indispensable, though difficult, sources for social history. The capitularies (as the legislation of the Merovingian kings and, after 751, their Carolingian successors are called) likewise contain much material on daily life.[37] So do the many Church councils held in the West, as the Church tried rigorously to suppress ancient heathen practices. One especially revealing compilation of disciplinary canons was put together by Regino, abbot of Prüm near Treves, about 906.[38] Finally, saints' lives, on the continent as in Ireland, afford often colorful insights into popular behavior.

Sexual Assignments

At the end of the first century A.D., Tacitus noted that the Germanic freemen shirked agricultural labor and that "all the bravest and most warlike do nothing, while the hearth and home and the care of the fields are given over to the women, the old men and the various infirm members of the family."[39]

Even among those Germans rich enough to own slaves and collect rents, "other duties, those of the household, are performed
by the lord's wife and children."[40]

Tacitus' words draw a distinction between an outer economy
of field work, usually though not exclusively done by men, and
an inner economy of household chores which formed the special domain of women. The *officia domus* included preparing
food, baking, cooking, brewing, and cloth making. The English
language bears relics of these ancient assignments. The word
"wife" may be etymologically related to "weave."[41] In Old
English or Anglo-Saxon, the ending "-ster" is a feminine form.
Words for occupations such as "webster" (weaver) or "brewster"
(brewer) thus originally denoted women. Only the word "spin-
ster" retains in modern English this ancient usage.

Women dried the harvested wheat. In the sixth century,
Gregory of Tours tells of a woman who piled wheat to dry on
the roof of the cell where St. Monegundis was living. She was
struck blind for violating the saint's privacy.[42] Women also win-
nowed the wheat. When St. Benedict, the father of western monasticism, first became a hermit, his nurse accompanied him.
"His nurse, in order to winnow the wheat, asked to borrow a fan
from neighboring women, which, carelessly left on the table,
was by accident broken."[43] Benedict miraculously repaired it.

Women turned the hand-held rotary mill, laboriously grinding grain into flour. Gregory of Tours relates that, in 589, a
lady named Septimina was convicted with her lover, Droctulfus,
of treason. (She had nursed the children of the Merovingian
king Childebert II.) Septimina was sent to the manor of
Marlenheim in lower Alsace "so that, working the mill, she
would prepare every day the flour needed for the food con-
sumed by the women in the textile works."[44]

One day, according to the miracles of St. Theodoric, a
woman named Gislaidis on a manor near Rheims decided to
mill her grain on a Saturday evening, in violation of the Sabbath. "...as she turned the mill by hand, of necessity in order to
grind the grain...the handle that she held, by which she turned
the mill, soon stuck to her hand, so that no one could free it."[45]
Only a prayer to the then deceased saint released her grip. In
Carolingian times, on a royal manor (perhaps Stephanswert
close to Utrecht), the wife of a tenant on a servile farm was re-

quired to "make malt."[46] Dependent farms often paid rents in beer on Carolingian manors, but only here does a survey associate its production specifically with a woman.[47]

In 789 Charlemagne issued a "General Admonition" to his subjects; in it he lists the types of "servile work" they must not perform on Sundays. Men are explicitly forbidden to do "rural labors," that is, cultivate vines, plow fields, plant hedges, clear woods, cut trees, quarry stones, or build houses.[48] Men also could not go to public assemblies or hunt. But they could carry three cartloads of supplies for the army, and, if necessary, bury the dead. The emperor also enumerates the kinds of work women are not to undertake: "They are not to do textile work on Sunday. They should not cut out clothes or sew. They should not wash clothes in public or shear sheep." The preparation of food is not mentioned, perhaps because cooking had to be done even on the Sabbath. Clearly, all phases of cloth making, from the shearing of sheep to the cutting, sewing, and washing of the finished garments, were in the woman's domain.

The Council of Meaux-Paris (June 845 and February 846) also gives a list of labors the faithful were not to perform on the octave days of Easter. Among them is *opus gynaeceum,* a variant form of our familiar "women's work"; the term was surely synonymous with all phases and types of textile production.[49]

Kings, Nobles, and Cloth

It is remarkable how little the cataclysm of Rome's fall in the West affected the millennial association of women and cloth making. St. Severus of Ravenna lived in the fourth century, though his legend was not written down until the ninth. In lay life he lived at home with his wife Vincentia and his daughter Innocentia. "With them to earn his bread, [Severus] performed women's labors. For he was accustomed to stitch and weave wool, after the manner of women, and hence he was popularly called *lanarius.*"[50] In the early medieval world, stitching, weaving, *lanificium* in general, remained women's work, which men shunned, except, as in Severus' case, out of need.

Even the ancient customs associated with weaving survived for a long time. Martin, bishop of Braga (modern Portugal) in the middle of the sixth century, condemns "women at their looms [who] call upon Minerva."[51] The Council of Braga over which he presided in 579 issued a similar condemnation. Regino of Prüm includes it in his compilation of canons in about 906.[52] He apparently thought that the warning to women weavers against invoking Minerva was still needed.

The kings and *potentes* of early medieval society met their own needs for cloth both by imposing rents in fabric upon their dependent cultivators and by organizing their own workshops. Payments in strips of linen are commonly listed among the dues owed by Carolingian serfs. On the royal manor of Stephanswert, the free farms (*mansi*) paid rents in both linen and linseed.[53] Strips of linen, often assigned a monetary value in the manorial records, seem also to have served as currency in this money-poor society.

We shall look more closely at the organization of the women's fabric shop in the following chapter. Here, we marshal further evidence of the survival of this distinctive institution from the ancient world into the Middle Ages.

Sometime between 555 and 560 Pope Pelagius I wrote to Julian, bishop of Cingoli in the Marches, the following letter:

> Concerning slaves be mindful of what we have commanded you, that you assign men who might be useful for a gynaeceum to them, but in such a way that the churches be compensated in cultivators for the value of their craftsmanship; nor is an artisan and serving boy of the same worth as against a peasant or cultivator;...see therefore that you do not give men who can maintain houses or cultivate, but take those who are useless....[54]

The pope expresses concern that the staffing of the cloth shops may deplete the ranks of cultivators. He seems to assume that the male workers assigned to the workshops will be children. The problem had to be common to catch the pope's attention and warrant this letter to the bishop of a small town.

The Lombard laws are one of the three Germanic codes that explicitly refer to these workshops. The oldest part of the laws, the Edict of Rothari, was promulgated in 643. If a free woman marries a slave, her parents have the right to kill her or to exile her.[55] If they fail to do so, then the king's officials, the gastald or the sculdais, are ordered "to take her to the court of the king and to place her among the woman slaves in the workshop." In this quote, the term used for workshop is *pisele,* a synonym for gynaeceum. The passage shows that the Lombard kings, like the Roman emperors before them, still operated state cloth works and, also like the Romans, were still using them as places of confinement for women.

It is also worth noting that the term *pisele* (or *pensilis*) meant a room with a fireplace. The later Lombard laws even state the wages that masons known as the Comacine masters should receive for building the fireplace or furnace.[56] The presence of a fireplace or furnace in the women's fabric shop almost certainly indicates that the women were dyeing the cloth.

In 821 or 822, the Carolingian king Lothair, ruling in Lombardy, promulgated a cartulary dealing with the nun who abandoned the religious life and took up prostitution. She was no longer to be confined to the women's workshop, "lest perhaps she, who before had intercourse with one man, now have the place for having intercourse with many."[57] Henceforth, the errant woman was to lose her property to the fisc and be subject to episcopal judgment. Presumably, before Lothair's revision, the gynaecea of Lombardy were also brothels; the parallel with the fabric works of Tyre in Palestine is striking.[58]

The laws of the Alamanni (recorded in their present form probably between 717 and 719) stipulate the fines to be paid by a man who has sexual relations with a slave girl (*ancilla*) who is either a *vestiaria* (wardrobe keeper) or a *genitiaria,* that is, a member of the women's fabric shop.[59] The reference to the woman cloth worker is ambiguous; it reads: "cum puella de genitio priore." This could mean either the head girl or a girl from a first or upper workshop, perhaps the one making the lord's own clothing. But as the text goes on to distinguish her from "other" girls working in the shop, the former interpretation seems preferable. The man who sleeps with the head girl must pay a fine of six shillings; if he sleeps with her apparent subordinates, he pays only three.

This passage invites several comments. The women's workshop has a recognized head, protected by a fine twice as large as that shielding the other girl workers. The group must have been fairly large, not merely a few servants helping the lord's lady to spin, weave, and sew. But another girl is also involved somehow with clothing, the *vestiaria.* She is not technically a member of the

workshop, and the penalty protecting her is the same as that protecting its head. Did she, as her name may imply, actually make
the clothes (*vestes*) from the cloth produced by the shop? At all
events, the organization of cloth making, showing three functional
divisions within the ranks of the women workers, was clearly quite
elaborate among the Alamanni. Moreover, the workshop mentioned in the laws is not a royal establishment. Presumably, few
Alamanni were rich enough to maintain their own workshops, but
the institution had to be common enough in society to merit the
legislator's attention.

The law of the Salian Franks also seems to assume a distinction between the head girl and her subordinates in the opera-
tion of the workshop.[60] The serving girl who "holds" either the
cellaria (presumably the food stores) or the workshop of her
lord is protected by a special fine. Both kitchen and cloth works
were under the supervision of women.

The Frankish kings and emperors issued several regulations
concerning these workshops. I cite only one of them here, as it indicates the range of cloth work the women were performing. An
unknown Frankish king, perhaps Charlemagne himself, issued a
set of directives concerned with estates, known as the capitulary *De
villis*. As no particular manor is mentioned, presumably the directives applied to estates across the entire kingdom (or empire). The
women working in the gynaeceum are to be supplied with "linen,
wool, woad, red dye, madder, carding implements, combs, soap,
soil, containers and other small things that are needed there."[61]
The list shows that women were working in both linen and wool;
they were carding and washing the wool and presumably weaving
it. And they were certainly dyeing the cloth. Again, women dominated all phases of the cloth making process.

The Council of Meaux-Paris (845–846) mentions women
fabric workers in the service of laymen. Men are not to commit
adultery in their houses "with their own slave girls or with girls
of the cloth shop."[62] The passage implies that an important
function of "slave girls" maintained in the lord's household was
the making of cloth. Moreover, those laymen who owned private churches were not to collect tithes, which were used to support their "dogs and women of the cloth shops."[63] The dogs
mentioned are presumably hunting dogs, and the women appear to be concubines rather than cloth workers. The man rich

enough to own churches was also likely to enjoy the services, sexual or domestic, of the *genitiariae*.

Clerics and Cloth

The Church also had great need for fabric, for sacerdotal vestments and for altar cloths, essential for the dignified celebration of the liturgy. But the old association of women with cloth making raised delicate moral problems for the celibate clergy. Where cloth was produced, there would be women; and where women, temptation.

One recourse was to ask the faithful to donate the needed fabrics. In a canon preserved in Regino's tract *On Ecclesiastical Discipline,* priests were to "preach throughout their parishes to the women that they should prepare linens for the altars."[64] But donations of this kind seem not to have been reliable, either in delivery or in quality. For the canons also contain regulations about women who lived apparently apart from their families in the vicinity of churches.

The Council of Meaux-Paris forbade women to reside in "any sort of habitation to which priests have access."[65] But Regino (or his sources) recognized that the priest may have need of the services women provide. He then should place the women (we should note the use of the plural) in a house in the village or estate, "and there he can supply them with all needed things."[66] Who are these women? The house that the priest is to find for them in a neighboring (but not too proximate) village or estate looks very much like a gynaeceum. And the reference to supplies is reminiscent of the capitulary *De villis.* The royal stewards are similarly directed to supply the women in the workshops with everything they need to produce cloth. The priest is apparently free to move these women about at will; they clearly were not working in family units.

Male monasteries were also dependent on women to make or mend the needed cloth. St. Lobin, a monk and later bishop of Chartres in the sixth century, gave his worn tunic to a girl in a female monastery who mended it for him but kept the old thread as a relic.[67]

The elites of early medieval society, both clerical and lay, needed fine cloths and clothing to display their status, to serve as gifts for their retainers, and to dignify the celebration of their liturgies and rituals. St. Radegundis did not like to wear, "in the barbarian fashion," the sumptuous garments set with gold and gems that marked her as a queen, but her asceticism was hardly typical.[68] The elites could not easily purchase fine fabrics, and they could not requisition them. They created their own fabric shops, staffed by trained and skilled women. The ancient gynaeceum survived because demand survived, even in barbarian Europe, for well-made, luxury clothing.

Magic

Tacitus observed that the Germans "believe that the [feminine] sex has a certain sanctity and prophetic gift, and they neither despise their counsels nor disparage their answers."[69] The northern barbarians cultivated a much richer culture of magic than did the Mediterranean peoples. Women in early medieval society retained a special affinity to the magical arts. Indeed, all the arts, which accomplished things that ordinary people could not do, radiated an aura of magic. Women at their looms, if they did not invoke Minerva, apparently were given to performing other rituals, which the Church regarded as superstitious:

> Let inquiry be made whether women in their wool working or in their weaving of cloth say anything or observe anything, but let them, as said above, do all things in the name of the lord.[70]

The Council of Braga (579) does not allow "in the collection of herbs that are medicinal that any practice or incantations be used," but only Christian prayers.[71] The council does not identify the sex of those gathering the medicinal herbs, but most likely they were women.

Regino of Prüm, in surveying society in the late ninth century and in gathering his canons, gives a good summary of the magical practices, which medieval folklore, and even theology, would long associate with women. He wants the parish priest to investigate the following:

> Inquiry is to be made whether there is any woman who through certain spells and incantations is said to be able to change the minds of men, that is, move them from hate to love, or from love to hate; or can damage or carry off the properties of men. Inquire too

whether there is one who says that together with a crowd of demons transformed into women she rides at night on certain beasts
and is numbered in their company. Such a woman by all means
should be expelled from the parish.[72]

The pagan goddess Diana often led the women, as they flew
about at night on the backs of beasts:

> ...certain wicked women, relapsing after Satan, seduced by the il-
> lusions and phantasms of the demons, believe and proclaim that
> they during nighttime hours ride with Diana the goddess of the pa-
> gans and an uncounted host of women on certain beasts, and in the
> dead silence of the night they pass over vast stretches of the world,
> and they obey [Diana's] commands as their leader, and on certain
> nights they are called forth to her service.[73]

Women also knew how to mix poisons:

> A woman, if she kills any persons by magical art, that is by drink or
> by any craft, let her do penance for seven years. But if she is poor,
> four years.[74]

The potions she prepared could also prevent a pregnancy:
"You have drunk some poison, that is herbs or other things, so
that you cannot have infants, or you have given it to another.[75]

Women in early medieval society tended the hearth and the
fire within it; they gathered the herbs needed for cooking, for
medicines, and for the dyeing of cloth. They were adept in arts
that many men did not fully understand. It is not surprising
that they seemed skilled in magic too.

Literacy

The practitioners of magic tended to be women of humble
background. We are much better informed about the learned,
rich women of early medieval society. They came overwhelm-
ingly from royal households or those of the high nobility. A
knowledge of letters was again essential for those destined for
careers in religion and apparently also for those prominent
women who remained in the world. The Merovingian queen
Radegundis learned to read as a little girl, as this art "suited her
sex."[76] Radegundis became an abbess late in life. She wrote repeatedly to the feuding kings of France, urging them to keep
the peace.[77] She carried on a correspondence with St. Germain,

bishop of Paris. Her nuns were also literate, and one of them, named Baudonivia, her "special student," wrote an extant life of her *magistra*.[78]

In sixth-century Gaul, Astrudis, the sister of St. Baldwin of Laon,

> ...was reared by her parents with zealous diligence, dedicated to the Christian religion, learning letters in the days of her tender childhood. She learned to sing praises to the son of the virgin. Through divine clemency, she also waxed strong of memory in listening and reading, and she exercised herself in the teaching of doctrine...she was full of eloquence, but much more of wisdom.[79]

Two eighth-century saints of northern Gaul (modern Belgium), named Harlindis and Renula, learned how to sing the psalms, how to read and write, and how to spin, weave, stitch, and sew. They even copied manuscripts, including the four gospels, the psalms, and "other writings." Perhaps they illuminated them too, as, according to their life, they also learned how to paint.[80] Their biographer identifies all these skills—reading, singing, copying, and painting—as arts usually done "by the hands of women." They were skills that women learned, and women passed on.

Two Merovingian girls, Madelberta and Aldetrudis, were sent to their maternal aunt Aldegundis to be "taught the sacred rule" and to be "nourished by spiritual milk."[81] Here is a continental parallel to the special relationship between maternal aunt and niece or nephew that we saw in Ireland.

Medicine

In typically vague fashion, Tacitus implies that Germanic women nursed the wounded. Mothers and wives inspected and counted the wounds of stricken warriors, brought the men food, and gave them encouragement.[82]

This association of women with the healing arts, characteristic of both barbarian and classical worlds, endures into the Middle Ages. Besides dispatching letters to kings and bishops and instructing her nuns, Radegundis ran a kind of hospital at her convent near Poitiers. Her chief therapy was the bath.[83] She herself washed the heads of the sick, cleaning away encrustations, scabs, and lice and removing worms. Wounds aggravated by scratching were treated with oil "in the Biblical fashion." Sick women were directed into a big tub, and Radegundis joined them. She washed each of them "from head to foot" with soap. Upon emerging, those in tattered garments were given new clothes. She fed all the sick, supplying each one with water and a napkin. She herself cleaned the faces and hands of those unable to wash themselves. Her patients then sat down to a three-course meal, and Radegundis herself brought "bread, meat and whatever was offered." The weak and the blind she fed with a spoon. She obviously set great store upon cleanliness, and her use of napkins and spoons at table is notable. She regarded care of the sick as a chief responsibility, even for women who had withdrawn from the world.

Another Merovingian saint, Monegundis, cured the afflicted by both poultices and prayers. She represents a type of feminine religious healer that remained common in the subsequent Middle Ages. Once, she detected poisonous worms in the stomach of a sick boy. She made a poultice of green vine leaf and spittle, applied it to his belly, and signed it with the sign of the cross. The sick child at first fell asleep—the pain had denied him sleep before; when he awoke, he passed the deadly worms. Many persons sought Monegundis' help for rashes or wounds. She prepared and applied poultices made from the leaves of herbs and trees, and these drew out the poisons.[84] Her therapies typically mixed religious practices and folk remedies.

Administration

Tacitus claims that Germanic males heard the advice of women with respect.[85] Women participated in the public assemblies of Merovingian France—so frequently, in fact, that they evoked the strictures of a Church council, meeting at Nantes in 660:

> …it is astounding that certain miserable women, acting shamelessly and impudently against divine and human laws, ceaselessly attend general assemblies and public meetings. They disturb more than they direct the affairs of the kingdom and the good of the commonwealth. For it is indecent and reprehensible even among the barbarian nations that women should discuss the issues that concern men. These women ought to be sitting among their girls of the

cloth shop and ought to be talking about their wool processing and their textile labors and about women. Instead, they usurp for themselves senatorial authority, sitting in public assembly as if in a court of law.[86]

Apparently, women were also appearing as advocates in lawsuits. At least, Regino of Prüm finds it relevant to cite the passage from the Theodosian Code that forbade women to act as advocates.[87]

If women faced disapproval in their public participation in assemblies and courts, they retained an unquestioned role in household management. For the great families, this was equivalent to the administration of estates and even realms. The unknown author of the capitulary *De villis* directs the estate stewards to obey "whatever we or the queen should command," or whatever a court official should command "in our name or that of the queen." If the stewards are convicted of negligence, they should accept whatever punishment "should please us or the queen."[88] The tract "On the Order of the Palace," written (or compiled) by Hincmar of Rheims, contains the following stipulation:

> The decor and decorum of the palace and especially the regal robes, and also the yearly gifts for the knights, apart from food, drink and horses, belong especially to the queen, and under her to the treasurer.... However, the gifts for the various legations pertain to the treasurer, unless by the king's order there is something appropriate for him to discuss with the queen.[89]

The yearly gifts to the knights invariably included fine fabrics and clothing, and the queen's authority surely reflects her role as supervisor of the shops that produced them. She also had a voice in determining the appropriate gifts (which might be of cloth) for foreign legations. Her involvement with cloth (and her supervision of the bedchamber) gave the Carolingian queen or princess responsibility too for guarding the royal treasury. In *Waltharius,* an anonymous Latin poem of the Carolingian period, the hero Waltharius plans to run off with Attila's daughter Hilgund, who is also the keeper of her father's treasury: "Waltharius thus spoke into the maiden's ear: 'Public authority made you the guard for these things.'"[90]

MODES OF PRODUCTION

The work assignments for women and men, which emerge clearly in the sources by the ninth century, are thus distinctive. Women dominated the inner economy—the household and its immediate environment, and all the productive activities carried on within or close to this space. Certain skills nurtured in the household—the arts of healing, literacy and religious learning, and even magic—also often won for women visibility in the larger society.

The work arrangements for women in the early Middle Ages do not seem to represent a "domestic mode of production." To be sure, the sources assume that most great households would have a gynaeceum. But the phrase "domestic mode of production" seems inappropriate from the perspective of the women cloth makers. Most of the women were not working with or for their natural families. They left their households of origin to take up this service and were specially trained for the task. They were specialized, full-time workers. The women in the gynaeceum at Marlenheim, according to Gregory of Tours, did not even do their own cooking.

Prospects

This chapter has reviewed women's work in the early Middle Ages, between the sixth and the ninth centuries. In this dark but pregnant age, Romans and barbarians—and thus the learned heritage of Mediterranean culture (including Christianity) and the folk traditions of the West (especially those of the northern barbarians)—met, mingled, and partially merged. From this integration came the world of the high, or central, Middle Ages.

NOTES

1. This is the conclusion of Chadwick, 1970, p. 255.
2. See the comments by Heist in the Introduction to *CS*, 1966, and my own remarks in Herlihy, 1985a, pp. 30–32.
3. Brigid had to assume "nunc coci, nunc pistoris, modo subulci, non numquam opilionis, aliquando messoris, sepe textricis officium, et alia atque alia hiis viliora." *CS*, 1966, p. 10.

4. "…sancta Brigida de frugibus suis colligendis operarios quosdam convenit, quos pro mercede paratos ad laborandum invenit." *CS*, 1966, p. 25.
5. *CS*, 1966, p. 89.
6. *CS*, 1966, p. 8.
7. Vita sancti Boecii. *CS*, 1966, p. 137: "Quadam autem die, cum ibi Lugidus audisset baltum ovis, dixit: 'In hoc loco non ero. Ubi enim fuerit ovis, ibi erit mulier, ubi furerit mulier, ibi peccatum; ubi vero peccatum, ibit erit dyabolus, et ubi dyabolus, ibi infernus erit.'"
8. *CS*, 1966, p. 136.
9. *CS*, 1966, p. 234: "Quodam die, hic sanctus puer, ludens in agro cum pastoribus ovium matertae sue…."
10. *CS*, 1966, p. 10. See also note 2.
11. *CS*, 1966, p. 20.
12. *Bethada*, 1922, II, 24.
13. *CS*, 1966, p. 239: "Veniens autem quedam juvencula, cuiusdam divitis filia, calcabat pannos pedibus suis."
14. *CS*, 1966, p. 10.
15. "Anus autem illa censum exilem vultu, leto et liberali dissimulans, ligna telis conficiendis idonea (textricis enim opus exercere consueverat) ipsa statim incidit, suis hospitibus ignem accendens tanto magis comodum quanto minus fumigantem." *CS*, 1966, p. 35.
16. "…invenibatur etiam in eadem domo ligna telaria, que formam exprimerent magnamque spectantibus ammirationem exhiberent." *CS*, 1966, p. 35.
17. *CS*, 1966, p. 366.
18. *Vitae sanctorum*, 1910, I, 95: "…quod color, quo clamidem regis consueverat intingere, illo anno deficeret. Quandam enim herbam ortensem antiqui habebant, nomine glassen, ex cuius succo tincturam pannorum suorum faciebant."
19. *Cáin Adamnáin*, 1905, p. 2.
20. *CS*, 1966, p. 9.
21. "…nam ille genera morborum et remedia curationum doctrina simul et exercitatione callebat." *CS*, 1966, p. 29.
22. *CS*, 1966, p. 84. She was a "portaria hospitalis."
23. *CS*, 1966, p. 21: "Nam et tunc et modo balneis tam Hybernientium quam Scotorum frequenter uti solent."
24. *CS*, 1966, p. 20: "…aquam sibi beata virgo fecit afferri…super corpus infirmantis respersit…."
25. *CS*, 1966, p. 21.
26. *CS*, 1966, p. 102: "…litterasque sibi competentes sub regimine sancti Finniani didiscit."
27. *CS*, 1966, p. 91: "…hospiciolo, ubi psalmos aliosque sibi necessarios perlegit libros."
28. *Vitae sanctorum*, 1910, II, 124: "Fuit quedam uirgo in campo Lyffe, Rychena nomine, que sanctum alumpnum cui nomine erat Columbanus habuit."

29. *Ibid.,* 164.
30. *Ibid.,* I, 119.
31. *ASS,* III Januarii, p. 296: "...nutricem suam, id est sororem matris...."
32. *CS,* 1966, pp. 81–83.
33. Life of St. Patrick by Joscelin of Furness. *ASS,* II Martii, p. 540.
34. *Cáin Adamnáin,* 1905, p. 5.
35. Tacitus, 1983.
36. See pages 35–37.
37. *MGH Capit.,* 1893–97.
38. Reginonis prumensis abbatis De ecclesiasticis disciplinis et religione Christiana libri duo. *PL,* CXXXII (1853), cols. 75–483.
39. Tacitus, 1983, cap. 15.
40. *Ibid.,* cap. 25.
41. Fell, 1984, p. 32. On cloth making in early England, see also Weinbaum, 1924–26, who concludes (p. 281): "Die Herstellung der Bekleidungsstücke lag gewiss in den Händen der Frauen."
42. *ASS,* I Julii, p. 279: "mulier, quae triticum super tectum suum siccandum posuerat, quasi de eminentiori loco...importune prospexit, moxque clausis lumine caruit."
43. From the Dialogues of Gregory the Great, cap. 4. *ASS O.S.B.,* 1935–40, I, "...praedicta nutrix illius ad purgandum triticum a vicinis mulieribus, sibi praestari, capisterium petiit, quod super mensam incaute derelictum, casu accidente confractum est."
44. Gregory of Tours, 1951, ix. 38 (p. 459): "...ut scilicet trahens molam his, qui in genitio erant positae, per dies singulos farinas ad victus necessarias praeparet."
45. *ASS,* I Julii, p. 63.
46. Brevium exempla. *MGH Capit.,* 1893–97, I, 252, cap. 8: "Uxor vero illius facit camisilem I et sarcilem; conficit bracem et coquit panem."
47. *St. Pierre,* 1868–71, I, 9, no. 6, dated 811–87. A farm (*mansus*) pays "de cervisa siglas xxx."
48. *MGH Capit,* 1893–97, I, 61, cap. 81.
49. *MGH Conc.* 1984, p. 126, cap. 80: "Dies quoque octo sacrosancte paschalis festivitatis omnibus Christianis feriatos esse decernimus ab omni opere rurali, fabrili, carpentario, gynaeceo, caementario, pictorio, venatorio, forensi, mercatorio, audientiali."
50. Vita auctore Luidolpho presbytero. *ASS,* I Februarii, p. 88: "cum quibus opera muliebria, victum quaeritans, operabatur. Nam lanam nere, more faeminarum atque texere solebat, unde vulgo lanarius vocabatur."
51. From the De correctione rusticorum. Martin of Braga, 1950, cap. 16.
52. Mansi, 1763–, 1902–, IX, col. 859, cited at the beginning of this chapter.
53. Specimen breviarii, cap. 24. *St. Germain,* 1844, 1886–95, II, 298. The *mansi ingenuiles* paid among other rents "de lino ad pisam seigam I...de semente lini sextarium I."

54. Jaffe, 1885, no. 956: "De mancipiis memor esto quia istud tibi iussimus, ut viros, qui forte gynicaeo utiles esse possunt, concedes illis, ita tamen, ut pro artificii ipsorum merito in agriculis compensentur ecclesiae; nec enim eiusdem aestimationis est artifex et ministerialis puer contra rusticum vel colonum;...vide ergo, ne tales des homines, qui vel continere casas vel colere possint, et illos tollas, qui inutiles sunt...."

55. Edictus Rothari, cap. 221. *Lombard Laws*, 1973, p. 95.

56. Grimoaldi sive Liutprandi memoratorium de mercedibus commacinorum, cap. 7. *Leges langobardorum*, 1868, p. 179: "Si vero furno in pensile cum cacabis fecerit...."

57. *MGH Capit.*, 1893–97, I, 317. Hlotharii capitulare olonnense. *Leges langobardorum*, 1868, p. 556, from the Liber legis langobardorum papiensis. "...ne forte, quae prius cum uno, postmodum cum pluribus locum habeat moechandi, sed eius possessio fisco redigatur et ipsa episcopali subiaceat iuditio."

58. See Chapter 1, note 74.

59. *Leges Alamannorum*, 1966, cap. 80 (p. 139): "De eo qui cum ancilla vestiaria et genitiaria concubuerit." *Laws of the Alamans*, 1977, p. 94, where *vestiaria* is translated as "chambermaid."

60. *Lex Salica*, 1949, cap. 1.

61. *MGH Capit.*, 1893–97, I, 83–91, cap. 43.

62. *PL*, CXXXII (1853), col. 285: "Si aliquis in sua domo consentit cum propriis ancillis vel geneciariis suis adulterium perpetrare...."

63. *MGH Capit.*, 1893–97, II, 42. *PL*, CXXXII (1853), col. 238: "Si autem laici capellas vestras habuerint, a ratione et ab auctoritate alienum habetur ut ipsi decimas accipiant et inde canes aut genitiariae eas accipiant."

64. "Presbyteri per paroechias suas feminis praedicent ut linteamina in altaria praeparent." *PL*, CXXXII (1853), col. 135.

65. *PL*, CXXXII (1853), col. 208.

66. *PL*, CXXXII (1853), col. 215: "Sed si quis de his habeat talem necessitatem patientem cui sit necessitas sustentatio presbyteri, habeat in vico aut in villa domum longe a presbyteri conversatione, et ibi eis subministret quae necessaria sunt."

67. Vita s. Leobini episcopi carnotensis. *ASS O.S.B.*, 1935–40, I, 127: "Quaedam Deo devota ex monasterio puellarum cum tunicam Leobini causa consuendi accipisset, et de novo filo resarciens refecisset, vetus filum ex ea accipiens ad suam zonam ex fide alligavit."

68. Vita auctore S. Venantio Fortunato. *ASS*, III Augusti, p. 69: "...more vestiebatur barbaro...."

69. Tacitus, 1983, cap. 8.

70. *PL*, CXXXII (1853), col. 285: "Quarendum etiam si mulieres in lanificiis suis vel in ordiendis telis aliquid dicant aut observent nisi, ut supra dictum est, omnia in nomine domini."

71. Mansi, 1763–, 1902–, col. 859: "Non licet in collectione herbarum quae medicinales sunt, aliquas observationes aut incantationes attendere nisi tantam cum symbolo divino, aut oratione dominica, aut tantum, Deus creator omnium, et dominus honoretur."
72. *PL*, CXXXII (1853), col. 286.
73. *PL*, CXXXII (1853), col. 352.
74. *PL*, CXXXII (1853), col. 301.
75. *PL*, CXXXII (1853), col. 250.
76. De s. Radegunde regina...auctore S. Venantio Fortunato. *ASS*, III Augusti, p. 68: "Quae puella inter alia opera, quae sexui ejus congruebat, litteris est erudita...."
77. *ASS*, III Augusti, p. 78.
78. *ASS*, III Augusti, p. 74: "Acta altera...auctore Baudonivia moniali coaeva et familiari Sanctae discipula."
79. *ASS*, I Januarii, p. 504: "Nutritur a progenitoribus suis haec cum magno studio totius diligentiae, tradita religioni Christianae, discens etiam litteras in diebus tenerae infantiae...laudes discit cantare filio virginis. Fit etiam per divinam clementiam capax memoriae audiendo et legendo, exercens se etiam in magisterio doctrinae...plena esse eloquentiae sed plus multo sapientiae."
80. *ASS*, III Martii, p. 384.
81. *ASS*, III Septembris, p. 109: "ad nutriendum lacte spirituali."
82. Tacitus, 1983, cap. 7 (p. 6): "...ad matres, ad coniuges uulnera ferunt; nec illae numerare aut exigere plagas pavent, cibosque et hortamina pugnantibus gestant."
83. Her services at the hospital are described in considerable length by Venantius Fortunatus, II, cap. 13. *ASS*, III Augusti, p. 70.
84. The story of the boy sickened with poisonous worms is from the Liber vitae patrum. Gregory of Tours, 1884–1969, II, 289. For her other cures, see the Liber in gloria confessorum. *Ibid.*, 313.
85. See note 61.
86. *PL*, CXXXII (1853), col. 317.
87. *CT*, 1952, 2.12.5 (p. 48), dated September 28, 393. *PL*, CXXXII (1853), col. 318.
88. *MGH Capit.*, 1893–97, II, 83–91, cap. 16. See also cap. 58, and the further comments in Herlihy, 1962.
89. Hincmar, 1980, cap. 5 (p. 72): "De honestate vero palatii seu specialiter ornamento regali nec non et de donis annuis militum, absque cibo et potu vel equis, ad reginam praecipue et sub ipsa ad camerarium pertinebat....De donis vero diversarum legationum ad camerarium aspiciebat, nisi forte iubetur rege tale aliquid esset, quod reginae ad tractandum cum ipso congrueret."
90. "Waltharius tandem sic virginis iniquit in aurem / Publica custodem rebus te nempe potestas fecerat." Goodman, 1985, p. 334.

CHAPTER 3

Countryside, Court, and Convent

Mon cuer, madame, si m'aprent
Que je ne face autre mestier
Le jour fors lire mon saultrier
Et fair euvre d'or ou de soie,
Oÿr de Thebes ou de Troye.
Et en ma harpe lays noter,
Et aux eschez autrui mater...

My heart, Madame, teaches me
That I should not do any other daily task
But read my psalter,
Make cloth of gold or of silk,
Hear tales of Thebes and of Troy,
Play lays upon my harp,
And mate others at chess...

—Fresne's declaration,
Galéran de Bretagne (ca. 1225)

The central Middle Ages, which we date here from roughly the year 900 to 1350, forms the high plateau of medieval social and cultural achievement. The population grew substantially; frontiers expanded; trade, moribund since ancient times, quickened; long-withered towns expanded in size and vitality. The European economy—and European civilization—acquired a different face. We enter a new and complicated world, the direct parent to our own.

Our task in this and in the following three chapters is to examine how in the central Middle Ages the new social and cultural environment altered the ancient work assignments for women and for men. For women, the epoch was one of both stability and change. They continued to fulfill—in countryside, court, and convent; in town employments and in the liberal professions—many of the traditional jobs they had performed since time immemorial. But in this same period, in several activities once regarded as women's exclusive domain, men appear as participants and partners. The employment of males in these tasks did not mean the exclusion of women—at least, not yet— but the ancient divisions of labor between the different sexes were shifting.

COUNTRYSIDE

Even as trade intensified and towns grew, most women continued to live and labor in rural surroundings.[1] The work of women in the countryside altered little between the early and the central Middle Ages. Women are chiefly visible in the "inner economy," close to the hearth. They raised vegetables and herbs, took care of the farm animals, sold their produce at market, cooked, and brewed.

Field Work

The rural economy did not allow strict divisions between the labors of women and of men. Heavy seasonal work might require the assistance of all available hands, and crises, both personal and social, might require that women perform work normally done by men. Thus, although women did not usually drive the plow or take in the harvest, they often were enlisted in the heavy work of harvesting. In Eadmer's life of St. Anselm of Canterbury, written in the early twelfth century, the saint himself, as a child growing up in Aosta in the Italian Alps, has a dream. In it he sees numerous women laboring in the fields, "the slaves of the king, taking in the harvest." But they gather the harvest "very carelessly and listlessly."[2] The boy journeys over the mountain to the king's palace, reports the poor performance, and is rewarded for his message. The king's palace turns out to be the heavenly court, but the lesson of the dream goes unexplained. Why did the child see only women harvesting the fields? Is Eadmer saying that these were not the right workers for the task, even as the leaders of the Church then were failing in their functions? Perhaps the Church needed a reform, a change of workers, which Anselm, in later life, would lead.

Again in the twelfth century, a noble woman of Pomerania on the Baltic coast rejected the preaching of the Christian missionaries in her land; she cleaved to heathenism. When the missionaries admonished their converts not to work on Sunday, she personally led her harvesters out to the fields to set an example. She rolled up her sleeves, belted up her dress, and gripped the sickle. But as she stooped over to mow the wheat, she became rigid, "like a marble statue." She could neither stand erect nor release the sickle.[3] She thus imparted a lesson to her workers, though not the one she intended. The tale points in two directions. Presumably, had she not been provoked, she would not have led the reapers. On the other hand, she knew how to handle a sickle and how to harvest the wheat. Women had to be prepared for field work, if only because emergencies (like threatened rain or strange beliefs) frequently interrupted the essential labors.

If the demanding work of plowing and harvesting was usually left to the males, women certainly participated as gleaners, picking up the stalks and kernels that the male harvesters left behind. On August 25, 964, a young French girl named Rotgildis, walking in the tracks of the reapers, gathered in the gleanings. However, upon inspecting them, she found that they were drenched in blood, for the reapers were working on a day dedicated to a saint.[4]

Women also weeded and cleaned the fields. As a little girl, St. Veronica, who came from a village near Milan, "often in the company of many women gave herself to cleaning the fields; but she was marvelously devoted to meditation; she fled her companions and preferred to labor alone."[5]

Family circumstances could also alter the conventional work assignments. The life of St. Alpaix illustrates the heavy burdens that a young peasant girl might be called upon to carry. Alpaix was born about 1155 at Cudot in the diocese of Sens, not far from Paris. She is one of the very few medieval saints (let alone women) of peasant stock—"reared," as says a contemporary chronicler, "and educated for the countryside and accustomed to rural labor."[6] She died in 1211, but was not canonized until 1878. She spent the last thirty years of her life as an invalid and a visionary;

even before her death, a contemporary Cistercian monk recorded her visions and also left an account of her childhood years.

Her father, named Bernard, was a poor man who earned his bread by the sweat of his brow. With the help of two oxen, he plowed his little field. As Alpaix was his firstborn, she was called upon to help from the tender age of twelve. Walking ahead of her father, she wielded the goad, pricking the oxen into greater effort.[7] She also carried on her shoulders baskets of manure and of sheep dung to field and garden. Because her arms could not sustain a heavy weight, she was harnessed to a sledge by a rope that passed over her arms and shoulders. Thus she dragged manure to the fields, "and equaled as best she could the efforts of her father."[8] Her childhood was labor.

Her brothers, because they were younger, guarded her father's cows and sheep in the pastures. On Sundays and festival days, when other girls foolishly gave themselves over to dancing and silly games, she led the cattle and sheep to pasture.[9]

Alpaix's hard and unrelieved labors eventually broke her slight frame. Sores erupted on her flesh, from the soles of her feet to her scalp. The stench they emitted was so great that not even the members of her family could tolerate her. They consigned her to an isolated hut and threw her black bread from a distance, "as if to a dog." Her brothers urged her mother to feed her no longer, to let her starve, as she was loathsome and an expense. But Alpaix besieged the Virgin with her prayers, and Mary finally showed mercy. Mary cured her ulcers and changed her stench into fragrance.

Animals

The care of animals was the special responsibility of peasant girls and women, as records from all over Europe amply illustrate. Where sheep and cows were many, as in Flanders, so were shepherdesses and milkmaids. In the twelfth century, the young Christina of St. Trond was forced by her two elder sisters to guard "the sheep going to pasture."[10] St. Juliane (1193–1258), born near Liège in Flanders, was the younger of two daughters (her sister was named Agnes). Both parents died when Juliane was only five. The two orphan girls were sent to a convent to be reared, and both were entrusted to an uncloistered religious woman named Sapientia. While still a child, Juliane asked for and was given the task of milking the convent's cows. "Juliane did this work so much the more diligently, the more she realized how many persons would use the milk drawn by her hands."[11] She was not an expert milker, as "many times" the animals kicked her and sent her sprawling on the earth, but a cry or a whimper never passed her lips. Once, her sister found her prostrate on the ground; Agnes reprimanded Juliane, warning her that she was likely to die in a dung heap. "But when [Juliane] heard her sister's voice, she was more greatly saddened by the spilling of the milk than by the injury of her own body."

In Tuscany in Italy, near the castle town of Santa Croce, Oringa (d. 1310) also guarded the cattle when she was a little girl. "It is said that when she was pasturing the cattle, she ordered them to take only wild grasses and to abstain from cultivated crops and the like; the animals obeyed...."[12]

An exemplum apparently first told by Jacques de Vitry and destined for a long afterlife in French literature illuminates the special relationship of women with animals.[13] An old woman carries her milk to market in an earthen jar; she daydreams on the way. With the three small coins from the sale of her milk, she will buy a chicken and raise it into a hen. From its eggs she will acquire many chickens, and from the profits of their sale

Women herding cows and a bull. *(Queen Mary's Psalter, Sir George Warner, ed. London: British Museum, 1912. British Museum, Royal MS 2 B.VII, plate 130)*

she will buy a pig. Once fattened and sold, the pig will earn her money to buy a colt, which will in time grow into a horse. In her musings she thinks of riding the horse to pasture. She cries "io! io!," and moves her feet to spur it forward. But the motion of her feet trips her, her milk spills upon the ground, "and as she had been poor before, so she became poorer now."

In the version of the same tale told by Etienne de Bourbon, the old lady becomes a young maid, who receives from her mistress "Sunday milk" as a gift. She carries it to market in a jar on her head. With the expected money she dreams of purchasing in turn a hen, pigs, sheep, and cows; her wealth will win for her a noble husband. She will ride in splendor to join him, but she too spurs the dream horse, trips, and spills her milk. These homely examples, while warning against counting chickens before they are hatched, show the array of animals that women raised. They show too that even poor rural women dreamed and hoped that the care of their animals could win for them a better life.

Brewing and Gardening

The brewing of ale also remained the particular task of women. In thirteenth-century England, the *Fleta,* a collection of legal texts, includes a set of instructions given to the steward of a manor. The instructions invite comparison with those given to Carolingian manorial stewards in the capitulary *De villis.*[14] The specialized women workers mentioned in the *Fleta* are dairy maids and alewives.[15] The English steward, unlike his Carolingian counterpart, seems to have had no responsibility for cloth making, and the female serfs are not required to work in a gynaeceum. The production of cloth, or at least of quality woolens, has left the English countryside.

Women were also losing their prominence in the milling of grain, chiefly for technological reasons. In 1073 on an estate near Ghent in Flanders, a serving girl named Siborch is still turning her flour mill by hand.[16] (She grinds on the feast of St. Amalberg, and, as is usual in such exempla, cannot let go of the handle.) But large water-powered and animal-powered grain mills were replacing hand grinding—and supplanting women in this important function. In England, the first water mill is mentioned in 762, and by the tenth century there were over 5,000 such mills.[17] Women, to be sure, retained some association with milling throughout the Middle Ages. There are five female millers (but fifty males) in the tax roll of Paris in 1292.

COURT

The central Middle Ages witnesses the great efflorescence of courtly culture and of the rich literary tradition associated with it. That tradition, initially expressed in French, makes manifest the arts and attainments noble ladies were expected to cultivate and display. Revealing among the accounts are those that describe the education of a noble girl.

Instruction

One such work is the story of Frêne, or Fresne in Old French spelling. Marie de France first told Fresne's tale in the twelfth century in one of her lays, but her version is short and spare.[18] A poet of the thirteenth century, perhaps Jean Renart, retold the story in the *Galéran de Bretagne,* and it is this longer version we examine here.[19]

Fresne, one of twin daughters, is abandoned by her mother, who fears that people will believe that the two girls were fathered by two different men. She wraps the baby in a rich cloth from Constantinople so that whoever takes the child will thereby recognize her noble origins, and she delivers the baby to a servant girl. The girl in turn places the baby in an ash tree, where the doorkeeper of a monastery finds her. He presents her to the abbess, who names the girl after the ash tree (*frêne*). She rears the baby together with her own nephew, Galéran, son of the count of Brittany. The skills both children are taught clearly show the sexual division of the arts in medieval, chivalric France.

Galéran is taught how to hunt with dogs, draw the bow, make arrows, and play at chess. He is being groomed in the martial arts. Fresne, on the other hand, learns (as Galéran does not) how to read; every day she reads the psalter. In life as in legend, noble women learned to read. In the middle of the eleventh century, Agnes, wife of Count Frederick of Goseck in Saxony, "after the manner of the ancients was beautifully instructed at Quidelinburg in letters and in diverse arts."[20] The abbey of Fontevrault in northern France contains funeral effigies of Plantagenet rulers, representatives of Europe's most powerful dynasty. The males, including King Henry II Plantagenet, are depicted sleeping, taking the rest of the warrior. Henry's wife, Eleanor of Aquitaine, is presented awake, reading a book. What she does in death, she and other noble women surely did in life.

Embroidery

Fresne also learns how to play the harp and sing to its music. She receives instruction on how to mate opponents at the noble game of chess. She is not, in other words, taught to be retiring or deferential to men but to interact, even aggressively, with them in chess and in social life. Her story certainly illustrates her independence and resourcefulness.

Finally, she learns how to make fabric, apparently how to weave as well as to sew and embroider. And as befits a heroine, she is unsurpassed in all the textile arts:

> Fresne had learned to work [cloth]:
> There is no [woman] worker from here to Apulia
> Who can weave and sew like she;

The tombs of the Plantagents at Fontrevault Abbey, showing Eleanor of Aquitaine reading a book. (*Giraudon/Art Resource*)

She knows how to make banners,
Lace and fabrics and purses,
and cloths worked from silk and gold
that are well worth a treasure.[21]

The two growing children fall in love, but Galéran is called
back to his high office, and the abbess warns Fresne that she, as
a girl of unknown birth, cannot aspire to a noble marriage.
Fresne determines to leave the convent. The abbess warns her
that "for bread you will have to card another's wool and at
home wash [another's] knit." Fresne, in the passage quoted at
the beginning of this chapter, haughtily replies that, besides
reading, playing music, and singing, she produces only quality
cloth. She departs, goes to Rouen, and persuades a widowed
bourgeoise, with a daughter named Rose, to take her in. She immediately turns the widow's house into a shop producing luxury
cloth. She teaches Rose how to make fabric of silk and gold, out
of which she "earns a goodly treasure," worth more than the
family's landed possessions. The household gains "great profit
from the drapes that she works and that she sells." Fresne labors
all day, enriching her hosts; but at appropriate times, in the
morning and after vespers, she plays on her harp and sings.

Meanwhile, her childhood sweetheart Galéran becomes engaged to marry her twin sister, whom Marie de France calls
Coudre, a name associated with the verb "to sew." She even puns
by having a character assert, "There is pleasure and profit in
Coudrier"; does this mean the girl, the art, or both? Fresne comes
to the wedding, but her mother recognizes her when she displays
the cloth in which she was wrapped as a baby. Women both make
cloth and communicate by it. The lovers are reunited; the twin sister is dismissed; and all, except for Coudre, are happy in the out-
come. Fresne's notable success is founded upon her skills, and
chief among them is her excellence as an *ouvrière* of cloth.

The French chivalric romances contain many references to
women and work in cloth. The references are, to be sure,
vague. Sewing and embroidery are emphasized, but it is almost
always hard to tell if women also wove the fabric. Fresne certainly did, in her daily labors at Rouen. But heroines and
queens are always distinguished by excellence in needlework.

Most noble girls learned their skills in the *chambre des dames*
(women's chamber), another manifestation of the ancient gyn-

aeceum. (Fresne was taught in a convent, but there too the nuns doubtless gathered together to work on their fabrics.) The "women's chamber" was not only a place of sewing but a school, in which older women, mothers or *maistres,* instructed young girls. The womanly skills, reading and music as well as sewing, were passed on in the feminine line. Sometimes the girl's instructor was her maternal aunt or grandmother.

For example, in her eleventh-century life, Matilda (d. 972), the future wife of Henry Fowler, king of Germany, was sent to her grandmother, an abbess, to be educated. There the future queen learned the Book of Psalms and other "sacred readings" and also "works of the hands," surely sewing and embroidery.[22] Empress Kunigunde, wife of Henry II, educated her sister's daughter Jutta, whom she "trained from her earliest years in every discipline as well as a knowledge of secular letters." This last example shows us again a feminine parallel to the avunculate relationship.

Chansons de Toile

A distinctive genre of Old French literature, known as the *chansons de toile* (cloth songs), offers tantalizing glimpses into the women's chamber, its functions and its culture. In the epic poem *Guillaume de Dole,* written by Jean Renart about 1228, Emperor Conrad of Germany hears his minstrel sing the praises of the blonde and beautiful Liënor, sister of the knight William of Dole. Although the emperor has not seen her, the minstrel's ravishing description wins his heart, and he falls madly in love with the girl. He sends a messenger to invite her to his court. The messenger arrives at the castle of Dole, and William takes him to the women's chamber, where his mother and sister are working. William boasts of their skills: "You see," he says, "what a marvelous worker is Madame; she knows all the arts, and her daughter likewise."

The women are making vestments for poor churches, working for charity, as is proper for noble ladies. William then asks his mother to sing, but she at first demurs: "Beautiful son, that was done in olden times (*en arriers*), when ladies and queens were accustomed to make their fabrics and to sing songs of history." But William persists, and she sings a *chanson de toile,* in fact the earliest surviving example of the genre. The common theme of these charming songs is love, but their usual setting includes women working at fabric. The songs also commonly show two generations of women, with the old instructing the young. In the passage below, the mother warns her daughter Aude that her love for Doon will only bring sorrow:

> Daughter and mother work at their finery.
> With golden thread they make golden crosses.
> The mother, of courteous heart, speaks to her child:
>   (How great is the love that Aude bears for Doon!)
> "Learn, my child, to sew and to spin,
> and to raise in finery crosses of gold.
> The love of Doon you had better forget."
>   (How great is the love that Aude bears for Doon!)[23]

Liënor, William's sister, also sings a *chanson de toile* with similar theme and scene; in this case, however, the girl depicted is embroidering cloth imported from England. Here is the song's first stanza; we should note the allusion to Aye's stern teacher:

> Aye the Fair sits at the feet of her stern mistress;
> in her lap she holds cloth that England has sent,
> with thread she traces many lovely designs.
> Alas, my love from another land,
> you hold, bind and surprise my heart.[24]

It is hard to know how well, if at all, these songs represent reality, or even whether they were ever truly sung by working women. But Alexander Neckam does describe a woman singing for the entertainment of a weaver.[25] And fine needlework in silk and gold thread was regarded as a noble art, suitable for noble women.

Government

Literacy was an indispensable attainment for noble women in chivalric Europe. They would often be called upon to advise their husbands, stand in for them during their frequent absences, and serve as regents when they were absent from home or departed from life. In Aragon in 1056, in the marriage donation (*sponsalitium*) made to Countess Adalmodis, her husband specifically mentions the *mobile,* or movables, "which by agreement are to be given to the châtelains each year."[26] Like the Carolingian courtiers who received their yearly gifts from the queen, these Spanish guardians of castles would be beholden to a woman for these yearly largesses. In Aragonese charters of investiture, it is also occasionally evident that a male principal is absent, and his wife must promise that her husband will agree to the transaction "thirty days after Alamannus her husband comes."[27]

Inheritance also could confer high office and administrative duties upon noble women, of which innumerable examples can be cited. In Léon-Castille, Queen Urraca (1109–1126) was a vigorous ruler; her recent biographer calls her "the indomitable queen."[28] Between 1227 and 1277, two women ruled in succession as countesses of Flanders and Hainaut: Jeanne of Constantinople (d. 1244) and her sister Margaret (d. 1279). We shall meet them again because of the role they played in founding houses for religious women (beguines) in their territories. Inheritance customs were especially liberal toward women in frontier regions, such as the crusading states of Palestine, the Morea in Greece, or the Iberian states, where warfare took a high toll of noble men. In contrast, republican governments, such as the city-states of Italy or of Flanders, where offices were filled by election or by lottery, virtually excluded women from public life.

Noble Women, Common Women

The prominence of women within the noble class in large part reflects the fact that high office was often interchangeable between the sexes. War was the chief business of the male, and the noble man had to be ready. The noble woman had also to be ready—to assume all his domestic functions, as administrator, supervisor, rent collector, judge, and sometimes even defender of the family castle. During the frequent and sometimes permanent absences of the male chiefs, and perhaps even when they were present, women kept the home fires fueled and burning.

The numerous skills, occasional power, and constant visibility of noble women had this further significance: The valued attributes of the noble woman had great influence on the rich tradition of chivalric literature, and that literature commanded an audience far beyond noble circles. The surveys of the Paris population (1292–1313) show a sprinkling of chivalric names even among the bourgeoisie: Guillaume Tristan, Oudart Percival.[29] Bietrix, one of the most common of Parisian women's names, probably evokes the memory of Charlemagne's mother in the epic stories. About 1242 in Italy, in the countryside of the small town of Pistoia, even peasant women bore courtly names, such as Finamore (Elegant Love) or Diadamore (Goddess of Love).[30] Visible and accomplished noble women, in fact and in fiction, surely encouraged other medieval women to think that they could be accomplished too.

CONVENT

Since ancient times, the Church had taught that a life of virginity represented the highest calling for a woman. But the history of women's religious communities in the Middle Ages is surprisingly troubled. As best we can tell, women's religious houses flourished in the early period. Queens and princesses, turned abbesses, presided over seemingly prosperous communities. Radegundis, considered in the previous chapter, became an abbess but kept an eye on the outer world and through letters instructed kings in their moral duties.[31]

The central Middle Ages presents a different picture. An index of the prominence of women in the Church is the number of female saints in relation to that of male saints. The index sinks to its lowest level in the years 1000 to 1150, when there are twelve male saints for every female saint (the ratio for the entire Middle Ages is 5.3 holy men per holy woman).[32] As the religious life was the chief avenue to recognized sainthood, this certainly indicates low visibility, and probably points to deeper problems, in feminine religious houses.

The sources leave the strong impression that in the central Middle Ages, women's convents were both few and poor. Hugh, bishop of Grenoble in France, who died in 1132, had investigated his diocese and found "that few were the monasteries of religious women."[33] St. Dominic was moved to found the first convent of Dominican nuns at Pouille in southern France when he found that the Albigensian heretics were receiving the daughters of poor nobles in schools, where they instructed them not only in literacy, but also in error.

Normandy

A unique source illustrates the state of women's religious houses in one important province—Normandy in northern France. Between 1248 and 1269, Eudes Rigaud, archbishop of Rouen, visited the religious houses of his archdiocese and counted the monks, canons regular, and nuns that he found in them.[34] The archdiocese included, besides Rouen, the suffragan sees of Séez, Avranches, Coutances, Bayeux, Lisieux, and Evreux. A rough addition of their numbers (not including canons and nuns attached to hospitals or the secular clergy) yields totals of 2,255 male religious and only 531 female—better than four men for every woman.[35] To be sure, the priories of Marmoutier, St.-Benoît-sur-Loire and Fécampin, the newer orders of Cistercians and Premonstratensians, and the Dominican and Franciscan friars were exempt from episcopal visitations, and Eudes gives no numbers for these communities. Their figures, if they could be included, would surely tilt the sex ratio among religious persons even further in favor of males. While several of the exempt religious orders—notably the Cistercian and Premonstratensian abbeys and the mendicant convents—included female houses, in their ranks too men far outnumbered women.[36] At the order's height in the early fourteenth century, the Premonstratensians, for example, included over 1,300 monasteries of men, but only 400 of women.[37]

The sixteen Norman convents for women, with an average size of slightly more than 33 nuns, were twice as large as the male houses (mean size, 16.5 persons). Many canons regular and some monks were performing pastoral work in very small and scattered priories or "obediences"—a fact which makes it difficult to count their true number. Eudes was adamant in insisting that no male religious live alone, but some male priories had only two, three, or four members. Religious women, excluded from pastoral services, never lived in communities smaller than ten nuns, and the largest of them, La-Trinité-de-Caen, had as many as eighty. Still, the number of male religious establishments, almost 140, was nearly nine times the count of those serving women.

Was the calling to the religious life so much more compelling for Norman men than for Norman women? The more likely explanation for this skewed sex ratio is that the Norman feminine houses were too few and too poor to accommodate all the women who sought to enter. Bishop Eudes heard many complaints about poverty in the convents he visited and several times forbade them to admit more postulants. He had, for example, strictly enjoined the nuns of St.-Aubin not to give the veil to anyone without his special mandate, since they were so poor. They disobeyed and admitted a daughter of a knight named Sir Robert Malvoisin. They explained that "urgent necessity and poverty had so compelled them," as Robert promised them an annual rent of 100 sous if they took his daughter. Bishop Eudes still demanded that the girl be returned to her father.[38] The impression is inescapable that poverty plagued women's religious houses throughout Europe. In 1215 the Fourth Lateran Council stated that women's houses in particular "admit as sisters hardly any woman without [requiring] payment"; they tried to excuse this vice by claims of poverty.[39]

Why were the Norman—and presumably the medieval—religious houses for women generally impoverished by the thirteenth century? There seem to be two chief reasons for this. Women in the earlier Middle Ages had inherited equally with their brothers; and queens, princesses, and rich women were the chief beneficiaries of feminine convents, which they themselves often founded or joined. In the thirteenth century, women, at least in elite society, were no longer inheriting equally with their brothers. The aristocratic family was now favoring male offspring and reserving its resources primarily for the support of its sons, often only the eldest son.

The new organization of elite kindreds is called the patrilineage. Under the new rules of inheritance, daughters received only the dowry they needed to attract a husband or the smaller dowry required to enter a convent. Unless she was the sole surviving offspring, a daughter would have no further claim on the property of her parents. She was, by test of inheritance, not a full-fledged member of her lineage of origin. After marriage, she was also not a full-fledged member of her husband's lineage (though her sons would be after her). She could not marshal substantial wealth either from her family of origin or from her family of marriage. She was not therefore in a position, as were her brothers (especially the eldest brother) to support with substantial donations the religious houses she favored.

Not likely to attract big donations, the feminine houses seem also to have had much more difficulty supporting themselves by their own labors than did their male counterparts. Bishop Eudes consistently prohibited communities of religious women from making silk purses, lace and lace collars, or other silk accessories; they were allowed to sew only liturgical cloths, which presumably they did not sell. Thus, on May 27, 1261, Eudes forbade the nuns of St.-Amand-de-Rouen "to make alms-bags, frill-collars, needle cases, and such things; nor should they do any work in silk except to make things pertaining to the Divine Service."[40] On January 22, 1262, he ordered the nuns of St-Saëns not "to work anything in silk unless it be such things as pertain to the church."[41] On September 17, 1267, in another visit to the nuns of St.-Amand-de-Rouen, he again admonished them: "we also forbade any work in silk to be done there, unless it was exclusively intended for the divine cult."[42]

The record of Eudes' visitations to the convents of Normandy contains one brief but illuminating reference to nuns involved in commercial activities. The ten "weak and aged sisters" serving at the Hôtel-Dieu at Caen "had occasionally sold bonnets or firewood and such things in order to procure certain articles which they needed."[43] The bishop ordered that there be given to the nuns "a sufficient supply of things needful to them so that they should not have to buy or sell anything at all in the town." He clearly believed that commercial activity of any sort was incompatible with the religious life for women.

Religious women could not, like their male counterparts, engage in plow agriculture. Nuns in the countryside did tend vines, and feminine houses did engage in dairy farming and the raising of animals.[44] In 1258, for example, the house at Villarceaux owned 8 cows, 4 calves, 6 horses, and 3 colts.[45] In 1265, its reported animals were 19 cows, 398 swine, 6 horses, 5 roosters, and 60 sheep.[46] Villarceaux, like other convents, characteristically lacked plow oxen.

Norman nuns did staff hospitals, maintaining the traditional association of women with the cure of bodies. Bishop Eudes visited hospitals (Hôtels-Dieu) at Bourgny, Caens, Bellencombre, Gournay, Les-Andelys, Mont-aux-Malades, Neufchâtel, Nogent, Pontoise, and Rouen. Characteristically, a rector and a community of canons resided at the hospital, and there was also present a larger community of nuns. (Hospitals were the only communities in Normandy with professed religious of both sexes.) Thus, at the Hôtel-Dieu at Rouen, Eudes found a prior, ten canons in residence, six other canons staying in outside obediences, and twenty sisters. But nursing nuns formed only a small minority of all religious women.

It is striking to observe the bishop's opposition to any teaching of lay students on the part of the sisters. He repeatedly ordered the convents of Normandy to dismiss the few young lay girls he found within them. In February 1267, he reported that there were "in the custody [of the nuns of Bondeville] some young girls, daughters of burghers of Rouen, which displeased us."[47] At the nuns' priory of Villarceaux, "there were also several secular girls under the custody, so to say, of certain nuns and this displeased us exceedingly."[48] In September 1269, he found some secular girls with the nuns of St.-Saëns; "we ordered them removed and sent back to their relatives...."[49]. The purity of the Norman nuns had to be vigorously guarded, even at the cost of poverty.

Why was Eudes so opposed to the nuns' selling the products of their labor or teaching children? A principal factor was surely the heritage of the Gregorian reform of the western Church, named for its greatest leader, Pope Gregory VII (1073–1085). The chief goal of the reform was clerical celibacy. The reformers, and the Church they reorganized, sought to distance the male clergy from women; sexuality was to be feared. They were adamant too that religious women should reduce their contacts with the outer world to an absolute minimum. The strict cloister the reformers imposed obstructed nuns in their economic activities, notably the making and selling of cloth. They were discouraged from attending public markets. Even the teaching of children brought them into dangerous contact with laypeople and with secular life. This exaggerated fear of sexual temptation had unfortunate consequences for the feminine religious houses. It deprived them of desperately needed means of support. And it deprived the medieval Church of the invaluable services that nuns might have performed in the teaching of children. No feminine religious order of the medieval period took teaching as its primary mission; this would have to await a later age.

With small endowments and little income from crafts, commerce, or agriculture (and none from education), feminine religious houses present a bleak picture. In Italy, Veronica of Binasco, born in the countryside, never learned to read. She journeyed to the nearby city of Milan and entered a convent; she helped support it by begging in the streets.[50] While this example occurred later in the Middle Ages—Veronica was born in 1445—from the twelfth century on, deprivation hovered like a dark cloud over the lives and communities of many religious women.

The Beguines

Even as the Church was failing to found sufficient numbers of religious houses for women, the incentives for women to enter the religious life seem to have mounted. The reasons for this are hard to identify and even harder to weigh. Spiritual motives were certainly fundamental. This was an age of great religious fervor, manifested in movements for Church reform, in the crusades, and in the founding of new religious orders. Women actively participated in, and at times were the leaders of this spiritual revival. But there were social reasons too that help explain why women in seemingly increasing numbers were seeking entry into convents. The population was expanding, and younger persons of both sexes encountered difficulties in finding stable places in adult society. The new ideals of chivalry exonerated women from fighting and in large part freed them from the risks of warfare; wars and crusades continued to take a heavy toll of men. For this and perhaps other reasons, women were surviving better and probably outliving men.[51] Finally, the age of first marriage for males was apparently advancing, and some males were choosing to remain permanent bachelors. Some women would now have no chance at all to find a suitable husband. Deprived of an opportunity for marriage (or for some, remarriage), they would encounter difficulties too in gaining admission into an approved religious house. Many of these solitary women drifted to the growing cities.

From about 1180, numbers of unattached women—single or widowed—become visible in the towns of Rhineland, Germany, and of the Low Countries. These women are called *beguines* (their male counterparts, always much fewer in numbers, are *beghards*).[52] The name apparently derives from Albigensian, and the association of the name with a principal heresy shows the suspicion with which the Church regarded these unmarried, uncloistered women. By the thirteenth century, they supposedly were counted in the thousands in the German and Flemish towns.[53] These women had counterparts under different names in many European regions. Eudes Rigaud in 1269 knows them as "daughters of God."[54] In Italy, where they appear beginning in the early thirteenth century, they are called *umiliate*, (humble women) or, in Tuscany, *pinzochere*.

The appearance of these women drifters has raised a classic problem in medieval social history, the *Frauenfrage*; the word means the "question of women" or, more nearly, of unattached women, unmarried and uncloistered. They took no solemn vows and followed no approved rule. They lived at home or in communities, wore no regular habit, and mingled freely with the lay world. Their presence created a major social problem for both Church and society. In medieval thought, the social world, like the physical world, was supposed to be ordered, with every object tranquilly resting in its assigned place. The idea of women without a place—without a family or a convent to anchor them in society—was extremely disturbing.

The Church suspected their morals and their orthodoxy and, from 1240, directed repeated condemnations against them. The Ecumenical Council of Vienne (1311–1312) expressed the culminating disapproval, condemning eight of their doctrinal errors. In a corresponding bull, Pope Clement V ordered that their communities be suppressed and that they themselves be regarded as heretics. The Council of Vienne attributed a number of strange errors to them, including this one: "To kiss a woman, since it is not a natural inclination, is a mortal sin; intercourse, however, since it is a natural inclination, is not a sin, especially when one is tempted to do so."[55]

The male-dominated hierarchy, with its disciplined organization and learned theology, clearly had difficulty coming to terms with this large but disorganized movement of irregular religious women. The Church's male theologians could not even determine what exactly these women really believed or how they really behaved in their spontaneously formed communities.

Clement's repressive policy proved unenforceable, and his successor, John XXII, revoked the measure in 1320. He asked only that the bishops of the Low Countries investigate how the beguines were behaving within their separate dioceses. Governments too had to worry about these female floaters. Between 1227 and 1277, the two women countesses of Flanders and Hainaut, Jeanne and Margaret (previously mentioned), established and endowed several beguine convents, or beguinages, within their territories. A memoir concerning (and an apology for) the beguines of Ghent, prepared for the bishop of Tournai in 1328, explains why these communities were founded:

> Those ladies of happy memory, Jeanne and her sister Margaret, in turn the countesses of Flanders and Hainaut, saw that the said land abounded in many women for whom for reason of their own condition and that of their friends [fiancés?], appropriate marriages were not possible.... Because of their number and the poverty of their parents they cannot easily obtain [marriages]. Honest girls and impoverished noble women thus must beg.[56]

The countesses "then founded, in various places of Flanders, certain spacious quarters, which are called Beguinages, in which the said women, daughters or girls, may be received."[57]

The saintly Louis IX of France was one of the most generous supporters of these irregular religious women. In 1264 he endowed a beguinage at Paris near the Porte de Barbeel.[58] It included 400 girls, most of them poor and many of them noble, whom Louis supported out of charity. He gave these beguines of Paris a further 100 pounds in his testament, to build larger quarters, and also bequeathed 100 pounds to beguines elsewhere in France. "He had houses of beguines set up in many of the towns, bourgs and castles of his kingdom."[59]

One of the best documented of the medieval beguinages is that of St. Elizabeth of Ghent. In 1235, Countess Jeanne donated a rent of 15 pounds in order to buy a hospital "for the use of poor religious women in Ghent."[60] In 1236, to build the hospital "for the use of the begging beguines," she donated an additional rent of 300 pounds per year.[61]

In 1328, the above-cited memoir in favor of the beguines of Ghent includes a doubtless idealized but nonetheless revealing description of how these women lived.[62] A *magna magistra* (chief mistress) supervises the entire community and sees to it that the rules are followed.[63] The girls and women wear the same clothing, but the memoir says nothing of vows. The "court" of the beguinage contains a central church, and is further divided into "many houses for the residence of the women, separated one from the others by an intervening ditch or hedges."[64] Each separate cottage has its own garden. In the cottages the girls and women live in community. They are poor, owning only their clothing and their beds. However, they are not a burden to anyone. "But by working with their hands, in washing wool and cleaning the cloths sent to them from the town, they daily earn enough so that, consuming modest fare, they pay their church obligations and grant from their few possessions small charities."[65] In each of the cottages there is one woman, called the *magistra operum,* who supervises the works and workers so that "all things are faithfully done according to God."

The memoir further describes the daily routine of the girls and women. After Mass in the morning at the central church, they return to their separate cottages, and there they silently do their work, "in which they are known to be useful to the entire commonwealth."[66] While they work, they do not cease from prayer. In each house, the two women best suited for this task read aloud the psalm, the *Miserere,* and the *Ave Maria,* one reading one verse, the other the next, "the others silently reading with them or paying diligent attention to what they read." At vespers they return for services to the central church.

> And through all these things, the [girls] are educated in morals and made skillful in domestic matters, so much so that great and good persons are accustomed to send their daughters to them to be educated, hoping that they will be found better than others no matter what the state to which they may later be called, whether in religion or in marriage.[67]

The beguinage of St. Elizabeth at Ghent shows distant similarities to the classical gynaeceum. Young women live and work together, supporting themselves by cleaning wool or cloth. The hope is that they will depart when they reach the age of marriage. But there are significant differences too. The work they perform is integrated into the textile economy of the town. The beguines wash the wool and cloth which are delivered to them from the city, but the tasks the women perform require little skill and earn them little remuneration. No mention is made of the central processes of cloth making—of weaving, fulling, and dyeing. Not even spinning is explicitly described, although it is hard to believe that the beguines did not spin the wool they had washed, as they listened to the prayers. The beguines do not compete—and doubtless were not allowed to compete—with the established, male-dominated textile guilds of the city. The classical gynaeceum, and the fundamental roles of women in cloth making, were changing.

Laypeople, laywomen in particular, supported the beguinages, and the beguines themselves remained on the margins of the officially approved religious life. But they were also free to develop their own religious insights, even as the old orders of nuns, beset by poverty, were declining in vitality. From roughly the late twelfth century, uncloistered women assume a remarkable visibility, even a leadership, in religious life.[68] We shall look at these charismatic women in Chapter 5.

The story of the beguines also directs our attention to the growing towns, where fundamental shifts in the sexual division of labor were occurring.

NOTES

1. On women in the medieval English countryside before the plague, see Bennett, 1987.
2. Eadmer, 1962, p. 4: "...mulieres, quae Regis erant ancillae, segestes metere."
3. Life of S. Otto bishop of Bamberg. *ASS*, I Julii, p. 353: "...moxque rebrachiatis manicis succinctaque veste, falcem dextra corripuit....Sed mirum dictu...ut erat inclinis, misera diriguit, et quasi marmoris efficies, nec semetipsam erigere nec falcem e manu dimittere potuit...."
4. Translatio prima s. Hunegundis virginis. *ASS*, V Augusti, p. 235: "Unde contigit, ut quaedam puella, Rotgildis nomine...jam dictos messores prosecuta est et spicas, quae de manibus eorum ceciderent, colligebat."
5. *ASS*, II Januarii, p. 172: "...purgandis agris plurimis comitata feminis sepius incumbebat. Erat autem mirum in modum cogitabunda, sodales fugiens solave operari peroptans."
6. *ASS*, II Novembris, p. 168: "...feminam editam et educatam ruri ruralique operi assuetam...."

7. *ASS,* II Novembris, p. 175: "…quae ante patrem suum boves arantes aculeo tangens sulcare cogebat."
8. *ASS,* II Novembris, p. 175: "…at, quia grave oneris pondus teneri eius lacerti sustentare non poterant funem ad duo antiora brachia cenovecotri ligaverat quem desuper humeros gestans, tam brachiis quam humeris onera deportando labores patris sui pro posse suo aequabat.…"
9. *Ibid.:* "Fratres vero eius, quia minores erant, vaccas et pecora patris sui in pascuis conservabant. Dominicis et festis diebus, quibus aliae virgines choreis deducendis et aliis inanibus iocis in se inaniter occupabant, ipsa boves et pecora ad pascua deducabat."
10. *ASS,* V Julii, p. 653.
11. *ASS,* I Aprilis, p. 444: "Agebat ergo Juliana hoc officium tanto devotius quanto plures lacte manibus suis extracto usuros cognoverat."
12. *ASS,* I Januarii, p. 659: "Ferunt eam boves pascentem, ut liberiori animo oratione se dederet, iis praecepisse segete aliisque satis abstinent. Parverunt brutae animantes.…"
13. Vitry's sermons are unpublished, but this exemplum is excerpted in Etienne de Bourbon, 1877, no. 271, p. 226, with Etienne's own version. It is also published in Crane, 1890.
14. See page 37.
15. *Fleta,* 1955–72, II, 122: "Et si pistor convictus fuerit vel braciatris.…" *Ibid.,* 257: "Nec etiam permittat quod aliquis vel aliqua ad caseatricem accedat.…"
16. *St. Pierre,* 1868–71, I, 103, no. 154: "…quaedam ancilla nomine Siborch…servile in mola pistrina ageret opus, lignum quo mole in girum ducatur ita manui eius desterae inhesit, ut sanguis sequeretur, nulla vi nullaque arte avelli posset."
17. According to Weinbaum, 1924–26, p. 289.
18. Marie de France, 1959, pp. 40–55, "Le Freisne."
19. Renart, 1925.
20. Chronicon gozencense, edited by R. Köpke. *MGH Ss.,* X (1852), p. 142. "Et quoniam eadem domina Agnes more antiquorum tam literis quam diversarum artium [sic] apud Quidelinburg pulchre fuit instructa.…"
21. Renart, 1925, lines 1158 ff: "Fresne avoit a ouvrer appris: / N'ot telle ouvriere jusqu'en Pouille / Com elle est de tistre et d'aguille; / Si sot faire ouevres de maniers, Laz et tissuz, et aulmosnieres, / Et draps ouvres de soye et d'or / Qui bien valoient ung tresor.…"
22. *ASS,* II Martii, p. 352: "…ut cum avia sua Abbatissa disceret psalmodialem librum, et industrias operum"; p. 354: "…ut illam doceret sacras lectiones et manuum operationes."
23. "Fille et la mere se sieent a l'orfrois / A un fil d'or i font orieuls croiz. / Parla la mere, qui le cuer ot cortois / Tant bon' amor fist [bele] Aude en Doon. / 'Apprenez, fille, a coudre et a filer, / et en l'orfois les oriex

crois lever. / L'amor Doon vos covient oublier.' / Tan bon' amor fist bele Aude en Doon." Text from Zink, 1978, p. 158.

24. "Siet soi bele Aye as piez sa male maistre / sor ses genouls un paile d'Engleterre, / [et] a un fil i fet coustures beles. / Hé! Hé! amors d'autre pais, / mon cuer avez et liez et souspris." Zink, 1978, p. 159.
25. See page 94.
26. *Liber feudorum*, 1945, I, no. 489: "Et dono tibi illud mobile quod est in conveniencia dandum castellanis per unumquemque annum."
27. *Ibid.*, no. 278, 10 November 1053.
28. Reilly, 1982, especially pp. 352–70.
29. Michaelsson, 1951, pp. 7 and 17, from the survey of 1313.
30. For further information, see Herlihy, 1988.
31. See page 40.
32. The figures are based on a count of those regarded as saints by the Bollandists and recorded in the *Bibliotheca Hagiographica Latina.* On the nature of the index, see Herlihy, 1985b, p. 3.
33. *ASS*, III Martii, p. 38: "...quia foeminarum religiosarum rara tunc erant monasteria."
34. Eudes of Rouen, 1964.
35. An exact count is not possible because some of the houses are not positively identified, because the numbers varied in the houses from one visit to the next, and because many of the members, especially monks and canons, were living elsewhere. This count includes the absentees but not the lay brothers and sisters and servants. The numbers must therefore be regarded as only an approximation of the true religious population.
36. On Cistercian nuns, see Thompson, 1978, pp. 227–52.
37. According to Geudens, 1911, p. 389. The count may be exaggerated, but the proportion is probably correct.
38. *Ibid.*, p. 411.
39. Mansi, 1759–98, XXII, col. 1051: "Quoniam simoniaca labes adeo moniales infecit, ut vix aliquas sine pretio recipiant in sorores, paupertatis praetextu volentes hujusmodi vitium paliare."
40. Eudes of Rouen, 1964, p. 457.
41. *Ibid.*, p. 513.
42. *Ibid.*, p. 678. For similar prohibitions, see *ibid.*, pp. 584, 591, and 608.
43. *Ibid.*, p. 662, April 28, 1268.
44. When Eudes Rigaud visited the nuns of St. Aubin in September 1267, he found thirteen in residence and "three were in the vineyards." *Ibid.*, p. 676.
45. *Ibid.*, p. 369, November 23, 1258.
46. *Ibid.*, p. 609, January 15, 1265.
47. *Ibid.*, p. 656.
48. *Ibid.*, p. 658.
49. *Ibid.*, p. 729.
50. *ASS*, II Januarii, p. 172. Veronica as a girl had tried repeatedly to learn her letters, but did not succeed because her father imposed

so many chores upon her; she was, moreover, assured in a dream that literacy was unnecessary for the religious life.
51. Herlihy, 1975.
52. McDonnell, 1954, 1969.
53. Tillemont, 1847–51, V, 308, gives the figure of up to 2000 at Cologne, apparently based on Matthew Paris.
54. Eudes of Rouen, 1964, p. 734: "November 15. This day we were at the Daughters of God, the Beguines, at Pré...."
55. Mansi, XXV (1782, 1903), col. 410: "Septimus, quod mulieris osculum (cum ad hoc non inclinet natura) est mortale peccatum: actus autem carnalis (cum ad hoc inclinet natura) non est peccatum: maxime cum tentatur exercens."
56. *Ste. Elisabet*, 1883, p. 74, n. 106, 14 May 1328, "Mémoire présenté aux délegués de l'éveque de Tournai en faveur des Beguines." "Sane bene memorie domine, Johanna et soror ejus, Margareta, successive Flandrie et Hanonie comitesse, considerantes quod terra predicta multum abundat mulieribus, quibus secundum conditiones earum et amicorum decentia matrimonia non paterent ...propter earum multitudinem vel parentum inopiam obtinere de facili non valerent; item quod honestas domicellas et nobiles depauperatas tamen opportet mendicare."
57. *Ibid.*: "In diversis locis Flandrie quedam spatiosa loca, quac vocantur Beghinarum curie, fundaverunt, in quibus predicte mulieres, filie seu domicelle, reciperentur."
58. This follows Tillemont, 1847–51, V, 312–13. Tillemont's great work of erudition was written probably between 1679 and 1684 and was based on a systematic survey of all the contemporary references to St. Louis that Tillemont could find. Not all the documents he consulted are extant today. Tillemont included in his comments on the king's career an extended discussion of the beguines and their history.
59. *Ibid.*, 313.
60. *Ste. Elisabet*, 1883, p. 1, no. 2.
61. *Ibid.*, no. 6.
62. *Ibid.*, p. 74.
63. Her mode of election and her duties are laid out in the statutes of the beguinage approved by Count Louis de Male in 1354. *Ibid.*, no. 130.
64. *Ibid.*, p. 74: "...plures domus pro dictarum mulierum inhabitione constitute, quarum quelibet ab alia fossati vel sepium interpositione distincta."
65. *Ibid.*: "...plures simul commorantes communiter, adeo sunt pauperes quod nichil habent nisi vestes et lectum cum cista, nec tamen cuiquam sunt onerose, sed operando manibus, mundando lanas et purgando pannos missos de villa, cotidie tantum lucrantur quod inde victum sumentes tenuem, ecclesiae iura persolvunt ac elemosinas modicas de modico largiuntur."
66. *Ibid.*: "...in quo toti patriae fore perutiles dinoscuntur."

67. *Ibid.*: "Et inter haec omnia, ita sunt in moribus composite ac rebus
    domesticis erudite, quod magne et honeste persone filias suas eis
    consueverint tradere nutriendas, sperantes quod id quemcumque
    satum forent postmodum vocate, sive religionis, sive matrimonii,
    invenirentur ceteris aptiores."
68. Support for this conclusion may be found in my typology of
    women saints, Herlihy, 1985b.

CHAPTER 4

Spinners, Weavers, Dyers

...Our work doesn't pay
Any of us even as much
As four pennies in a single day.
And that's not enough to feed us
Or put clothes on our backs...
...
And the ones we work for are rich
Because of what we produce.

—Complaint of the girl workers,
Yvain, lines 5306–5318

Among the many major changes in European life during the
central Middle Ages, one of the most significant was the rebirth
of urban life. The early medieval town in the Carolingian age
(eighth to ninth centuries) functioned principally as a burg or
fortress; the revival of trade from the late tenth century turned
many of the towns into lively centers of commercial exchange.
To supply their markets and to support their growing populations, some towns also began to nurture industries. By the late
thirteenth century, many towns attained the biggest size they
were to reach during the Middle Ages.

The making of cloth was one principal industry that experienced rapid growth within an urban setting. In this chapter, we
look at women in relation to cloth production. We first consider
the cultural values that continued to view the making of fabric
as preeminently women's work. We then take up the actual division of labor within the textile arts. We must begin in the
countryside and in a slightly earlier period than the one in the
previous chapter. The critical institution in the rural organization of textile work was the women's workshop, the by now familiar gynaeceum. We shall begin with an inspection of this in-

stitution in the Carolingian age, for the sources of this period contain the first reasonably full descriptions of the women's workshop. We shall then follow its history for as long as it has a history to follow—into the thirteenth century. Then we look at the shape of the textile trades within the towns, from their obscure beginnings in the eleventh century to their full efflorescence in the thirteenth.

VALUES

Throughout the central Middle Ages, into the thirteenth century, praise of women as fabric workers persist in the sources. The culture still honors women as the chief clothiers of the community. About 1100, Marbode, bishop of Rennes in Brittany and one of the leaders in the medieval renaissance of Latin letters, wrote a poem entitled the "Book of Ten Chapters." Chapter Four is a poem of praise for the married woman, the *matrona*. In describing her accomplishments, Marbode includes the following verses:

Who draws out the wool and the linen? Who turns the spindle?
Who prepares the skein [of yarn]? Who does the weaving?
These things accomplished for our benefit are so advantageous
That, if they were lacking, the quality of our life would decline.[1]

Even in rich households, the married woman was expected to participate in, and indeed, as we shall see, to direct, the work of spinning and weaving.

The legend of the English bishop and martyr Thomas Becket includes this picturesque story: Thomas is a young student pursuing his studies at Paris, about 1137. His schoolmates boast of the presents that their girls have given them on New Year's day. They tease Thomas, as he has received no similar gifts from a sweetheart. Thomas is hurt, and that night he prays to the Virgin, whom he has chosen as his bride and *amica*. Her statue responds with the gift of a tiny casket, full of episcopal robes. The vestments are "most skillfully and most subtly made." Thus the Virgin proves herself to be better and more skilled at cloth making than any earthly sweetheart.[2] Notable here too is the clergy's continued dependence on women for the making of vestments.

In later life, Thomas is forced into exile at Pontigny, and he has time to take from England only one hair shirt and drawers.

They soon become tattered, but he has no other garments. Then his Lady Mary comes; she greets him, comforts him, sits down beside him, and mends his tattered clothing. Skill in cloth making graces the Virgin, the most exalted of women. Like Minerva in the ancient world, Mary in this legend is the patroness of *lanificium,* the mistress of those that sew.[3]

Educators cited Mary's example to young girls to encourage them in cloth work. In the middle of the thirteenth century, Philippe de Navarre, in a tract on training children, insists that the daughters of both rich and poor learn "to spin and to sew; the poor girl will then have a skill, and the rich girl will know how others work." Mary, spinner and seamstress, should be their model: "Of this [work] no girl should be ashamed, as the glorious mother of God deigned to work cloth and to spin."[4]

THE WOMEN'S WORKSHOP

All across Europe during the reign of Charlemagne, and for three centuries thereafter, references to the women's workshop appear frequently in the sources, though the texts are never long. The Carolingian scholar Walafrid Strabo once enumerated the common words that he thought had passed out of Greek, through Latin, into the spoken German of his day. The examples he gives are the words for "cup," "father," "mother," and the "women's workshop."[5] The latter's adoption into the vernacular surely indicates that the term was used frequently in German society.

England

In England, Aelfric of Eynsham (d. ca. 1020) includes in his glossary of Latin and Anglo-Saxon terms the word *genitium.*[6] He defines it as a "towhus of wulle." *Tow* in Anglo-Saxon means "thread" or "material for spinning"; *hus* is "house"; and *wulle* is "wool." The phrase thus means "a house for spinning wool." Aelfric's Anglo-Saxon grammar also contains the probably related term *mearum ancillarum domus,* which means "the house of my women slaves"; the grammar contains no word for a house of men slaves. Aelfric's work also teaches its readers how to say these words of encouragement: "My girls, you are working better!"[7] However, I have not found a direct description of a gynaeceum in English sources of the Anglo-Saxon period. English manorial records are poor before the Norman Conquest, when the great estates were still loosely organized. Archeological evidence identifies within Anglo-Saxon settlements specialized huts given over to weaving.[8] The missing gynaecea in Anglo-Saxon England most likely reflect the scanty documentation.

The Continental Gynaeceum

On the continent, archeology is developing an ever clearer picture of the layout of early medieval villages, manorial complexes, and palaces. In what seems to be a common pattern, craft activities (the working of metal, stone, and even ivory; pottery making; cloth production; and so forth) were carried on in separate structures set apart from the main residences. Many of these ancillary structures were sunken huts; that is, they had earthen floors dug below ground level. Crafts that involved the use of fire are usually more easily identifiable in the archeological record than are spinning and weaving. However, the presence of loom weights (used to hold the warp threads taut on the vertical looms) or of postholes (marking where the frame of the looms once stood) indicates that cloth making was also carried on in ancillary structures. The processes of cloth making required fire too, in order to dye the cloth, but dye works have not yet, as far as I know, been positively identified in the archeological record.[9]

A palace of the Saxon kings and emperors (tenth century) at Tilleda in West Germany included in its *curia,* or court, two structures given over to cloth making, one measuring 24 meters by 6, and the other 15.5 meters by 4.5. According to the archeologist P. Grimm, who excavated the palace, the houses contained vertical looms; some twenty-two to twenty-four women worked in each of them. The fabric shops at Tilleda functioned into the twelfth century.[10]

The ninth-century Saxon serving woman Liutbirg, of whom more will be said presently, managed the household of Countess Gisla and of her son Bernhard. Later in life, Liutbirg was given her own separate cell, where she engaged in her religious exercises. She also operated within it a furnace "of burning coals," used for the "dyeing of [cloth] in various colors."[11] This small, separate structure with its dye works may well have been a sunken hut.

Records of the Carolingian age contain several descriptions of women's workshops, though all of them are vague and difficult to interpret. The abbot Adelhard of Corvey "built a dormitory and under it a heated room."[12] The heated room is certainly a gynaeceum. The women slept in the story above the work area; this suggests that the fire in the "heated room" was associated with their work rather than their physical comfort.

The capitulary *De villis* of an unknown Carolingian king directs the stewards on royal estates to achieve the following:

> Let our women's workshops be well ordered, in regard to houses, heated rooms, canopies, that is cellars, and let them have around them good hedges and strong gates, so that our work may be done well.[13]

The houses where the women lived are distinguished from the "heated rooms" (*pisla, pensilis*) where presumably they worked; again, the fire seems to have served industrial purposes. The *pisla* may well be the kind of separate cell which Liutbirg inhabited, where she maintained her furnace, her *igniculum carbonum*, for dyeing cloth. The phrase "canopies, that is cellars" may mean a covered sunken pit, used for spinning and weaving. *Turgurium* (canopy), used in the capitulary, appears also in the text of Liutbirg's life as a synonym for "hut."[14] Spinners and weavers seem to have worked at least seasonally in spaces open to air and light. Aelfric's glossary distinguishes "summer halls" from "winter halls."[15]

The survey of a Carolingian royal estate at Asnapium (perhaps Gennep in modern Holland) has several sections that refer to women's workshops; here are two:

> ...We find on the Asnapium fiscal demesne a royal hall excellently constructed of stone: three rooms, the whole house built around with second stories, with eleven heated rooms.

> ...We find in this fiscal demesne a royal house with two rooms, both equipped with fireplaces; one cellar; two porticos; a small enclosed courtyard strongly fortified with a fence inside, two rooms, with the same number of fireplaces; three houses of women, four storage barns....[16]

Here too, the work areas and the living areas were quite distinct, and the presence of three "houses" of women certainly proves that the estate was maintaining a large staff of female workers, undoubtedly engaged in textile production.

In 895 or a little later, an author named Wolfhardus described the miracles of the abbess St. Walburgis of Heidenheim, and included this account of a woman working in a fabric shop:

> There was a certain woman of the estate called Stopenheim by the name of Geila.... When the yearly festival honoring the dedication of [Walburgis'] basilica came around, she ignored it with an arrogant and irreverent countenance; she entered the winter work halls and began to weave with bent fingers the short tunic which earlier she had set up to weave. When after two times she passed the thread from the skein or ball that she held in her hand to the cloth, the ball stuck to her miserable hand. With the hand swelling, the mere women who were present could scarcely with great effort cut away her sleeve from the deceiving and swollen hand.[17]

This is a rare description of a woman operating the typical vertical loom of the early Middle Ages. She works at the loom alone, although there are other women present in the shop. With her fingers, she passes the woof thread through the warp. Her loom is set up in "winter work halls." Probably in good weather the women worked in open structures (Aelfric's "summer halls") or out-of-doors under canopies; they thus could take advantage of the long light of summer.

Another description of a women's workshop, by the twelfth-century poet Chrétien de Troyes, although fictional, also indicates that women worked at least part of the year in the open. In his chivalric romance *Yvain*, two wicked brothers, at their Castle of Infinite Misfortune, operate a women's workshop. This is its description:

> A great high hall, brand new,
> With a walled courtyard in front of it,
> And a wall of great sharpened stakes,
> And inside, behind the stakes,
>   [Yvain] saw three hundred girls
> All sewing away, some working
> With golden thread, some silk
> Working as hard as they could.[18]

The girls were working in an enclosed courtyard, although presumably in winter or in inclement weather they could retire into the hall behind it.

The Utrecht Psalter, a manuscript decorated with pen drawings between 817 and 834 in a monastery on the Marne, contains a sketch of women spinning and weaving.[19] They work under a canopy in the open air. It may be, of course, that the author wished to show all the activities of cloth making and did not want to hide some of them indoors. It is, however, more likely that women did indeed spin and weave for at least part of the year in the open air. The sketch gives no indication of where the women might be living.

Archeology, literary texts, and manuscript drawings all confirm that in the organization of the medieval gynaeceum work space was separated from living space and that the distinct phases of the cloth making process (notably weaving and dyeing) were carried out in special structures. The women's workshop was a large and complex enterprise.

Numbers

Chrétien's 300 girl workers, laboring as hard as they could at the Castle of Infinite Misfortune, surely existed only in the poet's imagination. The historical documents occasionally mention

St. Margaret spinning and tending sheep. (*The British Library*)

the number of women laboring in the shops, and it ranges between ten and forty. In 735 to 737, Count Eberhard, son of Adalbert, gave to the monastery of Murbach in Alsace "little girls, whom we have in our workshop, more or less forty."[20] The Carolingian royal estate thought to be Stephanswert had a workshop "in which there are 24 women."[21] An estate of Ingolstat in Bavaria, given to the monastery of Nideralteich in 840, contained "boys and women of the workshop in number twenty-two."[22] In 908, in an exchange of lands and serfs involving the church of Freising in Bavaria, among the serfs conveyed are one blacksmith, one shield maker, one baker, one fisherman "and twelve slave girls from the *genetium*."[23] The document does not reveal whether the twelve girls represented the entire gynaeceum. In 1018, Count Dodico donated an estate to the church of Paderborn in Westphalia, but he exempted by name and thereby freed ten women, "and the other women who formerly were assigned to the gynaeceum but are to be assigned there no longer."[24] The ten named women represent the minimum number actually working in the shop, which Count Dodico seems to have abolished, since he freed its workers.

Some estate descriptions mention the presence of a women's workshop but not the number of workers assigned to it. In 813, Bishop Rotaldus of Verona in Italy gave to the canons of his church a tenth of his revenues from a long list of his estates. The canons were to enjoy a tenth of wine, grain, vegetables, oil, salt, cheese, fish, linen, animals, and "of the garments that come from

Women shearing sheep, spinning, and weaving. (*Cambridge University, Trinity College, M.R. 17*)

the *pisele* or *giniceo*."[25] The women's workshops on his manors clearly provided a significant part of the bishop's revenues, though we do not know how many there were or how large they were.

The Flemish life of St. Macharius mentions a *genitium* of a count named Henry, but we are told nothing about its members, beyond mention of a little blind girl named Oda who was cured by the saint's intercession.[26] It is, however, worth noting that the blind Oda, but not apparently her mother, belonged to the shop. Presumably, even the blind could work at weaving, and the women employed in this shop seem to have been very young. Sometime about 1050 at Salzburg in modern Austria, Count Chadalloh and his wife Irmingard gave estates "with one *geniceum* and with the entire staff, that is, male and female slaves, both house servants and not, with all the tools...."[27]

Several estate surveys give the number or names of serfs attached to the manor house, though they do not place them explicitly in a gynaeceum. Still, women often predominate in these serf lists, and it is more than likely that the household staff included cloth workers. Thus, on the estate of Forçone in Lazio in central Italy, which belonged to the monastery of Farfa, the manor house contained seventy-three women and only twenty-three men.[28] The great survey of the estates of St.-Germain des Prés near Paris gives a list of fourteen slave girls (*ancillae*) and says that they make cloths (*camsilos*) if linen and supplies are given to them.[29] It is not stated where these girls work, but the reference to supplies recalls the directives regarding gynaecea contained in the capitulary *De villis*. Almost certainly the fourteen *ancillae* staffed a workshop. The same survey gives another list of nineteen *lidae,* women of a status lower than free but higher than servile.[30] They also make cloths for the monks, but we are not told where they labored. The monks would find it hard both to supply and to supervise these women if they were not working together.

The Woman Worker

The lady of the manor or castle and her daughters labored alongside their slaves and servants, and must have communicated with them. (We looked at sewing as a characteristically aristocratic activity in Chapter 3.) In a Flemish saint's life written after 980, a noble woman has a vision, and a girl in her workshop has the same dream; she reports it to her mistress, and thus confirms its veracity.[31]

Slaves and some half-free girls (*lidae*) made up the principal staff of the workshop. At the monastery of St. Sophia at Benevento in southern Italy, free women who married the monastery's slaves were also obligated to come with their sons and daughters to the manor house "to serve and direct," presumably to work in the gynaeceum.[32]

In *Yvain,* the wicked masters of the Castle of Infinite Misfortune received as tribute every year from the king of the Island of Virgins "thirty young girls," whom they put to work in their cloth shop.[33] It is hard, of course, to know whether women cloth workers were ever given as tribute, but they were certainly donated, especially to churches. In the life of St. John of Gorze, John at one time managed the properties and workshops of Count Requinus, and he also owned and dearly loved a church dedicated to St. Lawrence. He assigned to the church "a certain woman from the gynaeceum of his lord," and also found "a pilgrim, a priest of advanced years" who could perform the liturgy.[34] For the rest of her life the woman was to help ensure that the divine offices would be performed, a task that surely involved making or mending the needed altar cloths and vestments. Presumably, she was also a mature woman, lest her presence give scandal. Monastic chartularies make frequent references to women who either give themselves or are given to churches and monasteries. They are sometimes called "tributaries."[35] It is not clear how they were employed, but it is very likely that they, like the woman that John assigned to the church of St. Lawrence, made or mended altar cloths and vestments.

Besides using slaves and tributaries, the workshops, at least among the Lombards and Franks, harbored free women condemned for crimes.[36] The ancient gynaecea sometimes functioned as houses of prostitution, and their medieval counterparts seem also to have been sites of, if not prostitution, at least sexual irregularities. The medieval Latin word for a female shop worker, *gynaecearia,* is a synonym for "prostitute." Notker the Stutterer, a monk of St. Gall who compiled fabulous stories concerning Charlemagne and his son Louis the Pious, tells of two bastards who had been conceived in the workshop of

Kolmar in Alsace. Their father's name is not known, nor is the nature of his liaison with their mother, who passed on to them their servile status. The brothers became soldiers, fought bravely for Charlemagne, and "by their blood and that of the enemies they erased the mark of their servitude."[37]

According to a charter dated 821 from the church of Freising in Bavaria, a man named Tenil, whose wife had died, "driven by necessity had joined with a woman of the workshop, a servant of St. Mary's [of Freising], named Meripurga."[38] He conceived a son by her, named Hagunus, whom he came to love dearly. He therefore consulted with his relatives and friends about how he might acquire his *amica* Meripurga and her son from the bishop. He exchanged for them part of his inheritance. The charter does not explain how Tenil first gained sexual access to Meripurga, but clearly she was supervised very loosely in the bishop's workshop.

In the thirteenth century, Emperor Frederick II Hohenstaufen, the "wonder of the world," maintained staffs of women slaves at several palaces in southern Italy and Sicily, specifically at Lucera, Melfi, Canosa, and Messina.[39] Virtually all that we know about them comes from the administrative directives which Frederick, on campaign in Lombardy, sent to his southern officials in 1239 and 1240. He distinguishes among *ancille camere nostre* (slave girls of our chamber), *domicelle,* and *garcie,* the last term probably indicating young girls. Clothes are to be distributed to them, and the girls must be kept busy "at spinning or some other work, so that they do not consume the bread of idleness."[40] Many modern historians believe that the emperor's fabric shops doubled as his harems.[41] There is no proof of this. We can only observe that the girls of the gynaeceum seem often to have been sexually available.

The association of the workshops with slavery, imprisonment, and illicit sex gave these gatherings of women an unsavory reputation. In September 1183, the bishop of Salzburg in Austria donated to the canons serving in the church of St. Rupert a girl named Adelhaid, daughter of Diemdudis, and all her posterity.[42] She was, however, not to serve the church "in the work of making woolens or of the gynaeceum, but in the most honest offices of the said church." In the eyes of the bishop, cloth making in the gynaeceum was not the "most honest" employment.

Work and the Life Cycle

The pattern suggested by our sources is the following: Girls, mostly of servile status, entered the workshop at very young ages in order to learn the needed skills. Upon reaching adulthood, some would remain as instructors and supervisors, but many would pass from the gynaeceum, either to return to their families of origin, to marry, or to enter the service of a church. Thus, the Saxon woman Liutbirg trained girls "in singing psalms and in artful labors [surely including cloth making]." When they reached maturity, "giving them liberty she allowed them to return either to their relatives or wherever they wished to go."[43]

The miracles (recorded in 895) of the eighth-century abbess Walburgis of Heidesheim describe an older woman textile worker. Her name was Asnia. Presumably, Asnia had been trained in a gynaeceum when she was a young girl but left it at maturity. Stricken with epilepsy in adulthood, she prayed to St. Walburgis for a cure.[44] The saint cured her, but admonished her in a dream to go to her monastery "and receive from Eithilda the custodian of the church some work to be done with her own hands." She reluctantly obeyed and brought the work home, but she was distracted by other chores and neglected to perform it. Her eye then fell from its socket as a sign of the saint's displeasure. This cycle was repeated several times before Asnia faithfully performed the assigned labors. The work she did (or failed to do), though vaguely described, involved the making and mending of cloth. Surely the miracles were meant to be exemplary for the monastery's other scattered and negligent women cloth workers.

The service of young girls in the gynaeceum and their dismissal at older ages perhaps explain an otherwise perplexing feature of Carolingian manorial communities. The dependent families of St.-Germain, for example, show an extraordinary shortage of women in the ranks of the unfree. The sex ratio of the *servi* and *ancillae* recorded in the survey is a staggering 266 men for every 100 women. Among the free classes the same ratio is 119 men per 100 women.[45] Where are the missing servile women? It seems likely that many of them were young girls working in the monastic gynaecea, which are not otherwise described in the polyptych.

Conditions of Labor

The sources do not illuminate very well the conditions under which women worked in the fabric shops. Certainly, the shops had to be supplied with the needed materials and with food. The gynaeceum for which Septimania served as a cook (according to Gregory of Tours) must have had its own community kitchen.[46] The capitularies direct that the shops be secluded from the outside world by fences, hedges, and ditches, but the other sources cited above show that these barriers were often quite porous.

Chrétien de Troyes provides an imaginary, but intriguing, picture of these conditions of labor. The gynaeceum at the Castle of Infinite Misfortune produces silk and not wool; silk is the aristocratic fabric and the most common fabric mentioned in elegant courtly poetry. The gynaeceum otherwise operated fully within a commercial economy; it was indeed a medieval sweatshop. The 300 young girls complain to Yvain that they weave silk all day but are given only rags to wear:

> We'll spend our days poor
> And naked and hungry and thirsty,
> For they'll never pay us what we earn,
> Let us buy better food.[47]

They must purchase their food and clothing; we are not told where. No girl earns more than four pennies a day, and even those who are paid twenty sous a week are still miserable. "We work most nights, and we work all day, just to stay alive." Their diet consists of bread, "some in the morning and less at night." They are exploited: "And the ones we work for are rich, because of what we produce."

Writing about 1177, Chrétien is already disturbed by high prices. Later in the story, a noble damsel dresses Yvain:

> ...She took a pleated
> Shirt from her storage chest,
> And white stockings, and a needle
> And thread to sew on the sleeves,
> And did so. He was dressed: God keep
> This service from becoming too costly![48]

Could Chrétien's colorful depiction of a gynaeceum have had any correspondence with reality? Chrétien was writing even as the commercial production of and trade in cloth were rapidly developing. His striking amalgam of servile and salaried labor seems to combine elements of the old and the new economic orders.

Portraits

We have partial biographies of two persons, a woman and a man, who spent large portions of their lives in a gynaeceum. The woman is Liutbirg, a native of Saxony who died about 880. She was intimately associated with a line of Saxon counts. Charlemagne, after conquering Saxony and beginning its conversion to Christianity, named as count in the new territory a Saxon chief called Hessi. Hessi, whose only son died in adolescence, distributed his great wealth among his surviving daughters. Gisla, the firstborn of his daughters, married a count named Unuuan, who died in 804. They had one son, called Bernhard, and two daughters, Bilihilt and Hruothild, both of whom became abbesses. Gisla as a widow competently administered her vast domains, building many churches and establishing monasteries in lands only recently converted to Christianity. She is a good example of the woman administrator in Carolingian government.

On one of her many trips through her territories, she encountered at an unnamed convent a young girl, Liutbirg, who surpassed all the other girls in beauty, skill, and energy. Gisla inquired about her origins and learned that she had been born at Salzburg, a place not certainly identified. We are told nothing about Liutbirg's parents. Usually, saints' lives emphasize the noble origins of their holy subjects. The omission suggests that Liutbirg's parents were not nobles, perhaps not even free. Liutbirg never herself became a professed religious, though she honored nuns.[49] She first appears and passes her life as a servant. Her humble career almost surely indicates humble origins.

Her biographer lets fall one other significant particular about her early years. Once, later in her life, the devil "recalled to her memory how once in the years of her girlhood she had tricked a comrade of equal age."[50] Liutbirg had broken her needle in their common work; when her mate had gone out for a moment, she exchanged her own broken needle for the good one of her peer. She "congratulated herself on deceiving her, as if she had done something meritorious."[51] Liutbirg forgot the incident. But the devil in his cunning reminded her, and she recalled that this was done "in her childhood, when first she had learned the art of weaving."[52] Liutbirg and her comrade were surely in some sort of school, where young girls were learning the skills they would later exercise in the gynaeceum.

Gisla was so impressed by the young Liutbirg that she summoned her to serve in her own house, promising to treat her like a daughter. Her biographer celebrates Liutbirg's skills as a worker almost as much as her piety. This "girl of great endowment," "wise in counsel" and "constant in work," grew more capable as she matured. Her reputation spread. "She possessed such talent that she surpassed all others in the places where she lived and was reckoned to be a lady Daedalus of the diverse arts that are appropriate to the works of women."[53] She seems to have been a compulsive worker: "...as we have mentioned, she was master of many women's works, and never did she cease from work or some utility, either laboring with her hands or praying...."[54]

Countess Gisla, recognizing her abilities, made her the mistress of the palace; after the death of the countess, Liutbirg served Bernhard. "She had such a grasp of the administration of affairs that the governance of the palace rested almost entirely with her."[55] Among her skills was care of the sick. She also nurtured Bernhard's children (by two wives) so well that "she might have been called a mother rather than a nurse."[56]

Now tired by her ceaseless labors, she asked Bernhard for her own little cell, and there she passed the last thirty years of her life. Even in her cell, she kept her furnace for the dyeing of cloth. She directed from her cell a school for young girls, and she passed on to them the arts that had so distinguished her. Whatever time remained after her own work and her prayers, she devoted to teaching her disciples, "who were with her."[57] Her graduates were highly esteemed. Some she sent to holy Ansger, the archbishop of Bremen (831–865); they embellished his liturgies with their lovely singing and fine needlework.[58] They clearly had learned from Liutbirg how to read, sing, spin, weave, dye, and sew. As already mentioned, she freed other girls, allowing them to go back to their families or "wherever they wanted." The account of her life thus presents a clear example of the special education given to some young girls in early medieval society. It also shows the high prestige they could enjoy because of the skills which, in large part, they learned from older women.

The miracles of Bertin, abbot of Sithieu in Flanders, include the tale of a male worker in the gynaeceum. His name was Letfridus. As a child, he had somehow been committed to the house "of a certain, most noble man of the region." There, in the gynaeceum, he had been educated "until adulthood... in the art of sewing, cutting, weaving and every other kind of women's work."[59] But he did not remain there after maturity, probably because of possible scandal. We next encounter him watching sheep. One Sunday, he foolishly decided to guard the sheep instead of attending Mass, and he was struck blind. He appealed for help to the long-deceased St. Bertin, and the saint restored his sight. In gratitude he devoted himself to maintaining the wardrobe of Bertin's church. "Afterwards, whatever cloths there were in the said church to embellish or mend, or whatever ecclesiastical vestments there were to wash, he with great attention accomplished it. He prayed that just as he labored hard to wash away dirt from the vestments, so also divine clemency would wash away the stains of his sins." He served probably in much the same way as the unnamed woman in the life of John of Gorze served the church of St. Lawrence.

Letfridus, like the girls taught by Liutbirg, was a life-cycle textile worker, learning the arts as a child in a gynaeceum but being released as an adult to the larger world. He seems not to have utilized his skills as an adult, until he chose to do penance for his transgressions.

Output

The sources tell us nothing about the volume of output from the women's workshops. Still, references to the gynaeceum impress by their numbers, even as they disappoint by their vagueness. They are found in documents from Italy to England, and from the start of the Middle Ages until the early thirteenth century. The women's workshops undoubtedly played a central role in cloth production in many European regions over the first half of the Middle Ages.

Notker Balbulus, a monk of St. Gall, once described the annual distributions of cloth made by Emperor Louis the Pious (814–841). At Easter, Louis "gave gifts to all the palace ministers and all those serving at the royal court, according to rank."[60] To the more noble ministers he distributed belts and leggings and "the most precious robes brought from his most extensive empire." "Frisian cloth" (probably English or Flemish in origin but imported by Frisian merchants) dyed in different colors was given to the lower servants. He gave clothing of mixed linen and wool to "the keepers of the horses, to the bakers and cooks, as they had need." And finally, he distributed clothes to uncounted numbers of the poor.

A wag at his court twitted the emperor: "O you, happy Louis, who in a single day have been able to clothe so many men! By Christ, no one in Europe has today clothed more persons than you, except Atto."[61] It is, unfortunately, not known who this munificent Atto was, but clearly Emperor Louis impressed his courtiers with the quantities of cloth he had amassed. Where was this cloth produced in his "most extensive empire"? The only centers of cloth production that the documents mention are gynaecea.

THE BEGINNINGS OF CHANGE

The canons of the church of St. Nicholas, outside the walls of Passau in Bavaria, owned an estate named Entzenweis. A series of papal and imperial charters, confirming the canonry's possessions, refer to its existence. Thus, a charter issued by Pope Alexander II in 1073 mentions among the lands belonging to the canons the *curtis* Entzenweis with its gynaeceum.[62] The later charters continue to mention Entzenweis and its women's workshop, and one dated 1006 cites the presence of a mill. The latest of the charters mentioning the workshop was issued by Emperor Henry V in 1111. Then we are left without comparable charters until 1220, when Pope Honorius III confirmed once more the canons' ownership of Entzenweis. This last charter refers to the mill, but the gynaeceum goes unmentioned. As these solemn confirmations were usually copied from earlier charters, its disappearance is surely not an oversight. Sometime between 1111 and 1220, the estate or village of Entzenweis in Bavaria had lost its gynaeceum.

The Dispute between Sheep and Flax

There are other indications that the participation of women in cloth production was declining. Sometime probably between 1080 and 1083, an author who may have been Winric from Trier in the north Rhineland composed a Latin poem entitled "The Dispute between Sheep and Flax."[63] A fragment has survived; in it, Sheep and Flax dispute the relative merits of woolens and linens. The text makes several allusions to the work of men and women in cloth production. Sheep mocks Flax for the role women play in the making of linen. "Who can describe," taunts Sheep, "how many are the pains into which you are swept, twisted by women's hands...?" Moreover, Flax, once softened, is subject to the sport of women.[64] Would Sheep have derided Flax if women were playing a comparable role in the production of woolens? The poem implies that the preparation of linen cloth out of flax continued to be women's work; *lanificium,* on the other hand, the production of woolens, was not so any longer, at least not in the north Rhineland.

The Wheeled Ship

For the year 1137, the Deeds of the Abbots of St. Trond in Limburg, modern Belgium, relates a bizarre tale involving weavers:

> There is a race of hired persons whose business is to weave cloth from linen and wool. They are generally regarded as more impudent and haughty than other hired persons. To bring down their haughtiness and pride and to avenge a personal injury, a certain poor rustic from the village named Inda [Kornelimünster near Aachen] thought up this diabolical trick.[65]

With the cooperation of otherwise unnamed "judges" and "powers" and with the help of "frivolous" men, the rustic built a ship in a neighboring wood and equipped it with wheels so that it could roll over land. The "powers" then ordered the weavers to drag the ship by ropes from town to town, to Aachen and then to Maastricht, where it was further equipped with a mast and sails, and then to Tongres and to Looz. Its arrival was the occasion of celebrations lasting far into the night, during which men and women cavorted with each other shamelessly.

When Abbot Rudolph of St. Trond heard that the ship was going to roll through his village, he warned that it would bring disaster on the people. "But the village people welcomed [it] with the same enthusiasm and joy as the doomed Trojans received the fatal horse into their midst." The authorities commanded the local weavers of the town to stand guard over the ship night and day. "It's a wonder," says the monastic account, "that they weren't forced to offer sacrifices before the ship to Neptune, who usually holds dominion over ships." The weavers protested against the shameful service they were forced to perform. They did not deserve such shabby treatment, "since according to the right way of ancient Christians and Apostolic men, they lived by the labor of their own hands, working night and day so that they might be fed and clothed and could provide for their children." They had been unfairly singled out, "since among Christians there were many offices more despicable than theirs, for they saw nothing shameful in earning their bread without sin." "A rustic and poor weaver," they claimed, "is better than an urban and noble judge, who robs orphans and despoils widows."[66]

After calling at St. Trond, the ship was rolled into the lands of a neighboring count, against his expressed orders. The act provoked a war, and the region of St. Trond was devastated, even as Abbot Rudolph had predicted.

The story of the wheeled ship suggests that essentially pagan rites survived far into the Middle Ages. It also tells much about weavers in western Flanders in the middle of the twelfth century. The weavers mentioned are all males, forced to assume the male functions of towing the ship and of guarding it. They live in the countryside, and they contrast their own rustic honesty with the thieving ways of the urban judges. They seem to live exclusively by weaving, and they labor day and night. They are married, and through the work of their hands they support themselves and their children. As *mercenarii*, they receive money, probably from urban merchants who buy their products. They do not seem to enjoy free status. The "powers" can command them to tow the ship and guard it, force them, in other words, to perform a kind of corvée. They have also provoked the animosity of the persons, seemingly many, who devised this strange way of humiliating them. They loudly profess their own poverty, but could the money they were earning as weavers have kindled the jealousy of still poorer, unskilled neighbors?

The picture of Flemish weaving is significant too for what passes unmentioned. Women are nowhere described as specialized workers in cloth. They seem no longer to ply the arts that, in the same regions only a few years before, they had been exercising in the gynaecea.

Pictures and Words

Late in his life, Alexander Neckam (d. 1217), an English monk who had studied at Paris, wrote an essay entitled "On the Natures of Things," in which he included a description of various arts.[67] In one chapter, "De textore" (On the Weaver), the weaver appears seated at the loom, throwing the shuttlecock back and forth and marrying woof to warp to form the cloth. The use of a shuttlecock shows that this is a horizontal loom—an important technical advance over the vertical looms of the Carolingian age. A *textrix,* a lady weaver, appears in the same scene, but her contribution is clearly ancillary to the work of the *textor.* She combs the wool and burls the finished cloth, smoothing it and removing knots from it. She supplies the balls of yarn to the man at the loom. She spins the yarn, and as she does so, she sings sweet songs to relieve the tedium.[68] The male weaver has become the central figure; the *textrix* supplies him and serves him, even to the point of entertaining him with songs while he performs his monotonous work.

John of Garland, a teacher at Paris in the first half of the thirteenth century (he died in 1252) composed a dictionary (he was the first to use the word), through which his students could learn Latin terms for everyday activities and things.[69] The work is rich in information about trades and professions. It too shows that the domain of women's work was shrinking. "Certain men," John observes, "are usurping for themselves the offices of women," specifically the vending of napkins, towels, bedclothes, shirts, pants, and other wearing apparel.[70] Elsewhere in his dictionary, he gives a list of tools "suitable for women," including scissors and needles, thimbles and spindles, and various instruments for weaving linen. But a gloss on the original text adds: "Some of them are common to both sexes."[71] Whoever wrote the gloss (probably John himself) clearly recognized an enlarged male presence in the cloth trades.

According to John's dictionary, women dyers of cloth were rare in early thirteenth-century Paris. His treatment of the art assumes that all *tinctores* would be male. They have stained fingernails, "and for this reason are spurned by the beautiful women, unless they are accepted by reason of money."[72] Dyeing was among the most skilled of the cloth trades, as it required a knowledge of fabrics, dyes, and mordants. It seems also to be the first such skill which men took over, almost entirely.

Guilds

Toulouse in Languedoc claims a rich series of guild statutes, dated between 1270 and 1322.[73] Women were active participants in five guilds as weavers, finishers, candlemakers, merchants of wax, and dealers in small-weight merchandise (in effect, peddlers) which probably included old clothes. The statutes of the finishers and weavers, dated 1279, imply that all spinning was done by women.[74] Women at Toulouse were still engaged in weaving wool cloth and in dyeing it.[75] On the other hand, in a partial list of household heads resident in the Toulouse suburbs in 1335, not a single woman appears with an occupation.[76]

Barcelona in Catalonia was late in acquiring a wool industry, but it does appear as if women helped in its establishment. A report presented to King James II of Aragon in 1304 observes that the new industry was attracting to the city "from other hands numerous masters, both men and women."[77] At Barcelona during the first half of the fourteenth century, "women not only worked at the loom, but they were able to own their own shops, giving work to their employees and apprentices."[78]

The guild statutes of Italian towns also suggest that the labor force engaged in cloth production was mixed but that the participation of women was probably declining. The communal statutes of Bologna, dated 1288, mention "dyers, cleaners, shearers, finishers, weavers, burlers, stretchers of cloth, male combers and female combers, beaters, male spinners and female spinners, washers of wool."[79] The only two occupations cited in the feminine form are combers and spinners. Even the washers are treated as males.

Florentine statutes, dated 1296, of dealers in old clothes and workers in linen (*rigattieri e linaiuoli*), mention women vendors of clothes and workers in linen; the women are subject to the guild's authority and must post surety for their honest behavior. They were not, however, formally matriculated and were not full-fledged members of the guild.[80] A man who married the daughter or sister of a master could be matriculated for a lower fee into the guild, but this favor probably allowed guild members to pay a reduced dowry for their daughters' marriages. The guild statutes of the Florentine wool dealers (*lanaiuoli*), dated 1317 to 1319, continue to refer to weavers as both male and female.[81]

It does not seem possible to determine the number of women wool workers at Florence during the late thirteenth and early fourteenth centuries. The earliest notarial chartularies of Florence do contain fairly numerous references to women weavers. In 1288, for example, as seen in her will, a woman named Donata, an immigrant from Castellonzio in the countryside, supports herself by weaving cloths; after her death, her loom is to be sold and the proceeds given to the poor.[82] In 1299, another woman weaver, named Tessa, the wife of a shoemaker, accepts two brothers, ages eighteen and seventeen, respectively, as apprentices in order to teach them the art of weaving. They will remain with her for six years, and she will provide them with support as stipulated in the contract.[83] Male workers doubtless predominated in the Florentine textile industries, but women remained active even among the weavers.

The general pattern seems to be the following: By the thirteenth century in the textile towns of Europe, men were employed (seemingly in growing numbers) alongside women in the cloth trades that women once had dominated. But there are no indications of a systematic and effective exclusion of women.

Guilds and governments as yet had made no effort to limit women's work or to reserve or preserve jobs for men. In cloth making as in many other trades, women and men worked alongside one another without visible rivalry. The central Middle Ages remained a period of free enterprise and of open access to employment for both sexes.

As we now shall see, the experiences of women in the liberal professions show a comparable evolution.

NOTES

1. *PL*, CLXXI (1893), col. 1701: "Quis lanam, linumque trahet? Quis volvere fusum? / Reddere quis pensum, vel texere quis patietur? / Usus in nostros fiunt haec, tam commoda fiunt, / Ut si deficiant, vitae minuatur honestas."
2. *Thomas Becket*, 1875–85, II, 297: "Cum itaque S. Thomas scholaris juvenis adhuc exisistens scholas cum pueris aliis frequentaret, habuit magnam devotionem ad Virginem....Cum autem festum Circumcisionis Domini adesset, in quo novus incipere consuevit annus, et sodales sui quasi omnes gloriarentur de jocalibus pro novo anno a suis dilectis oblatis, ipse apud se turbatus est in animo suo...." The Virgin gives him "parvam pixidem porrexit, dicens: Hoc clemodium in pyside hac reclusum pro amore meo conserva." Thomas finds inside "praeparamentum operossissime et subtilissime elaboratum, in nullo deficiens." This version of the legend is from the chronicle of Hermannus Corneri, who wrote about 1430 but included much older materials.
3. *Ibid.*, 293. From Thomas Cantimpratensis (ca. 1255): "Cum esset Regina mundi, operis non ignara...salutat praesulem, comfortet ne timeat, de manibus ejus accipit vestem, resident juxta illum, et convenientissime reparat laceratam. Nec mora, opere completo, disparat."
4. Philippe de Navarre, 1888, p. 16: "Toutes fames doivent filer et coudre; car la povre aura mestier, et la riche conoistra miaus l'ovres des autres...de tou ce ne doit estre nule desdaignesse, car la gloriuse mere Dieu daigna et voit ovrer et filer."
5. De exordiis et incrementis rerum ecclesiasticarum. *MGH Capit.*, 1893–97, II, 473: "...Theotisci...a Grecis sequentes Latinos, ut chelih a calice, phater a patre, moter a matre, genez a genitio, quae Grece dicuntur cylex, pater, meter et genetion."
6. Aelfric, 1659, 1970, p. 79.
7. Aelfric, 1880, p. 101: "O meae ancillae, operamini melius."
8. The Anglo-Saxon settlement at West Stow (fifth to sixth century) included a sunken hut in which about 100 loom weights were

found, making it very likely that this was a weaving establishment. See Chapelot and Fossier, 1980, 1985, p. 112, and the specialist literature cited therein.

9. On this common type of structure, see *ibid.*, pp. 111–27.
10. Ennen, 1986, p. 88, citing Grimm's description of the Tilleda palace, which was published in 1963.
11. Vita Liutbirgis, 1937, p. 26: "Igniculum vero in ea cella carbonum ardentium propter diversorum tincturam colorum...."
12. Cited in *St. Germain*, 1844, 1886–95, II, 304: "Edificavit dormitarium subtus autem pisalem."
13. *MGH Capit.*, 1893–97, I, 87, cap. 49: "Ut genitia nostra bene sint ordinata, id est de casis, pislis, teguriis id est screonis; et sepes bonas in circuitu habeant et portas firmas, qualiter opera nostra bene peragere valeant."
14. Vita Liutbirgis, 1937, p. 25: "...in tam parvo domicilio veluti tugurio immissa."
15. Aelfric, 1659, 1970, p. 78: "zetas aestivales," "setas hyemales."
16. Brevium exempla, cap 25, *MGH Capit.*, 1893–97, I, 254: "Invenimus in Asnapio fisco dominico salam regalem ex lapide factam optime: cameras iii, solariis totam casam circumdatam, cum pisilibus xi...21. Invenimus in illo fisco dominico casam regalem cum cameriis ii, totidem caminatas, cellarium unum, porticus ii; curticulam interclusam, cum tunino strenue munitam; infra cameras ii, cum totidem pisilibus; mansiones foeminarum iii, spicaria iv...."
17. Ex Wolfhardi Haserensis miraculis S. Walburgis, edited by O. Holder-Egger, *MGH Ss.*, XV, 1 (1887), p. 543: "Fuit etiam mulier quaedam de villa quae dicitur Stopenheim nomine Geila....Nam cum dies festus eius basilicae dedicationis adveniret annuus...illa contumaci et inreverenti eam fronte despiciens, zetas hiemales et operosas ingrediens, curceboldum quem prius ad texendum erexerat, flexis digitulis texere coepit. Ubi dum duabus vicibus ex glomice sive tramea, quam manu tenebat, in tela fila transponeret, hesit miserae insertus manui glomex, et intumescente ea penitus cum lacerto, hae quae adfuere mulierculae mancellam ei a manu prevaricatrice et tumida dissuerunt."
18. Chrétien de Troyes, 1987, lines 5190–97.
19. Utrecht Psalter, University Library, Utrecht, MS 32, folio 84 recto; see Chapelot and Fossier, 1980, 1985, p. 120. The drawings were very influential in the post-Carolingian age, and three psalters inspired by them are in British libraries, one in Paris. See Dufrenne, 1978. The reproduction used here is from Cambridge, Trinity College, MS.R. 17.1. f. 263.
20. Charta Eberhardi. *St. Germain*, 1844, 1886–95, I, 621: "De mancipio nostro scopulicolas, quas in genicio nostro habuimus, plus minus quadraginta." Levison, 1901, p. 386, argues convincingly that *scopulicolas* should read *seu pulicolas*. He also upholds the document's authenticity and gives it the date 735–37.

21. Specimen breviarii rerum fiscalium Caroli Magni, cap. 4. *St. Germain,* 1844, 1886–95, II, 298: "Est ibi genicium, in quo sunt foeminae xxiv...."

22. Monumenta nideraltacensia. Diplomatorium miscellum. no. 7. *MB,* XI (Munich, 1771), p. 108: "Manicipia infra curtem inter pueros et feminas genecias, numero viginti-duo." Mention of them is also made in the confirmation by Abbot Gotbaldus, p. 110.

23. *Freising,* 1905–09, I, 788, no. 1045, exchange dated September 13, 908: "...atque de genetio ancillas xii."

24. *Westfalia,* 1847, p. 76, no. 95: "exceptis ministerialibus eius hominibus, Eilbehrt, Randuuihg, Acilia, Gela, Doda, Hoika, Mainza, Tamma, Hibuke, Hiaule, ceterisque mulieribus iam ad geniceum eis assumptis non ulterius assumendis."

25. *IS,* V (1720), col. 708: "...de vestimentis, quae de pisele veniunt, sive ginicro, decimam partem."

26. Ex vitis... Macharu, priore. *MGH Ss.,* XV, 1 (1887), p. 616: "Ex ginentio comitis Heinrici, de portu scilicet Einhamma erat puella nomine Oda caeca per annorum tempora...."

27. *Salzburg,* 1910, I, 245–46: "cum geniceo uno et cum omni familia, servis videlicet et ancillis tam curtilibus quam villanis...et cum omnibus utensilibus." I take this text to mean those attached to the *curtes,* or manors, and those on their own dependent farms.

28. *Farfa,* 1879–92, V, 254–63, a partial survey redacted sometime between 789 and 822.

29. *St. Germain,* 1844, 1886–95, xiii.109.

30. *Ibid.,* xiii.110.

31. Translatio sanctae Landrade virginis. *MGH Ss.,* XV, 1 (1887), p. 605: "...deliberanti adest quaedam ex ginetio eius puella cum eadem visione referens se monitam per haec eadem signa. Ea nunc in villa Godengohoro habitat."

32. Chronicon Beneventani monasterii s. Sophiae ordinis S. P. N. Benedicti. Printed in the Anecdota Ughelliana, *IS,* X (1722), col. 440, donation given by Pandolph and Landolph: "ut quomodo omnes legaliter ad nostrum sacrum devenire debuerunt palatium, sic illis in eodem monasterio deveniet ad serviendum et dominandum." The formula is repeated in several subsequent charters. I do not understand the sense of *dominandum.*

33. Chrétien de Troyes, 1987, lines 5256–85.

34. *ASS,* III Februarii, p. 698: "Ecclesiam porro S. Laurentii, quam diximus, unico amore excoluit,...ibi feminam quandam ex gynaeceo Domini sui divinis officiis sub levamine deputavit."

35. Many examples from Ghent are in *St. Pierre,* 1868–71. See, for example, no. 220, dated 1137, list of "tributaries," all women, serving St. Pierre.

36. See page 36.

37. Notker, 1962, pp. 91–92: "Erant quoque ibi duo nothi de genicio Columbrensi procreati...suo vel hostium sanguine servitutis notam diluerunt."

38. *Freising*, 1905–09, I, 385, no. 450: "...necessitate compulsus adherebat genitialis feminae sanctae Mariae famulae Meripure nomine et cum ipsa filium procreavit...."

39. For the sources mentioning the *ancillae*, see Kantorowicz, 1931, 1963, 1964, p. 523.

40. Huillard-Bréholles, 1859, V, 722: "ad filandum sive ad aliqua quecumque opera ut panem non comedant otiosum."

41. Frederick's principal biographer, Kantorowicz, 1957, p. 310, concludes that there is "no ground for assuming that the women were the odalisques of their lord."

42. *Salzburg*, 1910, p. 698, no. 237: "...non operi lanificii vel genescii sed honestissimis eiusdem ecclesie negociis parendum."

43. Vita Liutbirgis, 1937, p. 44: "...quas illa et in psalmodiis et in artificiosis operibus educaverat et edoctas libertate concessa seu ad propinquos, sive quo vellent, ire permisit."

44. *ASS*, III Februarii, p. 841.

45. Discussed in Herlihy, 1985a, p. 67.

46. See Chapter 2, note 43.

47. Chrétien de Troyes, 1987, lines 5298–5303.

48. *Ibid.*, lines 5420–5425.

49. This is indicated by the fact that she deferred to, and recognized as her superiors, women who were wearing a religious habit. Vita Liutbirgis, 1937, p. 44: "Quoscumque ergo viros sive mulieres in habitu religionis...conspexerat."

50. *Ibid.*, p. 32: "...ad memoriam revocans, quomodo illa puellari quondam aetate alteram coaetaneam suam ludificaverat...."

51. *Ibid.*: "...acum suam in communi eorum opere fractam, egressa namque compare sua eius integram acum clanculo surripere suamque confractam in loco eius connectere et sic eam de eius deceptione gratulari, quasi aliquid bene gestum haberet."

52. *Ibid.*: "...Haec illa ita gesta esse cuncta in infantia sua commemorat annis, quibus primum artem texturae didicerat...."

53. *Ibid.*, p. 13: "In tantum igitur capax ingenii fuerat, ut diversarum artium, quae muliebribus conveniunt operibus, illis, in quibus conversabatur, locis prae ceteris circumquaque habitantibus veluti daedala diffamabatur."

54. *Ibid.*, p. 26: "...sicut praediximus, multorum muliebrium operum artifex erat, nusquam ab alicuius utilitatis opere cessabat, nisi aut operando manibus aut orando...."

55. *Ibid.*, p. 15: "...rerumque suarum gubernacula in tantum possidebat, ut domus penes eam regimen constiterit penitus...."

56. *Ibid.*, p. 16: "...ut illis genitrix potius quam nutrix diceretur."

57. *Ibid.*, p. 26: "...si aliquod spatium temporis tantae strenuitati superfuit, eas, quae sibi aderant, instruendo...."

58. *Ibid.*, p. 44: "...puellas eleganti forma transmiserat, quas illa et in psalmodiis et in artificiosis operibus educaverat...."
59. *ASS O.S.B.*, 1935–40, III, 1, p. 131: "...in domo cuiusdam nobilissimi ejusdem regionis viri adultotenus educatus et altus fuit, atque in genaecio ipsius nendi, cutandi, texendi, omnique artificio muliebris operis educatus...."
60. Notker, 1962, p. 91: "In qua etiam cunctis in palatio ministrantibus et in curte regia servientibus iuxta singulorum personas donativa largitus est...."
61. *Ibid.*, p. 92: "...quidem de scurris ioculariter iniquit: 'O te beate Hludowice, qui tot homines una die vestire potuisti! Per Christum, nullus in Europe hodie plures vestivit quam tu praeter Atonem.'"
62. Monumenta san-Nicolaitana. *MB*, IV (1765), p. 288, no. 2. The subsequent confirmations are given in numbers 3, 5, 6, and 14, pp. 304–23.
63. For the date and authorship, I follow Van de Vyver and Verlinden, 1933. For the poem, see Conflictu, 1843. It has also been attributed to Herman of Reichnau, Hermannus Contrafactus.
64. Conflictu, 1843, p. 4381: "Quis queat in quantas rapieris dicere poenas, / femineis manibus vulsa solo penitus?" And again: "Cum jam perdideris quod habebas ante vigoris / ibis femineo dedita ludibrio...."
65. Gesta abbatum trudonensium. *MGH Ss.*, X (1852), p. 309: "Est enim genus hominum mercennariorum, quorum officium est ex lino et lana texere telas, hoc procax et superbum super alios mercenarios vulgo reputatur. Ad quorum procacitatem et superbiam humiliandam et propriam iniuriam de eis ulciscendam pauper quidam rusticus ex villa nomine Inda hanc diabolicam excogitavit tegnam."
66. *MGH Ss.*, X (1852), p. 309: "...meliorque sit rusticus textor et pauper, quam exactor orphanorum et spoliator viduarum urbanus et nobilis iudex."
67. Neckam, 1863, p. 281, cap. 171. For a technical interpretation of Neckam's text, see De Poerck, 1951, I, 313–15.
68. Neckam, 1863, p. 281. "Juxta liciatorium orditur textor, duplicique ordine distincto stamini trama interjecta maritabitur. Navicula autem intercurrens, pannum habebit in medio sui, spola vestituum, quae penso seu glomere materiam operi ministraturo operietur. Inde textrix telam stantem percurret pectine, aut mataxa circumvoluta globum filiorum ministrabit, aut dulci carmine taedium excludet, colum tenens laeva, dextraque nunc leniter lanam colo circumvolutam carpet, nunc filum subtiliter educet, usque dum fusum debita pensi quantitate rotundetur."
69. John of Garland, 1837. For a technical explication of the text, see De Poerck, 1951, I, 316–17.
70. John of Garland, 1837, p. 595: "Quidem homines usurpant sibi officia mulierum, qui vendunt nappas et manutergia, lintheamina,

et camisias et braccas, terista, supara, staminias et tellas, pepla et flammeola."

71. *Ibid.*, p. 606: "Haec sunt instrumenta mulieribus convenientia forcipes et acus, fusus et theca, vertebrum et colus, mataxa, trahale, girgillum, excudia et rupa, ferritorium, linipulus et culpatorium cum lexiva et laxvatorio, calotricatorium, licinitorium, quod monachi dicunt lucibrunciunculum." The gloss says: "Hae sunt instrumenta, etc. Quaedam sunt communia utrique sexui."

72. *Ibid.*, p. 600: "...et ideo contempnuntur a formosis mulieribus, nisi gratia numismatis acceptantur."

73. *Toulouse*, 1941.

74. *Ibid.*, p. 5: "...quod aliqua filandaria lane non recipiat ab aliquo homine vel femina lanam causa filandi...."

75. *Ibid.*, p. 6: "...omnes textores et omnes alii homines et femine huius ville Tholose possunt et liceat eis facere pannum..."; and p. 5: "...si aliquis tincturerius vel tinctureria...."

76. *Toulouse*, 1956. The survey contains nearly a thousand names of household heads and, according to its editor, Philippe Wolff, includes about a quarter of the city's population.

77. Carrère, 1967, p. 431. For further comment on this "carta del battle," with recent bibliography, see *Trabajo*, 1988, p. 260.

78. This conclusion follows from the interpretation of surviving guild statutes by the "Equip Broida" at Barcelona. *Trabajo*, 1988, p. 260.

79. *Bologna statuti*, 1939, II, 208: "tintores, battarii, tonditores, çimatores, tessarii, delapolatores, tiratores pannorum, petenatores et petenatrices, verghezatores, filatores et filattrices, lavatores lane."

80. *Arte dei rigattieri*, 1940, p. 9: "venditores et venditrices pannorum."

81. *Arte della lana*, 1940, p. 143: "quod nullus eorum [lanificum] det...aliquam telam alicui textori vel textrici ad tesendum."

82. See Herlihy and Klapisch-Zuber, 1978, p. 582.

83. *Ibid.*, p. 573.

CHAPTER 5

Doctors, Lawyers, Preachers

Sed consilio quorumdem inducta...pervenit ad quamdam feminam
sanctam, quae habebat gratiam curationum, et operibus misericordiae
plenam, quae plurimos diversis infirmitatibus pressos curavit. A
pauperibus nullam mercedem recepit, sed gratis eos pavit [palpavit?],
et medicinam quam potuit impendit.

But led by the advice of several persons, [the sick lady] went to a
certain holy woman, who had the grace of cures and was filled with
the works of mercy. She cured many persons oppressed by diverse
infirmities. She took no fee from the poor, but treated them for
nothing, and provided them with what medicine she could.

> Caesarius of Nuremberg,
> *Miraculas Erendrudis (1305)*

In the liberal arts—specifically those encompassing medicine,
law, and divinity—women's experiences were quite diverse
throughout the central Middle Ages. Women continued to exercise their traditional roles as society's nurses and healers. But
the growing professionalization of medicine brought a demand
that medical practitioners be formally instructed, examined,
and licensed. This insistence on certification restricted—though
it never entirely suppressed—the activities of women healers.
Probably because of the prohibition against women advocates
that was enshrined in the Theodosian Code, women had never
been very visible as lawyers, but even in this inhospitable art
they could not be entirely excluded. Their role in religion is the
most problematic of all. St. Paul's prohibition against women
preaching in the churches seemed to exclude them entirely
from religious teaching. In fact, they exerted a pervasive influence on styles of piety, though that influence is only partially
visible in the written records. Moreover, unlike their roles in
medicine and law, their importance in charismatic religion, as

mystics and visionaries, grew continuously as the Middle Ages progressed.

MEDICINE

Basic to the social history of the healing arts in the Middle Ages was the distinction between theoretical and empiric medicine, between *scientia* and *experientia,* or *theoria* and *practica.* The distinction is present, even if somewhat loosely, in the contrast between *medicina* and *cerugia* (surgery). Surgery in its common medieval meaning was not the performance of operations alone, but included all the practical techniques of healing.

The distinction, already present in ancient and early medieval medicine, became especially sharp in the central and late Middle Ages. From the twelfth century, the appropriation of the ancient medical texts (notably that of Galen) and the reception of Arabic medicine (principally through Avicenna) greatly enlarged and enriched the fund of medical theory. Newly founded medical schools systematically instructed students in the ancient principles. From the late thirteenth century, university-trained physicians were claiming the right to examine and to license all medical practitioners.[1]

Trotula

The most famous woman physician of medieval times is Trotula of Salerno; she is also an obscure and controversial figure.[2] She is the reputed author of the tract "On the Diseases of Women Before, During and After Childbirth," as well as a shorter disquisition on cosmetics.[3] Her major work on feminine infirmities survives only in an incomplete, early thirteenth-century copy made by a male, who cites her as an authority on the secret sufferings of women and claims that she is the true author of his work. Trotula enjoyed wide popularity in the late Middle Ages. She survives in a Middle English translation, and was known even to Chaucer.[4]

The medical school of Salerno, with which she is associated, can claim to be the oldest and for long the most prestigious medical school in the West. The first definite references to it date from the late tenth century.[5] Adalbero, bishop of Vienne in France, went there in search of a cure between 985 and 988, and Desiderius, the abbot of Monte Cassino who later became Pope Victor III (1086–1087), sought the help of its doctors in 1050. The Anglo-Norman historian Ordericus Vitalis was well informed about events in southern Italy, and he mentioned the "schools" of Salerno several times. In 1059, he related that a monk, Rudolf the Badly Tonsured, studied the science of physics (medicine) there and could not find anyone equal to him in the medical arts "except for a certain matron."[6] In 1085, Sichelgaita, wife of the Norman duke Robert Guiscard, tried to poison her brother-in-law Bohemond. She had been trained in poisons by the doctors of Salerno, who looked upon her as their *alumna,* or student.[7] The plot failed, and Sichelgaita even had to provide an antidote for the sickened Bohemond. But Bohemond remained pale and feeble for the rest of his life.

Women undoubtedly studied medicine and pharmaceutics at Salerno, and it is not inconceivable that the "learned matron" mentioned by Ordericus lectured publicly. How else could the breadth of her knowledge be widely known, even in distant England? The doctors of Salerno, beginning with Constantine the African (d. 1087), produced a steady series of tracts on diseases and healing. They several times cite the "women of Salerno" as the source of recommended cures. The women appear as experts not only on gynecological problems and on cosmetics, but also on such mundane infirmities as sunburn. The "women of Salerno" represent the tradition of empiric medicine, which the doctors of Salerno, presumably all males, were not hesitant to exploit.

There is, in sum, nothing implausible in the assumption that Trotula was a woman of Salerno experienced in the practice of medicine and in the secret diseases of women. In the last century, a Neapolitan historian of medicine, Salvatore de' Renzi, assigned her career to the middle of the eleventh century.[8] He points out that she was ignorant of the works of Constantine the African, who lectured at Salerno from 1077. She must have predated him, and may well have been the learned matron who, according to Ordericus, was in the city in 1059. De' Renzi went on to embellish her career with fanciful speculations, many of which persist in the recent literature.

In 1985 the late John F. Benton examined Trotula anew.[9]
He argued convincingly that she was not a male (as some historians have claimed, for the specious reason that no medieval woman could have acquired medical learning). Nor was
she a fictional figure. He thought that her real name was
Trota and that the diminutive Trotula was the title of her
writings. Somewhat surprisingly, he denied that she wrote
the works attributed to her. He too argued that only males
could have acquired the mastery of learned medicine that the
tracts reveal.

Benton was surely right in affirming Trotula's historicity;
women were indeed instructed by the doctors of Salerno and
were indeed celebrated for their medical knowledge. But his arguments against the authenticity of the works attributed to her
are not persuasive. Was it really the practice to apply a diminutive form of an author's name to his or her works? For example, the term *Clementina* is applied to the decretals of Clement
V, but it is surely not a diminutive; it is the third-person neuter
plural of the adjectival form, *clementinus*. It means "the things
of," that is, the collective decretals of, Clement, not "little Clement." Trotula's work on gynecology is often referred to as the
Trotula maior; in other words, the name is treated as a singular
noun. It cannot mean "the things of Trota," and surely not "big
little Trota." Trotula, as the tradition has always affirmed, is the
name of a woman, not of her writings.

Moreover, medieval readers respected famous names, and a
common way of attracting attention to a work was to attribute it
to a prestigious author. A condition of such attributions was
that the supposed author be a known person of established reputation. But Trotula had no independent reputation apart from
the few works that bear her name. There would be no advantage in assigning these essays to an otherwise unknown author.
A purely fictional person would serve as well. Benton's thesis
that Trotula was a real person, but that the works attributed to
her were written by males, is implausible. Either she was entirely fictional—and there is no evidence for this conclusion—or
she was the author of the works that bear her name.

It seems reasonable to conclude that Trotula was a true woman
of Salerno who lived sometime between the mid-eleventh and
early thirteenth centuries. Her reputation throughout Europe il-

lustrates the important and for long respected position that women held in medicine.

The schools of Salerno seem to have been entirely lay and secular in their membership. But monasteries too (after Carolingian times, all of them Benedictine) maintained a tradition of medical learning. Monks appear as medical experts—and so do nuns. The most prominent of the religious women trained in medicine was the German abbess and mystic Hildegard of Bingen (1098–1179).[10] Besides producing works on mystical theology and maintaining an extensive correspondence, she wrote a tract on *physica* (here, natural philosophy) and a work on cures. In her *physica*, she describes the characteristics of humans, animals, fish, plants, and metals. She is especially remarkable for her knowledge of herbs; in her works she describes some 485 herbs and plants. The importance of women—even religious women—in the "inner economy" of house and garden gave them opportunity to experiment with herbs, herbals, and pharmaceuticals; so did their traditional role as healers of the sick. Hildegard also shows the close relationship of medicine and religion—a kind of religious medicine characteristic of the therapeutic methods of the women empirics.

Jewish doctors too were prominent in the practice of medicine in the central Middle Ages, and their ranks also included women. I shall give examples later of some who practiced at Paris in 1292. Jewish women possessed a good knowledge of herbs and pharmaceuticals. According to her twelfth-century life, Christina of Markyate in England refused to accept Burthred, the choice of her parents, as her husband; to break her resistance, her parents hired a Jewish woman, who tried (of course unsuccessfully) to administer a love potion to the recalcitrant girl.[11]

Cerugia

In 1309 a French lawyer and official named Pierre Dubois presented to King Philip IV a project for the conquest of the Holy Land.[12] He recommended that a special endowment be established out of lands taken from lax monasteries and the military orders and that the endowment support, among other projects, special schools to train the personnel needed to reclaim Palestine. His proposals for the education of girls are especially revealing, as they illuminate the skills thought to be appropriate for women.

Recognizing the need to communicate with eastern potentates, Dubois recommended that "two or more" schools be founded for boys and "about the same number" for girls. The students of both sexes were to be selected from noble families when the children were four or five years old. Wise philosophers, skilled in recognizing a disposition toward learning, would choose them. The children would be educated free of charge, and they would not be returned to their parents unless all the costs of their training were reimbursed. Both the boys and the girls would be taught Latin and logic; then they would be trained either in Greek, in Arabic, or in some other oriental language. All would be instructed in theology. Some boys would then be sent to the Holy Land; these would undertake the cure of souls and would ultimately be ordained to the priesthood. Other boys would be trained in the law, both civil and canon; still others would be instructed in medicine, in the treatment and cure of men and of horses. These male doctors would maintain the health of the Christian army and people.

The curriculum proposed for the girls was quite distinctive. All the girls were to be taught medicine and surgery; they were also to be instructed in all the preliminary arts, including logic and natural philosophy, needed for a mastery of medicine. The smartest and prettiest of the noble girls would then be sent east; the Christian potentates would eagerly accept these beautiful and skilled young women into their households. Eventually, they would arrange the women's marriages to "the greater princes, clerics and the richer persons of the Orient." The medical training of the young women would make them especially desirable; the implication is that the ideal wife of a noble man is an expert healer. The endowment would cover the expenses incurred in negotiating the marriages, but the well-placed brides could be expected to reimburse the endowment from the wealth they would soon accumulate.

Out of love for their homeland, these wives would bring to their realms additional girls from the West, graduates of the special schools. The new arrivals would marry the sons of their hostesses and other great men of the region, including clerics destined for high Church offices. Learned and admired, they would gradually convert husbands, children, and acquaintances to the Roman faith. They could expect to be especially successful in converting eastern women, "whom they help by the practice of medicine and of surgery, and especially in regard to their secret ills and needs." Drawing great personal benefits from the medical skills of the western wives and maidens, the women of these eastern regions would come to admire and to love their benefactors; they would therefore want to join them in the Roman communion.

To be sure, Dubois believes that some boys and most girls would not be bright enough to master medical theory. Those males too dull to absorb the science of medicine could at least learn surgery; that is, the practical care of men and horses.[13] The girls should be instructed "in more intelligible, plainer and simpler science, as suits the fragility of their sex."[14] While disparaging the mental capacities of women, Dubois clearly looks upon surgery, or practical medicine, as a preeminently feminine skill. The male doctors and surgeons "should have wives similarly instructed, with the help of whom they can more fully look after the sick."[15]

The girls who were too unhealthy or homely to be useful in the Holy Land could still instruct others at home, "both in the science and the practice of surgery, and also of medicine, and of those things which are known to appertain to the art and work of apothecaries." In each school two girls should be retained who, "more knowledgeable than the others in medicine and surgery and their practices, shall instruct the other girls both in theory and in practice, so that the girls, when they shall leave the schools, will possess practical skill along with science."

Though practical medicine may be less intellectually demanding than medical theory, Dubois, following Aristotle, attributes to it an even higher social value. For without experience, he reminds us, "these [medical] sciences give little profit." As the Philosopher maintains, those who have experience without science are worth far more than those who have science without experience. Women medical practitioners, even if deficient in theory, knew how to heal.

Dubois' ingenious scheme was never implemented, though the Council of Vienne (1311–1312) did stipulate that schools of Hebrew, Greek, Arabic, and Chaldaic be established at the Roman court and at the universities of Paris, Oxford, Bologna, and Salamanca, each language to be taught by two masters.[16] Dubois' assumption, that the ideal wife or daughter of a noble man should be skilled in medicine, finds solid confirmation in the great mirrors of noble society, the chivalric romances.

Heroines and Healers

According to Chrétien de Troyes, author of the oldest surviving French romances, the wounded Yvain—and his wounded lion—were both nursed back to health by "two young girls…both of them wonderfully skilled in medicine."[17]

Many wounded heroes in the chivalric romances are treated and healed by women. In the twelfth-century romance *Tristan and Iseult*, the mother of the heroine, also named Iseult, is queen of Ireland. "In all the world physician was there none so knowing of all manner and arts of healing, for she knew how to help all manner of diseases and wounds wherewith men be visited."[18] Her reputation extended overseas to Cornwall and to Britain, and twice she cured the hero Tristan. He had done battle in Cornwall with the Morhaut, a fierce monsterlike person (and the brother of Queen Iseult) who came every three years to receive in tribute thirty youths and thirty maidens.

Tristan prevailed in the fierce combat, but he was wounded by the Morhaut's poisoned sword. The wound festered, and from it there issued a stench so nauseating that all fled his company. He sailed to Ireland to Queen Iseult, who alone knew how to cure him. She placed a plaster on the wound, drained the poison out of it, washed it with soothing balms, and laid on other plasters that healed it entirely in forty days. Later, Tristan slew a dragon in Ireland, but he foolishly put its poisoned tongue into his shoe. Its noxious vapors overwhelmed him, but the two Iseults healed him again, through ointments and medicinal baths. We should note the high proficiency of the two Iseults, mother and daughter, in the healing arts. The romance implies that medical knowledge, the special property of women, was passed down through the generations in the feminine line.

Marie of France, countess of Champagne, was both a patron of the new poetry and herself an author.[19] In one of her romances, a king tries to prevent his beautiful daughter from marrying, although she is in love with a noble young man. The king stipulates that only the man who can carry the girl to a pinnacle of a high mountain without resting may marry her. The young man accepts the challenge. To aid her suitor, the princess sends a letter of appeal to her aunt, who has been studying medicine for thirty years at Salerno. The aunt prepares a philter, which will give the young man strength and endurance in the ascent. He carries the girl up the mountain, but haughtily refuses to take the potion. Upon reaching the top, he collapses and dies of exhaustion. The philter spills on the ground and, Marie says, medicinal herbs now grow from the earth that it moistened. Women, it should be noted, have a special knowledge of herbs and pharmaceuticals.

In another French romance, *Aucassin and Nicolette*, Nicolette, who is a Saracen girl, cures a sick pilgrim simply by allowing him to glimpse her shapely ankle.[20] Once, her lover Aucassin was so excited at meeting her that he fell from his horse and dislocated his shoulder. Nicolette skillfully resets the shoulder, applies a poultice, and cures the sprain.

The German chivalric romances are no less rich than the French in allusions to women healers. In Wolfram von Eschenbach's *Parzaval* (written between 1200 and 1210), a queen and her maidens cure the wounded hero.[21] In Hartmann von Aue's *Erec*, the king's sister Famurgon at her death passes on her medical knowledge to another woman. In Gottfried von Strassburg's version of *Tristan and Iseult,* the male physicians who had cared for the stricken hero abandon him; only Queen Iseult knows how to cure him.

In Heinrich von dem Türlin's *The Crown* (written between 1210 and 1240), Queen Ginover (Guinevere) has learned from a Latin book, *Theoria medicinae* (The Theory of Medicine) that women are naturally colder than men, but she does not believe it.[22] The Lady Anzansnuse treats Gawein's (Gawain's) wounds with a plaster: "she knew very well how to make it, having learned the secret from Isolde [Iseult] of Ireland."[23] A noble maiden goes off into the woods to gather medicinal herbs needed to treat a wounded knight.[24]

The chief business of the noble man was making war. The sexual division of labor among the nobility is thus quite distinctive. Noble boys were trained to inflict wounds, and noble girls to heal them. Noble women were taught, usually by other women, to mend the mayhem their men had made.

Religious Medicine

Women were equally prominent as healers among the common people, probably providing most of the care that sick people received. Like St. Monegundis in the sixth century, they often combined folk medicine with prayers and appeals for miraculous help. An account of the miracles of St. Erendrude, composed by the chaplain Caesarius before 1305, offers an example of this common type of healer. St. Erendrude herself was a Bavarian abbess who died about 718. In one of her miracles, a rich lady was stricken so badly by pustules erupting on her loins that she could not walk; she was further afflicted by "elephantine leprosy."[25] Doctors were called from the universities (the *studia generalia*), and so was a monk physician, a Master Simon, "whose name is even today held famous." The woman's wealth, in other words, ensured for her the best care and counsel the universities and the monasteries could provide. But the doctors could accomplish nothing. In desperation, the lady sought out a "holy woman" who had cured many and charged little for her services.[26] Master Simon accompanied her on her visit to the healer, who recommended that she pray to St. Erendrude. She did, and she was miraculously cured. The "holy woman" worked her cures not only by administering medicinals, but also, when it appeared necessary, by gaining the intervention of the saints. Even the learned Master Simon praised her arts.

Midwives

Woman empirics and, of course, midwives were especially important in gynecology. The conviction was widespread that only women could decently inquire of other women about their feminine complaints. Women alone attended women in childbirth, for the reason, as one late collection of miracles puts it, "that they understand these things more correctly than do men."[27] In the late thirteenth century, Margaret of Cortona in Italy, a widow with a child to support, found employment in "diligently attending the noble women of Cortona in childbirth."[28] She also helped them bathe, prepared delicious dishes, and joined with others in singing "for the solace of the convalescing woman." Occasionally, however, pious thoughts reduced her to sobs and interrupted her in her therapeutic singing.

Physicians and Empirics

In France, the profession of medicine offers an early, clear example of the tension between the university-trained physicians and the women empirics. At Paris, as everywhere, women could not easily acquire formal training in medical theory. They were not admitted to the medical schools, and most were not usually taught Latin. Some female practitioners, as we shall see, could not read at all. Of 7647 physicians known to have practiced in France after 1200, only 121 were women (1.6 percent).[29] About one-third of these were midwives or nurses, and none lived in the thirteenth century. (However, this compilation of names cannot have included the several women physicians practicing at Paris in 1292, a topic to be considered in Chapter 6.)

As early as 1271 the medical faculty of the University of Paris, claiming precedent going back to at least 1220, insisted that all practitioners of medicine be examined and certified.[30] Repeatedly throughout the fourteenth century, the faculty appealed to the popes to condemn the unlicensed practice of medicine at Paris. In 1312 and again in 1322, the dean of the medical faculty prosecuted unlicensed women practitioners. The first was Clarice of Rouen, wife of another practitioner, Pierre Faverel, who was also indicted; the second was named Jacqueline Felicie de Almania.[31]

In 1312, on the dean's complaint, Clarice was arrested, fined, and excommunicated. Jacqueline's prosecution ten years later is recorded in greater detail.[32] A woman about thirty years old, she was accused of visiting many sick persons, both in Paris and its suburbs. She examined their urine, took their pulse, and palpated their bodies. She then told them, "I shall heal you with God's help," and stated her fee. She returned many times and again examined the urine "in the manner of physicians and doctors." She prescribed tonics to drink, "sedatives, laxatives, digestives, both liquid and non-liquid, and aromatics." In spite of repeated warnings from the university doctors, she continued to practice.

At her trial for the unlicensed practice of medicine, several former patients came forward to testify to Jacqueline's skill. They sought her counsel only after the licensed physicians had failed to help them; some frustrated physicians even referred difficult cases to her. She treated one patient with warm baths, poultices, and ointments; for others she prescribed various herbs, such as camomile. Jacqueline herself maintained that the prohibition against unlicensed practice was directed at foolish and ignorant persons. She, on the other hand, was expert in the medical arts and trained in their precepts. Moreover, it was "better and more honest" that a "wise and expert woman" should visit a sick person of her own sex, examine her, and inquire after "the secrets of nature." Trotula and Pierre Dubois had made the same point: that women physicians are more knowledgeable than men in treating women patients.

The faculty argued that just as women could not be advocates or even witnesses in criminal cases, so *a fortiori* they ought not be allowed to practice medicine. Jacqueline had not attended the medical lectures; she was not even literate. The court accepted the faculty's argument, ruled Jacqueline guilty of unlicensed practice, fined her, and confirmed her excommunication.

But the victory of the university physicians over the women empirics at Paris was far from total. The licensed physicians were simply not numerous enough to meet the needs of the entire population. And the onslaught of the great epidemics, from the middle of the fourteenth century, would immeasurably increase the demand for medical services. The licensed physicians might win condemnations of unlicensed medical practice from papacy and monarchy, and they might win suits at court. But at the bedside of the sick, women, perhaps even more frequently than men, would remain in attendance.

LAW

Medieval Europe lived under two different legal systems, based, respectively, on custom and on written (Roman) law. Roman legal precedents also profoundly shaped the canon law of the Church. With the intellectual revival of the twelfth century, Roman law gained in prestige and gradually extended its domain throughout most areas of the European continent.

The Roman legal tradition confronted women with formidable obstacles in the practice of law. The Theodosian Code (2.12.5 and 9.1.3) explicitly prohibited women from presenting criminal accusations in court (except in regard to crimes committed against their own persons); nor could they serve as patrons or advocates in another's trial. Church councils held at Paris in 1212 and at Rouen in 1214 excluded women from the corporation of lawyers practicing before the ecclesiastical courts.[33] In 1322, as we have just seen, the faculty of medicine at Paris used this prohibition as a precedent in its effort to exclude female empirics from medical practice.

Women were much more visible in courts of customary law. Noble women continued to inherit offices which empowered them to serve as judges or advocates. At least in romantic fiction, they presided over the "courts of love," deciding delicate issues of sentimental etiquette. Also at least in fiction, they could learn even Roman law and pass on their knowledge to students. On the religious level, the faithful were instructed to address the Virgin Mary as *advocata*, the gracious advocate of sinners before the court of heaven. Finally, in all courts, women were allowed to speak in their own defense.

Women frequently appear as lords and vassals in the feudal records of southern France and Spain. The frequent absence of husbands and fathers on crusade added to their visibility. Thus, sometime between 1098 and 1113 in Aragon, a woman named Sibila, wife of Ficapal, who is said to be "on pilgrimage," swears fidelity to a count named Peter.[34] She will serve him "as a man should his best and firmest lord." Other Aragonese charters use the phrase "as a faithful woman should her lord."[35] Sibila will even participate in his military campaigns and attend the sessions of his court.[36] As mentioned in another charter, she holds the lordship over "knights and vassals."[37] The active role of women as lords and vassals inevitably involved them in the business of feudal courts.

In 1130 in Germany, a lady named Eilica, countess of Goseck near Merseburg in Saxony, obtained from Albero of Bremen the office of advocate over the recently founded monastery of Goseck.[38] She soon became involved in a protracted struggle with the abbot Bertold. She accused him "of many unspeakable crimes" and summoned him to trial "at the face of the church." But her accusations were dismissed "as those of a woman against an abbot." Roman precedent was obviously affecting judicial procedure even in Saxony. After Bertold's death, Eilica persisted, argued with lawyers, appealed to the archbishop of Bremen, called together an assembly, addressed the gathering, and "all the people shouted in her praise."[39] Eilica was not unique in her service as advocate of an ecclesiastical institution. In 1104 in Bavaria a lady named Adelheit bears the title, and in 1134 one named Lewkardis does so also.[40] All these women gained the powers they exercised by inheritance.

Not even the Theodosian Code prohibited women from studying law. In a tale that cannot be substantiated, in 1236 at Bologna a woman named Vitisia, or Betesia, Gozzodini lectured at her home on the Institutes of Justinian to more than thirty students.[41] She bears the name of a distinguished family of Bolognese jurists, but otherwise I have not been able to identify the source of the story.[42]

Women could not have been entirely separated from the study of law. In the cathedral of Pistoia in Italy, the tomb of the jurist Cino (d. 1339) displays a relief sculpture that portrays Cino lecturing on law to rows of students. In the very back row, listening and learning, is the figure of a woman. No text, to my knowledge, tells us who she is or why she is learning the law. The sculptured panel commemorates Cino, and surely it indicates that at some moment in his career, in some forum, he had taught law to women.

Dramatic trial scenes involving women are frequent in medieval legend and literature. One tells of Empress Cunigundis and her husband, Henry II (d. 1025), both historical characters and both saints.[43] Cunigundis and Henry have vowed to preserve their virginity, even within marriage. The devil tries repeatedly to break their resolve, but fails. Then he devises a clever ruse. He takes the form of a handsome young knight, and one morning he leaves the empress's bedroom, in full view of her servants. They conclude that the young man has passed the night with Cunigundis, and report her suspected adultery to the emperor. Deeply hurt, Henry decides to shun his wife. Cunigundis, abashed by her husband's remoteness, learns of his suspicions. She demands a formal trial before the princes of the empire. They gather in court, and Henry commissions them to make judgment "recalling the laws and decrees of our ancestors." Cunigundis eloquently affirms her innocence, and asks that her case be decided through ordeal by fire. Twelve red-hot irons are laid out, and Cunigundis in bare feet walks over them. She treads on the burning irons "as if they were flowers." She even stands an extra moment on the twelfth iron and intones praises to God. She thus establishes her innocence before the court and her husband.

There are many other medieval tales portraying women who make dramatic court appearances or who lecture on the law before a male audience. But the exploitation of these themes in fiction probably shows how rare such incidents must have been in real life. The widespread reception of Roman law throughout Europe from the twelfth century created a nearly insuperable obstacle for women who might wish to serve as advocates.

RELIGION

Religious interests and values saturated medieval culture, and individuals who possessed special knowledge of religious matters inevitably earned a special prestige and influence. In spite of ancient prejudices and contemporary obstacles, medieval women were able to achieve great visibility in the fields of sacred learning and pious practice.

Theology

Girls in towns could occasionally receive instruction, though outside the new schools and universities. Perhaps the best-known example is Eloise, niece of Fulbert, a canon of the Church of Paris. In one of history's most celebrated love affairs, she becomes involved with her tutor, Abelard. Supposedly, her reputation as a learned girl first attracted her future lover. In order to gain access to her, Abelard offered to give her private lessons for a modest fee, and this appealed to her miserly uncle.[44] (It would be interesting to know whether Fulbert, "who loved his niece dearly," was her uncle in the maternal or paternal line.) Supposedly, Eloise mastered Greek and Hebrew as well as Latin; later, after both had retired to monasteries, she carried on a learned correspondence with her former lover. Excluded from the new schools, medieval women faced major obstacles in acquiring formal training. Nevertheless, some did so, either with the help of relatives or tutors or through their own unaided, but at times inspired, efforts.

Counselors and Sages

That any medieval woman could have functioned as a spiritual counselor or sage may seem surprising. As already noted, in two crucial passages (1 Timothy 2:11–15 and 1 Corinthians 14:34–35), Paul seems to have excluded women altogether from the teaching mission of the Church. In fact, this prohibition was less sweeping than it may appear. Although women could not teach formal doctrine to adult males within a church, they could still teach in other settings: in the home, in small gatherings outside church, and even in public squares. They could teach children, other women, and, privately, adult males. And they could instruct by example as well as word.

Women's place in medieval society in fact ensured that they would play a special role in religious instruction. They were the nurses of society, and the cure of bodies was closely tied, in the medieval perspective, to the cure of souls. "Bodily sickness," the Fourth Lateran Council observed in 1215, "sometimes is caused by sin"; and the council insisted that the soul be treated before the body.[45] Women were the first teachers of children and for many males a source of counsel throughout their lives. Perhaps they were, as Christine de Pisan believed, more given to charity and care for their neighbors' ills than were men. But the kind of sacred information they commanded was also distinctive. It was in largest part rooted in oral tradition, much like the knowledge of empiric cures. Again, the written sources offer only glimpses of its nature and content. But the glimpses are enough to establish its importance—and women's importance—in medieval religious life.

As spiritual counselors, women sometimes exerted influence on the highest levels of lay society. Christina the "marvelous" (d. 1226), an uncloistered religious, really a Flemish beguine, seems to have been illiterate. But according to her contemporary biographer, Thomas of Cantimpré, "she understood all latinity, and she fully grasped the sense of Holy Scripture." She "unlocked most clearly the most obscure questions [of Scripture] for certain spiritual friends, when she was asked."[46] Thomas is careful to mention that "she did this most reluctantly, saying that it was the office of the clergy to expound on Holy Scripture, and that this was not her ministry."[47] Still, she was on occasion persuaded to unravel the divine mysteries.

Louis, count of Loen, heard of her mastery of holy wisdom, visited her, and began "to love her and to adhere sincerely to her counsel and instructions." He called her his mother, and she often admonished him and directed him on the paths of justice. She predicted political events. In 1218, when he felt death approaching, he summoned her, sent his courtiers away, arose from his sickbed, prostrated himself before her, and recited "all his sins from the eleventh year of his life."[48] He made, in other words, a general confession to Christina. Her biographer, recognizing that her seeming administration of a sacrament might give scandal, assures the reader that the confession was not made "for absolution." But, by his own account, there was no priest present at the count's deathbed and no other confession was made—or at least mentioned. For Count Louis, Christina played the role of father confessor as well as spiritual mother.

After confessing his sins, the sick man summoned his courtiers back into his chamber and disposed "all his possessions according to Christina's counsel." At his death, she saw in a vision that his soul was carried off to purgatory, "to be tortured by most cruel pains." But Christina pitied her spiritual child, and petitioned God that the sufferings be visited on her instead of him. Her prayer was answered.

Many holy women appear as spiritual advisors to men as well as women, and many of their clients were socially prominent. The women also functioned as the leaders within small groups of "spiritual friends." Indeed, this is how their reputation spread and how they were able to attract biographers, who were almost always males. The two regions of Europe in which these women saints are most prominent are Flanders and the Rhineland (from the late twelfth century) and Italy (from the thirteenth). The many cities in both regions facilitated social interactions and the formation of small conventicles, in which women often were the dominating presence.

Thus, in Flanders Lutgard, though a nun, acceded to the request of a knight, sullied by many sins, that she become his spiritual director; he, her spiritual son.[49] Yvette of Huy, a Flemish widow who died in 1228, became renowned for her sanctity and attracted "men and women, seeking to be instructed by the teachings of this most holy woman."[50] In Italy, Margaret of Cortona (d. 1297), a widow whose father would not allow her to return to her house, and who lived for a while as a prostitute, gained a similar reputation. "Who can count," asks her biographer, "how many were the Spaniards, Apulians, Romans and others who came to her, that they might be instructed."[51] Christ himself rewarded her with the title *mater peccatorum,* the mother of sinners.[52]

Though often unlettered, these women constantly amazed their male biographers with their knowledge of theology. The blind St. Sibillina of Pavia (d. 1367) discoursed profusely about the sacred mysteries. According to a religious man who heard her, "she could not have been more eloquent in the expression of theological words, had she attentively read the meditations of St. Bernard or the soliloquies of St. Augustine."[53]

The life of Christina of Stommeln (a village near Cologne in Germany), who died in 1312, affords a picture of the kind of conventicle which these holy women led. Her biographer, Peter of Dacia, was invited to visit the holy woman in her home outside Cologne. He recorded the presence there of Hilda de Monte, her sister-in-law; Gertrude, the sister of the parish priest; a woman named Aleidis, "who by weeping (it is believed) lost her eyes"; and an unnamed little girl.[54] Peter himself became a frequent visitor, as did other men of the neighborhood, including the parish priest who had brought him. No rule joined together these little groups, and no liturgy was performed. They engaged in pious discussions, and a woman was the leader.

Priests and Preachers

The sector of religious life that the orthodox Church kept tightly closed to women was the priesthood and the performance of sacerdotal functions. But, from about 1100, powerful heretical movements challenged the Church's supremacy in many parts of Europe, and some of the heresies were willing to accept women as priests. This perhaps was one reason that the heresies proved attractive to women. They appear among the heretics with a frequency hardly to be matched in any other branch of medieval cultural history.

In the thirteenth century, Etienne de Bourbon, a French Dominican who had had much contact with the heretics of the South, principally Albigensians and Waldensians, reported that the heretics condemned marriage as a carnal sin. They allowed married women to obtain divorces, even over the opposition of their husbands, in order to follow their sect or to pursue a life of continence.[55] Peter Waldo, founder of the Poor Men of Lyons, or the Waldensians, sent his followers, including women, through the villages surrounding Lyons to preach to the people. "They, both men and women, simple and illiterate, scurrying through the villages and penetrating the households and preaching in the squares and even in the churches, won others to [their belief]."[56] The heretics, the Dominican noted, were divided on the question of whether or not women could serve as priests, but some accepted them:

> Some [heretics] discriminate on the basis of sex, saying that the [priestly] order requires the male sex. Others do not make a distinction so that a woman, if she is good, can exercise the office of a priest. I saw a woman heretic, who was burnt; she believed that, having the power, she could try to offer consecration upon a box prepared in the form of an altar.[57]

If heretical women could preach in public, spreading their errors, ought not orthodox women respond, similarly in public? The legend of the thirteenth-century saint Rose of Viterbo includes an extraordinary tale of public debate on religious issues, in which women were the participants. The Albigensian heresy had penetrated into Italy, and Rose set out to refute it publicly:

> In the simplicity of her heart she daily preached Christ Jesus to the people.... Against the heretics she raged fiercely, and she confounded their heresies with logical reasons, refuting their own arguments as false, and, as everyone listened, she showed the falsity of their contentions by clear and open reasons. And so to all who heard her it was crystal clear, and true in fact, that the [Holy] Spirit was speaking through her mouth.[58]

But the heretics were strong at Viterbo, and they pressured the communal government into exiling Rose and her relatives. The exiles took refuge in a castle called Vitorchiana, 4 miles from the city. However, there too a woman heretic was preaching against the Catholic faith. Rose engaged her in public disputations, confounded her with the logic of her reasoning, and clinched the case through opportune miracles.[59] The source of this account is not contemporary, but the legend still presents an arresting picture. In the thirteenth century, in a small castle town of central Italy, two women publicly dispute the fundamental questions of faith.

The biographers of women saints, sensitive to Pauline strictures, are hesitant to present their holy subjects as public preachers. But occasionally the theme slips through. Margaret of Faenza moved to Florence as a young girl and made her career in that city, dying there in 1330. She acquired, as she aged, a reputation for holy eloquence. Christ himself instructed her to go "through diverse places" and to offer consolation to those laymen who came to her.[60] She complained, "[I am] a simple woman, and I must live and speak with the learned and the foolish." Christ in response touched her tongue "so that from that moment she should have such effect and power, that truly God was recognized in her speech." As the fame of her eloquence spread, both men and women flocked from far and near to hear her. The enraptured crowds included "counts and barons, prelates and religious, drawn by the sweetness of her words." "No matter how many heard her, they all returned consoled to their homes." She still had doubts about her eloquence, but Christ reassured her:

> Do not doubt, daughter, that I am always with you in all things, and never shall leave you. I place my words in your mouth, and through your words I penetrate the hearts of the listeners, so that they know that without doubt I speak through you.[61]

The life is not explicit in describing where and in what circumstances Margaret addressed the "counts and barons" and other laymen. The entire tone of the life, the repeated emphasis on her eloquence and "sweetness of speech," indicates that she was preaching to large assemblies.

The prominence of women as spiritual advisors, as sages, and even on occasion as preachers was doubtless disturbing to many Church officials and explains the reticence with which the biographers describe women as interpreters of the Scriptures or as preachers. Occasionally, a biographer will directly confront the sensitive issue of the role of women within the Church. One of them was Hugh of Fleury, author of the life of Yvette of Huy (d. 1228). Writing in the Low Countries, a vibrant center of feminine piety at the time, he concluded the life with an extraordinary chapter. It is entitled "A Useful Admonition for Those Who Disparage the Virtues of the Saints of Our Day."[62] The "saints of our day," as his context makes clear, were women. Their critics were male clerics. "For much more now than earlier there are found in the Church of God many carnal men, not possessing spirit, who will not or cannot grant to others what they do not feel within themselves...."

> They at once judge impossible, what they hear of these saints, or they think that it should be reckoned frivolous, falsely stating that no faith ought to be given to those who [the pronoun is feminine] do not rely on the authority of the Fathers. [They claim], that what old or poor miserable women and lowly persons report to be visions of God are entirely dreams or tricks; [these persons], they maintain, are affected in the head because of the night vigils and think that phantasms of their imaginations are revelations of mysteries. And thus the carnal man does not understand those things which are of the Spirit of God.[63]

Hugh countered these criticisms with a biblical text (Matthew 11:25): "I confess to you Father, Lord of heaven and earth, because you have hidden these things from the wise and the prudent, and have revealed them to the poor." Who, he asks, are the poor? They are surely the poor in spirit, and theirs is the kingdom of heaven. The ranks of the poor, Hugh implies, are filled with women.

NOTES

1. Bullough, 1966, on the professionalization of medicine in the central Middle Ages.
2. Benton, 1985.
3. English translation in Trotula, 1940.
4. The Middle English text and a modern translation are available in Trotula, 1981.

5. Kristeller, 1945, reviews with a critical eye the early references to medical practice at Salerno; the citations are from his article, pp. 145–46.

6. Ordericus Vitalis, 1969–80, II, 76: "Physicae quoque scientiam tam copiose habuit ut in urbe Psalernitana ubi maxime medicorum scolae ab antiquo tempore habentur neminem in medicinali arte praeter quandam matronam sibi parem inveniret."

7. *Ibid.*, IV, 30: "...inter quos enutrita fuerat et a quibus veneficiorum eruditionem perceperat. Protinus ipsi voluntatem dominae et alumnae suae cognoverunt."

8. *Collectio salernitana*, 1852, 1967, I, 149–57.

9. Benton, 1985.

10. On Hildegard, see Ketsch, 1983–84, I, 261.

11. *Christina of Markyate*, 1959, p. 74.

12. Dubois, 1891.

13. *Ibid.*, p. 72: "Qui vero in addiscendo fuerint rudiores...cerurgiam hominum et equorum audiunt."

14. *Ibid.*, p. 70: "...scientia modo quo fieri poterit sensibiliori, planiori et faciliori, propter sexus fragilitatem."

15. *Ibid.*, p. 62: "Isti medici et cerurgici uxores habeant similiter instructas, cum quarum auxiliis egrotantibus plenius subveniant."

16. *Chartularium*, 1889–97, II, 154, no. 695. See also *ibid.*, 293, no. 857, July 25, 1326, in which Pope John XXII inquires about language instruction at Paris.

17. Chrétien de Troyes, 1987, lines 4697–98.

18. Hughes, 1943, p. 7.

19. *Ibid.*, p. 13.

20. *Ibid.*, p. 15.

21. Examples are taken from Ketsch, 1983–84, I, 267–69.

22. Heinrich von dem Türlin, 1989, lines 3374–76: "That which I have often heard read...may well be false."

23. *Ibid.*, lines 6720–23.

24. *Ibid.*, lines 9542–44.

25. *ASS O.S.B.*, 1939, pp. 350–55.

26. See the passage cited at the beginning of this chapter.

27. *ASS*, III Septembris, p. 247: "quia puer procedebat contra naturam quam rem mulieres rectius intelligunt quam viri...," account of a miracle of St. Adrian, dated 1 May 1516.

28. *ASS*, III Februarii, p. 306: "Et quoniam de suarum manuum labore se et filium decreverat alere, coepit nobilas Dominas de Cortona humilis Margarita diligenter custodire in puerperio."

29. Jacquart, 1981, p. 13. Jacquart's calculations are based on a dictionary of medieval French physicians originally compiled by Ernest Wickersheimer which she supplemented. Of 8219 physicians, she excluded 172 who lived before the twelfth century and 572 for other reasons.

30. Kirbe, 1953, pp. 5–6.
31. See especially Kirbe, 1953.
32. *Chartularium*, 1889–97, II, 255, nos. 811 to 816, "Lis Facultatis Medicinae Parisiensis contra practicantes illicite medicinam."
33. Fournier, 1880, pp. 32–41, "Des avocats."
34. *Liber feudorum*, 1945, I, 105, no. 197.
35. *Ibid.*, 508, no. 477, lines 1053–77: "...sicut fidelis femina debet esse suo seniori...." For a contemporary depiction of Viscountess Maria paying homage to Alfonso the Chaste of Castile for her lands of Bearn and Gascony, see, in the same book, plate 12.
36. *Ibid.*, 105: "...et faciat ad eum...hostes et cavalcatas et placitos per directa fide...quomodo homo debet factere ad suum solidum et meliorem seniorem."
37. *Ibid.*, 211, no 199. Sibilla sells to Ildefonso, king of Arragon, the castle of Galin, "cum senioratico militum et hominum."
38. Chronicon gozecense. *MGH Ss.*, X (1852), pp. 154–56.
39. *MGH Ss.*, X (1852), p. 155: "...haec ut cum legisperitis disputando certavit..."; p. 156: "Post perceptam archepiscopi legationem, post advocatissae serenissimam allocutionem, omnis populus in eius laudem conclamavit."
40. Monumenta oberatacensia. Codex traditionum. *MB*, XIII (1777), p. 15, an. 1104: "quod quidam prepotentes et timorati homines, videlicet Adelheit advocata et tres fili eius...." Monumenta mallerstorafensia. *MB*, XV (1787), p. 258, an. 1134: "...domina Lewkardis advocata mater Friderici....Eodem anno predicta matrona videlicet Lewkardis advocata...."
41. The source is Fort, 1883, 1970, p. 372, citing Ghirardacci, 1596–1657, I, 159.
42. *Chartularium studii Bononiensis*, 1909, I, 115, 24 February 1251, "Consilium...Napolionis de Gozadinis."
43. *MGH Ss.*, IV (1841), pp. 819–20.
44. Abelard, 1840, cap. 6; *PL*, CLVIII (1885), col. 127: "For since this good (I mean a knowledge of letters) is rarely found in women, so much more did it distinguish the girl and made her famous in the entire kingdom." The "knowledge of letters" to which he refers probably means the Latin language.
45. Mansi, XXII (1778, 1903), col. 1010: "Cum infirmitas corporalis nonnumquam ex peccato proveniat...."
46. *ASS*, V Julii, p. 657: "Intelligebat autem ipsa omnem latinitatem, et sensum in Scriptura divina plenissime noverat, licet ipsa a nativitate litteras penitus ignoraret, et earum obscurissimas quaestiones spiritualibus quibusdam amicis, cum interrogaretur, enodatissime reserabat."
47. *ASS*, V Julii, p. 657: "Invitissime tamen facere voluit; dicens Scripturas sanctas exponere, proprium esse clericorum, nec ad se hujusmodi ministerium pertinere."

48. *ASS,* V Julii, p. 657: "…et supplex ante pedes Christinae peccata sua ab anno aetatis suae undecimo usque ad diem illam… recitavit."

49. *ASS,* IV Junii, p. 201: "in spiritualem filium recipi postularet."

50. *ASS,* II Januarii, p. 157: "…et alii quidam promiscui sexus et aetatis, viri et feminae, cupientes sanctissimae mulieris institui disciplinis."

51. *ASS,* III Februarii, p. 317: "…et quis potest numerare Hispanos, Apulos, Romanos et ceteros, venientes ad eam, ut instruerentur salutaribus monitis?"

52. *ASS,* III Februarii, p. 342: "Ego enim feci tibi peccatorum mater."

53. *ASS,* III Martii, p. 70: "Mirandum est…quod mulier idiota de divinis tam ubertim tam promte, arcana quandoque tam idoneis loqueretur verbis, adeo ut per quemdam Reliogiosum dicebatur in vita ejus, si meditiones B. Bernardi vel sololoquia B. Augustini attente legisset, non debuisset plus abundari divinorum verborum sententiis."

54. *ASS,* V Junii, p. 245: "…quae plorando (ut creditur) oculos amiserat…."

55. Etienne de Bourbon, 1877, pp. 299–300: "Item, in matrimonio carnali, dicunt quod uxor potest a viro recedere eo invito et e contrario, et sequi eorum societatem vel viam continencie."

56. *Ibid.,* p. 292: "Qui etiam, tam homines quam mulieres, idiotae et illiterati, per villas discurrentes et domos penetrantes et in plateis predicantes et eciam in ecclesiis, ad idem alios provocabant."

57. *Ibid.,* p. 296.

58. *ASS,* II Septembris, p. 437: "In simplicitate nempe cordis Christum Jesum quotidie gentibus praedicabat, bonis bona pronuntianda aeterna, et malis supplicia sempiterna. Contra haereticos autem horribiliter saeviebat, et eorum haereses argumentis sensibilibus confutabat, argumenta illorum falso replicabat, et cunctis audientibus, dictorum argumentorum falsam apparentiam apertis rationibus clarius ostendabat. Itaque cunctis audientibus liquido videbatur, et erat, quod per eius os loqueretur Spiritus…."

59. *ASS,* II Septembris, p. 437: "Praeterea autem in eodem, quod diximus, castro Vitorchiani erat quaedam haeretica perfida, quae contra Fidem Catholicam quotidie horrenda latrabat…."

60. *ASS,* V Augusti, pp. 845–54.

61. *ASS,* V Augusti, p. 850: "Non dubites, filia, quia tecum in omnibus semper sum, nec in perpetuum derelinquam…ego ponam verba mea in ore tuo, et per verba tua penetrabo corda audientium, ut cognoscant me in te sine dubio loqui."

62. *ASS,* III Januarii, p. 165.

63. *ASS,* III Januarii, p. 165.

CHAPTER 6

Paris, 1292–1313

Quoniam, disponente et causante celestis armonie benivolencia, generati, nati et nutriti in regno Francorum, presertim prope Parisius, in moribus, constancia, fortitudine et pulcritudine, natos in aliis regionibus naturaliter plurimum precellunt, sicut naturaliter probavit experiencia, que est summa rerum magistra...

Since, by the benevolence and through the power of celestial harmonies, the persons conceived, born and nurtured in the kingdom of the French, and especially near Paris, naturally far surpass those born in other regions in morals, determination, strength and beauty, as experience naturally shows, the best of teachers...

—Pierre Dubois (1305–1307),
De recuperatione Terre Sancte

The city I have selected to illustrate the work of women at the close of the thirteenth century is Paris. The city is of interest for several reasons. It was the capital of the most powerful monarchy in the West and the seat of its oldest and most renowned university. It was almost certainly the largest city in Europe. Moreover, there have survived from the years 1292 to 1313, during the reign of King Philip IV the Fair, seven tax rolls, surveys of the urban population; four of them are published and can be readily accessed.[1] The tax imposed was known as the *taille*, and the rolls themselves are officially called the "Books of the Taille of the City of Paris." Moreover, about 1270, the provost of merchants of the city, Etienne Boileau, copied into one great collection the statutes of the principal guilds of the city.[2] No other medieval town offers so many guild statutes from so early a date. All these sources give a view of labor and laborers, of working men and women, unequaled for this period anywhere in Europe.

POPULATION

Numbers

How big was Paris at the end of the thirteenth century? Many estimates have been made, ranging from fewer than 50,000 to more than 300,000 inhabitants. The ambiguity of a single record or, rather, a single entry in a record explains the discrepancies. In 1328, Philip VI of Valois, the newly chosen king of France, ordered that a count be made of all the parishes and hearths in his realm. A document giving the summary totals of that vast undertaking has survived. It bears the title "The Parishes and Hearths of the Baillies and Senauchausées of France." Regarding Paris, the document reports: "The city of Paris and St. Marcel represent 35 parishes and 61,098 hearths.[3] St. Marcel was a Parisian *bourg*, or suburb, a physical extension of the city. The number of parishes, thirty-five, assigned to Paris, is correct. But the supposed count of 61,098 Parisian hearths has startled historians.

If the number is accurate, Paris would have been a very large city indeed in 1328. To convert a count of hearths into an estimate of total population, an estimate must be made of the average number of persons resident in each hearth, or household. Five is a common estimate, but this would set the population of Paris in 1328 at more than 300,000 persons—a fabulous count. However, rather consistently, hearths within cities are smaller than those in the countryside, reflecting characteristically low urban birthrates and high death rates. Moreover, the study of many hearth lists shows that wherever women appear in significant numbers as heads of households, the average household size is likely to be small. Many women heads of households will be widows, and many will be living alone. For example, at Florence in 1427, women presided over 14.3 percent of the households, and the average size of all Florentine households was only 3.8 persons.

At Paris, in the taille of 1292, the percentage of women appearing at the head of an apparent hearth is even higher—15.4 percent. The average household size was thus probably even below 3.8 persons. A reduced multiplier of 3.5 still sets the population of Paris in 1328 at upward of 210,000 persons.[4]

Even this estimate of 210,000 strikes some historians as unacceptably large. In 1956, Philippe Dollinger argued that the population of Paris in 1328 could have been only 80,000. He gave four reasons for rejecting the larger figure.[5] First, the circle of walls enclosing Paris was small. Philip II Augustus had constructed these walls between 1190 and 1209, and they enclosed only 273 hectares. A century later, Charles V expanded the fortified and enclosed area of the city by 166 hectares. But the total enclosure of 439 hectares remained comparatively modest by medieval standards. The walls of Ghent, for example, encompassed 644 hectares, and its population was only about 60,000.[6] Second, not one of the seven extant Books of the Taille yields hearth counts surpassing 15,000—well below the 61,098 recorded in 1328.

Third, Paris could not have been substantially bigger than other northwestern European towns—than London, with probably only 40,000 persons; Ghent, with 60,000; or Cologne, with perhaps 57,000.[7] A population of 210,000 places Paris well above the order of magnitude expected of medieval cities.

Finally, in Dollinger's view, the Parisian economy, lacking major export industries, could not have supported so large a population. The estimate of 210,000 for the population of Paris in 1328 is, in his view, "abnormal, stupefying, in contradiction with everything we know of the urban development of the period."[8] The figure of 61,000 hearths recorded in 1328 had to be "an error pure and simple."

In the same year, 1956, in his big survey of urban populations in late medieval and early modern Europe, the Belgian historian Roger Mols also concluded that the count of 61,000 hearths at Paris had to be erroneous. He thought that the figure exceeded by too much the estimated populations of other northern cities in the same period. Mols suggested that the scribe must have intended to write 61,000 persons instead of hearths.[9]

But can these objections outweigh the testimony of a contemporary record? In 1966 a French historian, Raymond Cazelles, reviewed the evidence once again and affirmed the accuracy of the higher count.[10] The figure of 61,098 hearths derives not from the guess of a casual chronicler but from a fiscal accounting done to illuminate the king's resources. Would the budget officials have let pass an egregious blunder involving thousands of hearths? Cazelles also rejected the argument that the circle of walls around Paris was too small to shelter a population of 200,000. Walls do not necessarily include the entire citizenry. And at Paris, settlement had expanded well out into suburbs. Moreover, the Books of the Taille, with their low count of hearths, could not have included the entire population, only those both obligated and able to pay the tax.

Finally, the contemporary descriptions of the city are quite consistent with the high estimate of 200,000 people. In his praises of the city of Paris, written in 1323, Jean of Jandun, master of the College of Navarre, observed that its artisans were packed so closely together that, wherever the eye should fall, it could not find two contiguous houses not packed with people.[11] As for the houses themselves, they were, he alleges, countless:

> If anyone should wish to count the number of ... houses of Paris, he would, it seems, labor in vain, hardly less than he who would try to count the hairs on the heads of hairy persons, or the stalks in a great field, or the leaves of a gigantic forest.[12]

The chronicle of Jean of St.-Victor describes the celebrations held at Paris in 1313, when Philip IV the Fair knighted his eldest son.[13] There paraded before the royal family 20,000 men on horseback and 30,000 on foot. The English ambassadors were supposedly stunned by the turnout. This total of 50,000 adult males, probably between eighteen and sixty years of age, corresponds perfectly with a total population of 210,000, or with the 61,000 hearths of the tax list of 1328.

Could the Parisian economy have supported such numbers? Many descriptions of the city dwell not only upon its large size but upon its overflowing markets, true horns of plenty. In 1164 a cleric, Peter of Celles, recently sent to Paris for study, wrote back to his bishop, John of Salisbury: "You have chosen for me, my dear friend, a very pleasant exile, where joys, though frivolous, abound, and where the supply of bread and wine is even more abundant than in my homeland...."[14]

Botero

Much later, in 1588, in a tract called "The Greatness of Cities," an Italian savant named Giovanni Botero explained Paris's huge size, then 450,000 people. In the quaint English of a Tudor translation, the city "in people and in abundance of all things exceedeth far all other cities whatsoever within the scope of Christendom." Moreover, it "feedeth them with such plenty of victuals and with such abundance of all delicate and dainty things as he that hath not seen it cannot by any means imagine it."[15]

Botero does not believe that the fertility of the city's region— the Paris basin—explains the plenty of its markets. Tourraine, he observes, was more pleasant, Saintonge and Poitiers more fertile, Languedoc more varied in its fruits, Normandy more open to the sea, Burgundy more flowing in wine, and Brittany and the territory of Bourges more crowded with cattle. Paris' critical advantage was rather "the easiness and commodiousness of conduct, the carrying out and bringing in, I mean, of commodities and wares to and fro."

Paris, in sum, was served by an unsurpassed network of land and water routes. The flat Paris basin was easily traversed. It was not divided by close-in political frontiers, obstructing movement. Its crucial asset was the Seine:

> ...And Seine, a mean river in France, beareth ships of such bulk, and carrieth burdens so great, that he who sees it not would not believe it; and there is not a river in the world that for proportion is able to bear the like burden. So that although it exceed not a mediocrity and be but a small river, yet notwithstanding it supplieth wonderfully all the necessities and wants of Paris....[16]

Although Botero was describing sixteenth-century Paris, surely the same factor of easy transport explains—and supported—the city's size in medieval times.

THE BOOKS OF THE TAILLE

The seven extant tailles of Paris, dating between 1292 and 1313, offer an exceptional profile of the city, its people, and their labors. To meet a mounting need for money, Louis IX (1214–1270) collected special "aides," or tailles, from his subjects. As early as the 1270s, just after Louis' death, the Brabant poet Adenet le Roi related how the land and the city of Paris were already burdened by "many a bad tax...taille and tariffs."[17] The seven tailles that have survived are only a late segment of a long skein of impositions.

Certain groups within society enjoyed a traditional exemption from this direct tax: the nobles who served in the army, the clergy, members of religious orders, students (very numerous in this university city), and anyone whom the king favored. Other, still larger groups enjoyed a practical exemption: They had not sufficient money to pay the tax.

Methods

In imposing the taille, the officials of the royal fisc first set the total amount to be collected in the city. Assessors divided that sum among the population. They classified the people both by status and by residence. In 1292, three groups were assessed separately from the rest of the city's population. These were the "Lombards"—in fact, all Italians in Paris were regarded as Lombards; the *menus genz* (lesser people), a nondescript collection of poor but apparently taxable persons; and the Jews. In later tailles, the assessors also placed in special categories the mint workers, the grain merchants, and the dead.[18] In 1313 the dead were further divided into those who had paid before their demise and those who still owed. Even the departed were not forgotten or forgiven their fiscal obligations.

Most persons in the Books of the Taille fell into the category of *gros genz* (big people). The assessors listed them according to their residences and households. The largest unit was the *queste,* or *quête,* usually a division of an urban parish. In the four published surveys I have utilized, the quêtes appear in approximately the same order, indicating that the assessors were working from a master list of the city's principal administrative divisions. In each survey, they further divided the quêtes into smaller units, usually identified by street names. These names and their order of appearance vary from one survey to another. The assessors probably inserted these small divisions for their own convenience as they proceeded.

Units of Assessment

Most of the entries in the Books of the Taille carry the name and the assessment of an individual taxpayer. A few entries refer to groups, such as "the beguines in the house of Laurence of

Saint-Marcel."[19] And a few entries assign an assessment to commercial companies, notably those of the Lombards, or institutions, such as the convents of the Knights Templars.

About 5 percent of the entries mention additional names or refer to children or other relatives of the apparent head of household.[20] The surveys do not, in other words, give an exact count of the numbers represented in these multiple entries. Thus, in 1292 we encounter "Beatrice the poulterer and her daughters," with no exact count given of her daughters.[21] The allusions to household members are both vague and varying. For example, Aalis la Bourdonne appears with four infants in her assessment of 1296, but alone in 1297; it is hardly likely that she lost all four offspring in a year's interval.[22] The assessors were consistent in identifying only the person they held responsible for the tax; they might or might not allude to others. The following analysis therefore counts only the first-named person in every entry, the one held responsible for the tax.

What type of social unit did these entries represent? The assessors themselves referred to the entries as "hearths" (*foca*), and I shall use their terminology here.[23] But they were also using the term very loosely. Quite frequently, the surveyors separately assessed persons who almost certainly were living together—parents and children, sisters and brothers, even, though rarely, a husband and wife. Thus, in 1313, Morise the Breton bears an assessment of 70 sous, and his wife Jaqueline is separately charged with 48 sous.[24] In 1292, Symon du Pont is assessed 8 sous, and his three unnamed children bear an even higher assessment, 18 sous.[25] Marguerite Euvout also has three unnamed children, separately assessed; they were surely very young, as they were living with a nurse.[26] Masters and their servants or apprentices were usually separately assessed. Thus, André Bigue, his two daughters, and his male servant all appear with separate assessments, though surely they formed a single household.[27] Even servants received a humble salary, and the assessors taxed them for it. The entries, in sum, do not represent true hearths, and they cannot be used for making estimates of the total population.

In the following analysis, I classify each entry, or hearth, by the sex of the responsible taxpayer. The sex of the taxpayers is usually easily identifiable through their personal names. However, there are some ambiguities. Names such as Denise, Gile, or Huistace were used by both sexes, and even normally masculine names such as Philippe, Guillaume, and Alixandre were occasionally borne by women. Usually, however, the sex is easily recognized through the masculine or feminine form of a modifier, an occupation or nationality. In the absence of evidence to the contrary, we can only assume that normally masculine names such as Philippe or Guillaume identify a male. The count of hearths I present below probably slightly understates the true number headed by women.

The manner in which women appear as heads of hearths illuminates their status. In the largest survey of 1292, 2238 women appear as apparent heads of hearths. Of these, 114 were widows (the names of their deceased husbands are given) and another 79 were or had been married (the names of their husbands are given). Probably most women in this latter group were also widows. The marital status of the vast majority—some 91 percent—of the female taxpayers is uncertain. Marital status of women seems not to have mattered very much to the assessors. In other words, in identifying responsible taxpayers, the assessors did not routinely subsume women under their husbands' names or households. In the eyes of the tax collectors, the women they assessed enjoyed (or were burdened by) fiscal, and surely in some measure economic, independence.

Whether headed by men or by women, the Parisian hearths were very unstable. Table 6.1 gives an overview of the earliest and latest surviving tailles, those of 1292 and 1313, respectively.

The total number of hearths declined by 56 percent (from 14,516 in 1292 and to 6,324 in 1313). Feminine hearths disappeared in relatively greater numbers than did masculine hearths. They were 15 percent of the total in 1292, but only 11 percent in 1313.

The stablest element in the tax surveys, which governed all other variables, was the sum that the assessors hoped to collect. It was roughly 12,000 livres, or pounds, in 1292, 10,000 in 1296 and 1297, and 13,000 in 1313.[28] To compensate for the diminished number of hearths, the assessors had to increase the average assessment; it was two times higher in 1313 than it had been in 1292. Clearly, the collectors, pressing to meet their quotas, were concentrating their efforts on recording persons who were most capable of paying. The returns to be expected from

Table 6.1   Entries in the Tailles of Paris, 1292 and 1313

Type	1292			1313		
	Number	Percent	Average*	Number	Percent	Average*
Men	12,279	84.58	0/17/3	5589	88.36	2/3/2
Women	2,238	15.41	0/12/7	735	11.64	1/11/4
Indeterminate	2		1/12/0	—	—	—
Group	22		0/19/11	3		20/10/0
Institutions	9		14/15/7	—	—	—
Total assessment			12,222/11/0			13,284/11/2
Average assessment			0/16/9.24			2/1/11.9

*Values are given in livres/sous/deniers of Paris; figures are rounded to the nearest denier.
SOURCE: Géraud, 1837, and Michaelsson, 1951.

the poor did not justify the costs of a rigorous scrutiny. It is, moreover, very likely that the nonextant earlier tailles, imposed since the reign of Louis IX, showed a larger count of hearths than the 15,000 recorded in 1292.

The tracking of the same taxpayers from one survey to another also shows high instability. I have done this for the parish of St.-Germain-l'Auxerrois. Predictably, the rich emerge as the most stable and most visible contingent. Gautier Morel, who appears in 1292 and 1296, is almost certainly the same as Gautier Moriau in 1297 and 1313.[29] He was a wealthy man, assessed for large sums in all four surveys. But only in the survey of 1313 do we learn his occupation: He kept an inn or tavern. His record, and many more that could be cited, also shows that occupational names were not consistently stated. Thus, another rich man, Guillaume from Rheims, appears as a *mestre avocat*, (master lawyer) in 1292, simply a *mestre* in 1296 and 1313, and simply an *avocat* in 1297.[30] Hearths headed by women are especially elusive. I could not find in the parish of St.-Germain a single woman who appeared in all four surveys, and it is rare to find a woman in 1297 who also appears in 1313. It is likely, however, that Marie de Dreues of 1297 is the same as Marie de Dreus of 1313; from the later survey we also learn her occupation: a *hostelière*; she was either a shopkeeper or an innkeeper.[31]

Are the tailles of Paris really representative of the city's population? Clearly, they do not offer a random sample of the urban hearths. The powerful, the poor and mobile, students and the clergy—rich men, poor men, beggar men, thieves—largely escaped the scrutiny. Still, the thousands of taxpayers listed in the tailles formed the heart of the Parisian economy; they were the men and women who sustained the city's prosperity.

The tailles help illuminate a subject even harder to investigate than women's occupations: their patterns of immigration.

IMMIGRATION

The information on immigration into Paris provided by the tailles is abundant but ambiguous. The names themselves yield two kinds of evidence. Some names are followed by a *de*, meaning "from," and then the name of a place (never the name of a person). Other personal names are accompanied by what can be called ethnic adjectives, such as Breton, Lombard, Norman, Picard, Fleming, and German. Names with *de* seem most frequently to identify immigrants from nearby towns and villages, from places whose names were quite familiar to Parisians. Ethnic adjectives, on the other hand, are the preferred form for immigrants from more distant provinces; for many, the exact place of origin would not be readily recognizable in the city.

Place names within the taille lists are often hard to identify and even to interpret. Some places of origin were within the city, and even the form "from Paris" appears. Thus, Auberi "from Paris" lives in the second quête of the parish of St.-Germain-l'Auxerrois in 1292.[32] We are not told why he appears with this unhelpful pointer to his origins. Ethnic adjectives give better evidence of origins. Table 6.2 shows the crude count of names of origin, of the type "de N.," for the surveys of 1292 and 1313.

In both surveys, about four out of ten Parisian males, and three out of ten females, were apparently immigrants to the city. This estimate is admittedly very crude. Some Parisians, who give with their names a place of origin, may not have been recent immigrants. And some true immigrants doubtless go unidentified. In spite of wide margins of uncertainty, the population of Paris under Philip the Fair certainly included a large contingent of persons born elsewhere.

Table 6.2 Immigrants in Paris, 1292 and 1313

	MEN			WOMEN		
	Number	/1000	Wealth*	Number	/1000	Wealth*
Totals:						
1292	12,279	1000	0/17/3	2238	1000	0/12/7
1313	5,589	1000	2/3/3	735	1000	1/11/12
"De N.":						
1292	3,424	279	0/18/1	547	244.4	0/13/10
1313	1,686	302	2/15/1	198	269.4	2/6/2
Ethnic adjectives:						
1292	1,306	106	1/13/5	121	54.1	0/13/8
1313	566	101	1/13/7	49	66.6	0/12/3

*Averages are rounded to the nearest denier.

There is, however, a significant difference between the two kinds of names identifying immigrants. Women appear more often as new arrivals from named places than as bearers of ethnic adjectives. In 1292, the sex ratio (number of men per hundred women) among those with a stated place of origin was 626, but among those bearing ethnic adjectives it was 1079. In other words, Parisian women frequently moved, but most came from nearby towns and villages. Men, on the other hand, came in proportionately greater numbers from distant provinces and countries.

We can further illustrate the differing immigration patterns of the two sexes by comparing immigrants from two clusters of towns, one nearby and the other distant. The first cluster consists of towns in the Paris basin, specifically Beauvais, Compiègne, Laon, Senliz, and Soissons. The second includes towns from Picardy and Flanders, specifically Amiens, Bruges, Brussels, Cambrai, Ghent, Lille, and Liège. The statistics are presented in Table 6.3.

Table 6.3 Immigrants in Paris from Towns of the Paris Basin and from Picardy and Flanders, 1292

	MEN		WOMEN		
Region	Number	Wealth	Number	Wealth	Sex Ratio
Ile-de-France	184	0/13/8.7	42	0/6/0.29	438
Picardy and Flanders	72	1/11/1	4	0/5/9	1800

The sex ratio for immigrants from towns of the Paris basin was a comparatively low 438 men per 100 women—lower even than that of the entire set of household heads (548). The women from the nearby towns and villages were also poorer than women in general in the city; this suggests that they filled low-paying jobs as household servants and unskilled workers. Even the men from the nearby areas were poorer than the average Parisian male taxpayer. On the other hand, comparatively few women were drawn to Paris from the more distant Picardy and Flanders. Picard and Flemish males were also much wealthier than the average Parisian. Paris was drawing from the textile towns of those provinces rich drapers or cloth merchants and skilled male workers. In 1313, the richest male in the survey, with an assessment of 150 livres, was a draper from Ghent named Wasselin.[33] Some women too were also cloth merchants or skilled workers and carried a high assessment. The richest woman in the survey of 1313 was a dame Isabeau, a *drapière*, or cloth merchant, from the village of Tremblay, probably Tremblay in Normandy; she bore an assessment of 75 livres.[34] As distances increased between the natal province and the city, proportionately fewer women came to Paris.

The ethnic adjectives, and the numbers of people who bore them, help delineate the demographic catchment basin of the Paris population, from which the city was drawing substantial numbers of its people. Table 6.4 shows the numbers of Parisian heads of households who display an ethnic adjective (among the categories that contain twenty-five or more persons).

Rather surprisingly, the largest category of immigrants identified by ethnic adjectives is the English. They are followed in descending order of frequency by the Bretons, Lombards, Normans, Picards, Germans, Burgundians, Flemings, Jews (though an ethnic, not an immigrant, group), Scots, and Lotharingians. Also present in large numbers are the Welsh and people from Cornwall (or Cornouaille in Brittany), and there are even a few people from Ireland. One of the Irish, named Jehan, is found managing a tavern in 1297.[35] A sprinkling of Danes and Norwegians adds to this northern contingent of immigrants.

We can summarize our evidence on immigration as follows: Paris of course drew heavily from nearby provinces; the city's lure also extended all across the western continent and even beyond. It is interesting to note the presence in Paris in 1292 of

Table 6.4 Parisian Heads of Hearths with Ethnic Names, 1292 and 1313

Immigrants	MEN			WOMEN			Sex Ratio
	Number	/1000	Wealth	Number	/1000	Wealth	
Bretons:							
1292	242	19.7	0/13/10.2	16	7.12	0/18/10.5	1513
1313	131	23.5	1/12/4.5	10	13.6	1/13/3.5	1310
Burgundians:							
1292	62	5.1	0/11/1.93	13	5.8	0/9/3.69	477
1313	41	7.4	1/4/8.29	4	5.4	0/3/7.5	450
English:							
1292	290	23.6	0/7/11.3	15	6.68	0/3/11.2	1933
1313	141	25.2	1/0/7.67	9	12.3	0/4/1.11	1567
Flemings:							
1292	60	4.9	3/0/3	8	3.6	2/0/9	750
1313	30	5.4	6/17/8.59	5	6.8	0/4/2.4	600
Germans:							
1292	108	8.5	0/14/0.44	6	2.3	1/10/6	2080
1313	31	5.4	1/4/5.18	3	4.1	0/15/0	1000
Jews:							
1292	58	4.7	1/6/8.8	28	12.5	1/16/4.71	207
1313				(Jews expelled, 1306)			
Lombards:							
1292	171	13.9	8/2/1.4	9	4.0	1/6/8	1900
1313	27	4.9	3/12/3.8	2	2.7	0/15/9	1350
Lotharingians:							
1292	11	0.9	0/10/7.6	0	0.0	0/0/0	
1313	25	4.4	1/6/11.7	1	1.4	0/8/0	2500
Normans:							
1292	119	9.7.	0/9/10.7	20	8.9	0/12/7.19	595
1313	38	6.0	0/12/6.78	4	5.4	0/16/1.5	950
Picards:							
1292	105	8.6	0/13/3.19	14	6.2	0/4/3.42	750
1313	38	6.0	1/15/9.89	4	5.4	0/4/10.5	950
Scots:							
1292	57	4.6	0/6/11.3	5	2.3	0/11/2.39	1140
1313	29	5.2	1/0/3.1	2	2.7	0/5/3	1450

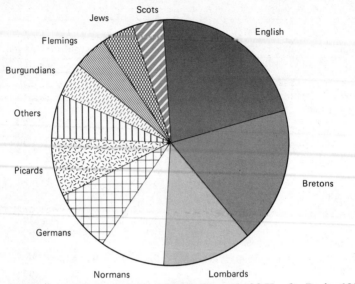

Figure 6.1   Ethnic Origins of Male Household Heads, Paris, 1292.

persons, including women, *d'outre mer* (from beyond the seas).[36] Presumably, they were refugees from the crusading state of Palestine, the last outpost of which, Acre, had fallen one year before, in 1291. Hungarians are also represented.[37] From beyond the Pyrenees come immigrants from Aragon, Navarre, and Spain.[38] The immigrant from Navarre is a physician, and one Spanish arrival works in Cordovan leather. Two immigrants in 1292 identify themselves as "Provençal" and one as "Gascon."[39] Several towns of southern France contribute to the stream: Bordeaux (one in 1292), Marseilles (two), Carcassonne (one), Cahors (three), and Montpellier (two).[40]

The Lombards formed the biggest southern contingent, but they are distinctive. They are the richest of the national groups, but they include very few women. The Lombards seem to have been chiefly bankers and big merchants who traded in Paris but did not intend to make the city their permanent home and did not bring women with them. One Lombard in 1292 is named Bouchacin. He is almost certainly the father of Giovanni Boccaccio, who, according to one version of his origins, was sired illegitimately in Paris.[41]

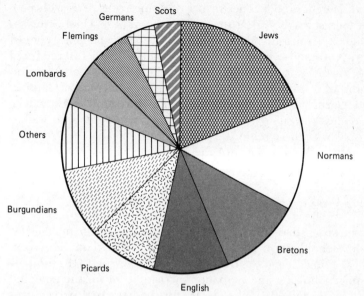

Figure 6.2 Ethnic Origins of Female Household Heads, Paris, 1292.

Although the entire western continent is represented in the Paris population, the groups from the distant south, with the exception of the Lombards, are very small, and most of them (Gascons and Provenceaux, and those from Bordeaux, Marseilles, Carcassonne, and Montpellier) disappear altogether in the survey of 1313. By numbers, the big and consistent contributors to the population are the northern zones. Not only are the English the largest ethnic group, but in 1292 the city of London itself contributes an additional twenty men and three women. Not even Lyons in central France sends as many (nine in 1292, eight in 1313).

Notable and curious are the many Celtic immigrants— Bretons, Cornishmen (from Cornwall or possibly Cornouaille in Brittany), Welsh, Scots, and Irish. These regions lacked major urban centers, and those who wanted an urban experience seem to have made Paris their capital. In the previous century, a great figure from Brittany, Abelard, made the schools of Paris the stage on which to display his brilliance. If the same pattern held in the early twelfth century as existed in the late thirteenth, he did not come alone.

The geographic zones principally supplying Paris with people unmistakably reflect the configuration of its chief artery of trade and transport, the Seine. The river provided easy contact with Normandy; beyond its mouth, the English Channel and the North Sea opened avenues to Brittany, Wales, and Ireland to the west, to England and Scotland to the north, to Flanders and Germany to the east, and even to distant Scandinavia. Doubtless the city exchanged food and commodities, as well as people, with these regions. Paris was unmistakably the great metropolis and magnet city of the north.

OCCUPATIONS

In the large survey of 1292, nearly 48 percent of the male heads of households show an occupation, as do more than 39 percent of the female heads.[42] In the smaller survey of 1313, the percentages showing an occupation increase to 74 for the men and 47 for the women.[43] The reason for the increased percentages seems again to be the omission of many poor persons and presumably the unemployed in the later survey.

The occupational names present some difficulties. Were some of them really nicknames or family names? Probably, yes; for example, many Parisians bear two occupational names, but it seems unlikely that most of them worked at two jobs. In 1313 we meet Raoul le coustellier coustellier, Raoul the Cutler, a cutler.[44] Probably the form "le coustellier" was either a nickname or a family name. Accordingly, when a taxpayer appears with two occupations, only the second one is included in the following analysis. On the other hand, it is not likely that many of the single occupational names were in fact nicknames or family names. The use of surnames was still far from general in Paris around 1300. The gender of the name always agrees with the sex of the bearer—a phenomenon not to be expected of authentic surnames.

The occupational names borne by women present even more difficulties. Again, some may have been nicknames. There are two priestesses heading hearths at Paris in 1292. What did these women do? There is also one *clergesse*, a feminine cleric, but perhaps her title indicated literacy and employment as a scribe or sec-

retary. (There is also one *escrivaine*, or lady copyist.) Did the occupational names that women bore perhaps represent the trade of a
deceased husband, which the widow did not even exercise? This
apparently was the practice in some late medieval German
surveys.[45] Women do appear with unusual occupations in the
Paris tailles—in jobs, that is, normally performed by men. One
woman smith or blacksmith (*fevresse*), one maker of stirrups or
harnesses (*lormière*), and three women masons stand out in 1313.
In 1292 we even encounter a female dealer in gravel and sand
(*gravelière*). It may well be that these women entered these normally male professions as helpers to their husbands, though the
entries themselves do not state this. On the other hand, it is inconceivable that these feminine occupational names were fictional and
that the women who bore them were not engaged in the specified
line of work. As we have seen, the assessors only occasionally identified a woman by her husband's name. Would they then identify
her exclusively by her husband's occupation? Married couples
sometimes appear in the lists with different occupations.[46] All the
evidence indicates that Parisian women really were active in the
trades whose names they bore. In the following analysis, I do not
assign to women the occupations borne by their husbands, living
or deceased. Only names feminine in gender are counted as
women's occupations.

Women and the Parisian Economy

What was the contribution of women in the large and complex economy of Paris? The numbers I cite in the following
section may appear small, but considering the low represen-
tation of women in the surveys (between 11 and 15 percent of
all taxpayers), the fact that women are even represented in
the occupation is more important than their absolute numbers.

In 1292, women appear in 172 occupations; in 1313, they
are seen in 130 occupations. (The comparable figures for men
are 325 occupations in the earlier year and 276 in the later.)
Women are thus represented in a large number of trades and in
all the principal economic sectors. As drapers, money changers,
jewelers, and mercers, they appear among the richest professions. There are even women moneyers, or mint workers.[47]

They are copyists and artists. There are women tavern keepers, firewood dealers, and even masons, shoemakers, girdle makers, millers, smiths, shield makers, and archers. Like men, women trained apprentices, who were not necessarily other women. Thus, in 1292 a "valet" named Oudet works in the household of Aveline, a milliner.[48] A lady juggler and dancer are present among the taxpayers of 1292. Very few occupations seem to have been composed exclusively of males. Those which involved either distant travel or heavy hauling—such as the occupations of sailors and porters—appear without women. Women were also excluded from some licensed professions, such as those of notary and lawyer. However, in these fields, even male practitioners were surprisingly few. Although women show a wide distribution across the occupations, they also show a marked

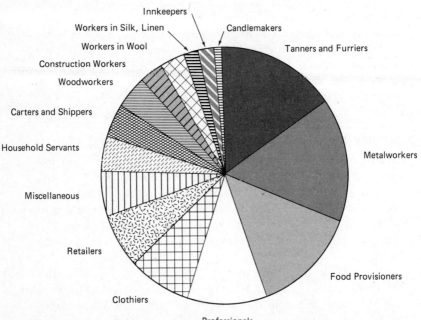

Figure 6.3   Distribution of Occupations by Categories, Male Household Heads, Paris, 1292.

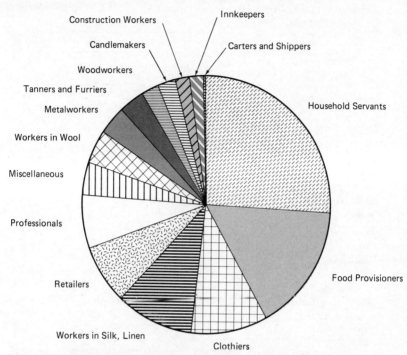

Figure 6.4 Distribution of Occupations by Categories, Female Household Heads, Paris, 1292.

tendency to specialize in particular trades. Table 6.5 shows the fifteen most numerous professions for Parisian women in 1292 and 1313.

Not surprisingly, the vast majority of household servants were female (they were also omitted in the survey of 1313). Male valets were also numerous (287), but presumably these were apprentices distributed throughout many professions. Most household servants were probably young girls newly immigrated from the countryside.

Women were important in the preparation and sale of food. There are five women "friers" (*fritières*), five millers, five sellers of milk, four soup makers, four sellers of oil, three brewers, three sellers of cheese, two wine dealers, and several types of bakers (nine *pastaières*, three *oublaières*) in the taille of 1292. Somewhat

Table 6.5   The Fifteen Largest Feminine Occupations in the Paris Tailles, 1292 and 1313

1292		1313	
Profession*	No. of Women	Profession*	No. of Women
Household servant	197	Tavern keeper	23
Peddler	50	Peddler	20
Dressmaker	46	Hostel keeper	18
Laundress	38	Dressmaker	11
Beguine (religious)	29	Laundress	10
Hairdresser	22	Silk spinner	10
Silk thread worker	20	Candlemaker	10
Silk worker	14	Mercer	9
Barber	13	Silk thread worker	7
Nurse	12	Woolworker	7
Hostel keeper	12	Linen worker	7
Fishmonger	11	Hairdresser	7
Wax worker	10	Wax worker	7
Candlemaker	10	Poultry dealer, firewood	5
Old-Clothes dealer, weaver, milliner, pastry maker, baker	9	dealer, goldsmith	

Key: baker = *fournière*, candlemaker = *chandelière*, dressmaker = *cousturière*, firewood dealer = *buchière*, fishmonger = *poissonière*, goldsmith = *orfevresse*, household servant = *chamberière*, hairdresser = *coiffrière*, hostel keeper = *hostelière*, laundress = *lavandière*, linen worker = *linière*, mercer = *mercière*, milliner = *chapelière*, nurse = *nourrice*, old-clothes dealer = *ferpière*, pastry maker = *pastaière*, peddler = *regratière*, poultry dealer = *poulaillière*, silk thread worker = *crespinière*, silk worker = *ouvrière de soie*, wax worker = *cirière*, weaver = *tesserande*, woolworker = *lanière*.
SOURCE: Géraud, 1837, and Michaelsson, 1962.

surprisingly, professional cooks (*cuisiniers* or *keus*) were usually men—11 out of 12 in 1313.

Women were prominent as *regratières*, peddlers who sold food-stuffs and salt. They were also numerous among the peddlers of rags and old clothes (*ferpières*). Women washed the clothes, al-though eight male *lavandiers* also appear in the taille of 1292.

Women were also very prominent in the care of the sick and the prescription of medicine. There are eight lady doctors and two *ventrières*, or midwives, at Paris in 1292. Three other women with the title of *mestresse* (mistress) may have been doctors. Not counted among the doctors in the taille, as she was not head of her household, is a Jewess named Sarre, or Sarah, a *mirgesse* (physician) and an apparent refugee from England. She lived with her husband, Vivant, who was not himself a doctor. Barbers too performed medical services, such as bloodletting or the setting of bones; thirteen were women in both 1292 and 1313. The many nurses (twelve *nourrices* in 1292) in the tax lists were all female. Spice dealers were also pharmacists; two were women in 1292 and two again in 1313. Finally, women administered the women's bathhouses at Paris (there were three *estuveresses* [keepers of hot baths] in 1313), which adult males were not supposed to enter.

Notable among the industries that employed women in significant numbers were the sale of wax and candlemaking. Women candle and wax dealers (*cirières*) outnumber the men ten to eight in 1292, and they are well represented (ten women, sixty-seven men) among the candlemakers (*chandelières*).

An industry that women dominated was the making of silk cloth. The raw silk had to be imported, chiefly by Lombard and Jewish merchants, from southern Europe, but women almost exclusively were engaged in producing the silk fabric. There is only one male spinner of silk to be found in 1292; the named women *filleresses de soie* are eight. The great corpus of guild statutes gathered by Etienne Boileau about 1270 identifies five silk guilds, whose membership seems to have been chiefly female. These were the spinners of silk by big distaff, spinners of silk by small distaff, workers (*ouvrières*) of silk fabric (who seem to have done weaving), weavers of silk, and makers of silk caps.[49] Probably, the numerous women simply called "weavers" in 1313 were working in silk. These female silk guilds show the same structure as the predominantly male guilds. Their statutes mention *preudes fames* (good women) charged with enforcing regulations. Spinners could not employ more than three girl apprentices and had to employ them for not fewer than seven years. The girls could then become mistresses of the trade in their own right.

As the chief spinners and weavers of silk, women were very visible in the making of luxury fabrics and clothes. They embroidered cloths (eight *broderesses* in 1292) and made lace (six *lacières*), purses (four *boursières*), pillow cases and altar cloths (twenty *crespinères*), and ribbons, coifs, and hats.

Why were women so important in the working of silk? One reason may be that most silk products—purses, coifs, ribbons, and the like—were made specifically for women. It is, however, also likely that their smaller fingers and greater manual dexterity gave them an advantage over men in spinning and weaving the fine silk threads. They were surely also more adept in lace making and embroidery than were men. Gold thread was often used in embroidery, and this probably explains the appearance of women as goldsmiths. (There were six *orfevresses* in 1292.)

Women were visible too in the production of another fabric: linen. The guild statutes, while mentioning only male *liniers*, assumes that both apprentices and workers in a linen shop will be female.[50] There were eight female *linières* registered at Paris in 1292 (as compared with eleven males) and four linen weavers (*telières*). While males may have sold the finished cloth, the workers who produced it were chiefly women. Flax was a garden crop, probably grown chiefly in the suburbs. Since time immemorial, gardens were the preserve of women. (A sixteenth-century English work, the "Book of Husbandry," assigns the growing of flax, the retting of the fibers, and the spinning and weaving of linen to the husbandman's wife.)[51] Some rural girls or women who settled in the city would have brought these skills with them.

It is further worth noting that at Paris these *ouvrières* in silk and linen seem to have worked in their masters' shop or house and not their own.

Patterns of employment are different in regard to woolens, by far the largest of the fabric industries. There were seventy-three male weavers at Paris in 1292 but only nine female, and these latter may have been working in silk or linen. In 1313 the comparable figures for weavers are sixty-three males and only four females. Among dyers, the sexual division is even more unbalanced. There were fifteen male dyers and one female dyer in 1292; twenty-five males and one female in 1313. Women doubtless spun the wool into yarn, but there are only six spinners (*filandières*) identified at Paris in 1292, and we cannot be certain that they were spinning wool rather than flax or silk. It almost appears as if the spinning of wool, though widely done by Parisian women, was not considered a primary profession worth naming in the surveys.

Wealth

Two further comments may be made on the status of women workers at Paris. They were consistently assessed at lower amounts than were men in the same profession. Table 6.6 compares the average wealth of men and women in representative occupations; the statistics are based on the survey of 1313.

Women workers consistently had fewer assets than their male counterparts. The two averages for all professions show that women's wealth was about two-thirds that of men. In the long run, the limited resources of women probably weakened their influence in the regulation of the trades. Moreover, women's participation in the Parisian work force seems to have declined between the two surveys of 1292 and 1313. Women constitute 13 percent of all taxpayers showing an occupation in 1292, but only 8 percent in 1313. To be sure, the latter survey excludes all household servants. But even if we leave the servants out of the calculation, the appearances of female workers drop from 13 to 10 percent of all taxpayers showing an occupation. Women's contribution to the total tax burden also diminishes from 9 percent in 1292 to 5 percent in 1313. Possibly, these small changes are purely artifacts of the document, engendered by the greater effort on the part of the assessors to

Table 6.6 Average Wealth of Parisians in Typical Occupations, 1313

Occupation*	Men		Women	
	Number	Average Wealth†	Number	Average Wealth†
All occupations	4147	423.5	348	277.8
Money changer	23	2089.2	2	638
Tavern keeper	535	438.7	23	153.4
Doctor	7	120.9	3	84
Dressmaker	55	89.4	11	80
Goldsmith	157	540.2	5	68.4
Peddler	59	105.4	20	46.1
Candlemaker	47	181.3	10	42.8
Launderer, -ess	5	40	10	39.2

*Key: As in Table 6.5.
†Values are in deniers.
SOURCE: Michaelsson, 1962.

snare the wealthy. But possibly too, these slippages portend the direction of future change.

Conclusion

The surveys of the city of Paris from 1292 to 1313 show that many women participated in an extraordinary variety of employments (172 in 1292). Women also appear in large numbers as independent artisans, working in shops or households outside their own homes. A "domestic mode of production," in which women work as part of a family unit and are subject to the authority of its usually male chief, is often supposed to be normative in the preindustrial European world. But it seems not to have characterized industry at Paris during the reign of Philip the Fair. If it had, it would have rendered most working women invisible to the tax assessors.

Though represented in nearly all the major economic sectors, women held special prominence as innkeepers, sellers and preparers of all manner of foods, peddlers of new and used clothing, wax dealers, spinners and weavers (especially of silk or linen), dressmakers, milliners and embroiderers, doctors, nurses, pharmacists, and bath attendants. In spite of the remarkable range of work they accomplished, women show on the average only two-thirds the wealth of men in the same occupations. This doubtless increased their social insecurity during the closing Middle Ages when violent plagues, famines, and wars profoundly disturbed the economy and community.

In spite of somber portents, Paris in about 1300 remained a fairly open community—open to immigrants and (before 1306) to Jews. Its big and bustling economy was even open to women. In its size, prosperity, tolerance, and culture, the Paris of this period embodies the finest achievements of the medieval urban revival.

NOTES

1. Géraud, 1837, edited the taille of 1292; see Michaelsson, 1951, 1958, and 1962, for the tailles of 1313, 1296, and 1297, respectively.
2. Boileau, 1870.

3. "La ville de Paris et de Sanct-Marcel figure pour 35 paroisses et 61,098 feux." Cited in Géraud, 1837, p. 477.
4. The exact estimate would be 213,843.
5. Dollinger, 1956.
6. The figure for the population of Ghent is the recent estimate in Nicholas, 1987, p. 17.
7. These particular estimates are from Chandler and Fox, 1974.
8. Dollinger, 1956, p. 35.
9. Mols, 1954–56.
10. Cazelles, 1966.
11. Jean de Jandun, 1867, p. 52: "...tante spissitudinis vicinitate compressi sunt, ut, undique perlustrantibus oculis, vix ipsorum continencie due domus contigue videantur expertes."
12. *Ibid.*: "At vero si quis omnem ceterarum domorum Parisius numerum summare vellet, fortassis laboraret in irritum, paulo minus illo qui multorum undique hyspidorum capitum pilos, aut agri magni stipulas, aut ingentis silve folia dinumerare temptaret."
13. Cited in Géraud, 1837, p. 467.
14. *Chartularium*, 1889–97, I, 24, no. 22: "Satis amenum delegisti, mi carissime, exilium, ubi superabundant gaudia licet vana, ubi exuberat plus quam in patria panis et vini copia...."
15. Botero, 1956, p. 271, from the translation made in 1606 by Robert Paterson.
16. *Ibid.*, p. 236.
17. Adenet le Roi, 1946, lines 1475 ff:
    "Mainte mal coustume ot cele establie;
    Taille et tonlieus assist ou pays par maistri
    De quoi la povre gent estoit molt mal baillie,
    Et la terre en fu molt en maint lieu apovrie,
    Encor le maintient on a Paris la garnie,
    Despuis en fu la vile assés plus asservie
    Qu'ele n'estoit devant, puis n'en fu netiie."
18. Michaelsson, 1962.
19. "Les béguines de chiés Lorenz de Saint-Marcel," Géraud, 1837, p. 63.
20. Thus, Géraud estimates the number of named individuals to be "close to 15,200," but there are only 14,516 entries based on personal names; see *ibid.*, p. 197.
21. *Ibid.*, p. 19: "Béatriz la pouletièere et ses filles."
22. Michaelsson, 1958 (taille of 1296), p. 25, and 1962 (taille of 1297), p. 21.
23. See Michaelsson, 1951 (taille of 1313), p. 9: "usque huc lxxviii foca."
24. *Ibid.*, p. 49.
25. Géraud, 1837, p. 11.
26. *Ibid.*, p. 12.
27. *Ibid.*, p. 17.

28. Michaelsson, 1958, p. 307, gives a total of 10,507/5/0 for 1296; *ibid.*, 1962, p. 451, gives a total of 10,585/11/6 for 1297.
29. Géraud, 1837 (1292), p. 16 (70 sous); and Michaelsson, 1958 (1296), p. 12 (1 livre 21 sous); 1962 (1297), p. 13 (3 livres); 1951 (1313), p. 14 (1 livre 10 sous).
30. Géraud, 1837 (1292), p. 26; and Michaelsson, 1958 (1296), p. 30; 1962 (1297), p. 29; 1951 (1313), p. 92. Guillaume's assessment grew from 30 sous to 6 livres, then to 7 livres 15 sous, and finally to 22 livres 10 sous.
31. Michaelsson, 1962 (1297), p. 9; 1951 (1313), p. 11.
32. Géraud, 1837, p. 5. On the problem of place names, see the discussion in Michaelsson, 1950.
33. Michaelsson, 1951 (1313), p. 18.
34. *Ibid.*, p. 202.
35. Michaelsson, 1962, p. 20.
36. See Géraud, 1837, p. 21, for Ysabeau d'Outre-Mer, her two sons, Jehannot and Henri, and her daughter, Marguerot, all separately assessed.
37. Three are present in 1292: Guillaume Hongrie, Phelippe le Hongre, and Chardot, his nephew. Géraud, 1837, pp. 6 and 146.
38. Four are from Aragon in 1292 (Géraud, 1837, pp. 49, 108, and 151), four also in 1313 (Michaelsson, 1951, pp. 32, 104, 321, and 322). Mestre Jehan, a physician from Navarre, is entered in Géraud, 1837, p. 152. There are five entries "de Espaigne" in 1292 (Géraud, 1837, pp. 52, 62, 63, and 169), but only one in 1313 (Michaelsson, 1951, p. 16).
39. Géraud, 1837, pp. 82, 88, and 149. Neither province is represented in 1313.
40. *Ibid.*, pp. 26 (Bordeaux), 87 and 168 (Marseilles), 47 (Carcassonne), 95 and 105 (Cahors), and 28 (Montpellier).
41. *Ibid.*, p. 2, Bouchacin, chiès Marie de Senz.
42. The exact figures are 5876 out of 12,279 hearths for the men and 883 out of 2238 for the women.
43. The exact figures are 4147 out of 5589 for the men and 347 out of 735 for the women.
44. Michaelsson, 1962, p. 243.
45. See Wesoly, 1980, p. 117, for the argument that women in German hearth lists carried the names of occupations they did not exercise.
46. Géraud, 1837, p. 6, Gautier le charretier and his wife, Dame Anès l'escuière. *Ibid.*, p. 114, Jehan de Montereul with no declared occupation and his wife, Dame Aalès la barbière.
47. See the survey of 1297, Michaelsson, 1962, p. 428, Jehanne la moussete, and p. 430, Eremborc, both listed among the moneyers.
48. Géraud, 1837, p. 95.
49. The statutes are in Boileau, 1879: p. 68, fileresses de soye a grans fuiseaux; p. 70, fileresses de soye a petits fuiseaux; p. 74, ouvrières

de tissuz de soie; p. 83, tisserandes de soie; p. 207, chapeliers et chapelières d'orfois. The text of these last statutes makes it apparent that the membership was chiefly female. It mentions, for example, the employment of only female workers or apprentices.

50. Boileau, 1879, p. 118: "Nus liniers de Paris ne puet ne doit avoir que i. aprentice...la quele aprentice il ne puent ne doivent prendre a mainz de vi anz de service...." "Li linniers de Paris prent tant d'ouvrieres comme il voudront...."

51. See the remarks concerning flax and hemp by James Greig in Astill and Grant, 1988, p. 114. The sixteenth-century author is Master Fitzherbert (1534).

CHAPTER 7

Late Medieval Society (ca. 1350–1500)

Ars lanificii bona est, et victui necessaria.

The art of making woolens is good, and needed for sustenance.
—Lidwina of Schiedam to a widow (before 1433),
Vita S. Lidwine

The late Middle Ages has been traditionally viewed as a golden age for working men. From the middle of the fourteenth century, famines, wars, and above all plagues radically reduced populations all over Europe. Losses in many European regions ranged as high as two-thirds of the population. Numbers stabilized at low levels from the early fifteenth century, and remained so for another fifty years. Not until roughly 1470 and after was growth renewed. The dearth of workers and heightened competition for their services drove wages up to two or three times what they had been before the first onslaught of plague in 1348.

If working men benefited from their own falling numbers, what were the experiences of working women?

ITALY

Late medieval Italy is a land rich in the documentation of social history, both literary and statistical. Among the works of literature, a poem entitled "The Conduct and Customs of Women" offers a list of feminine occupations. The poem was written by Francesco da Barberino (Barberino is a small town in the Florentine countryside).[1] He died a victim to the

154

plague of 1348, but he may have written his poem as early as the 1320s.

In the fifteenth part of the poem, he warns against the temptations and sins involved in the typical occupations that women held. The occupations he mentions are those of barber, baker, seller of fruits and vegetables (*treccola*), seller of eggs or chickens (*pollaiuola*) or cheese (*caciauola*), beggar (*accattatrice*, literally "a woman who receives"), innkeeper or cook, hawker of charms, mercer, and uncloistered religious (*conversa*). The mention of the barber's art and the allusion to sorcery recall the medieval woman's ancient association with the medical or magical treatment of ills. Women appear in his list in the familiar role of innkeeper, offering travelers lodging and food (they are not to provide, Francesco insists, additional comforts). Most of the named occupations involve sales of food and clothing. The sins he mentions in discussing women's occupations include the cheating of customers but never the bad treatment of apprentices or employees. The women he describes are peddlers or workers but not masters or employers.

Statistical records, specifically Italy's many and large fiscal surveys, show us the active, taxpaying population and, partially, the women within it. Later than Francesco's poem, they suggest that even the number of feminine occupations he describes was shrinking over the late Middle Ages.

Bologna

A survey, dated 1395, survives from the university town of Bologna. It lists all household members, and it gives their ages and occupations but not an estimate of wealth. A few women appear with occupations. Madonna Zohana, age eighty, "who spins," lives with her daughter Bertolomia, age sixty; the two old women are surviving in the city by the work of their hands.[2] Another old lady, named Fiore, age sixty, is a *revenderixe*, a retailer of rags and old clothing. Margherita, age forty, who is not given the title *dona* and may therefore not be married, is a spinner of linen. Four other women spinners of linen are her neighbors. They are the widow Dona Mina Pifari, age fifty, who lives with her daughter, age eleven; Dona Francesca, age forty, appar-

Selling chickens. (*Scala/Art Resource*)

ently a widow with a family of two girls, ages fifteen and four-teen, and two boys, ages five and three; and another widow, named Armelina, age forty-five. Armelina presides over a large family of five persons: Two boys, ages sixteen and twelve, are learning how to make keys; their younger brother is three years of age; and her two daughters are also young, ages nine and six. Three unmarried girls, presumably young though their ages are not explicitly stated, are *fanti,* servants. Another unmarried girl is a *famula,* also a servant. One older women, addressed as *dóna* and presumably a widow, serves as a *massaria,* a house-keeper. These fourteen or fifteen women are the only ones in the survey who show an occupation, and none of their jobs seems notably prestigious or remunerative.

This and other surveys frequently name both widows, their late husbands, and the husbands' occupations. At Bologna, for example, the occupations once filled by the deceased husbands were those of baker (*fornaro*), gardener (*ortolano*), mercer (*merzero*), tailor (*sarto*), armorer (*armailolo*), shoemaker (*chalcalaro*), hose or girdle maker (*challegaro*), and the like. It is possible, but not provable, that the widows continued their husbands' work. Women participated minimally in the Bolognese work force, and then only in such specialized work as the spinning of linen.

If women workers are few at Bologna, women beggars are many—some married, most widowed or single. The laborer Iohannes of Padua and his wife, Guaxia, of unstated ages, are both described as "poor and beggars."[3] Ser Iohannes de Fregano—his title indicates that he was once a notary—and his wife, Nobilis, are both "poor, sick, who beg and live from charities."[4] Two poor women, probably widows, Dona Fiore, age seventy, and Dona Pina (called "her companion"), age eighty, apparently share their common poverty.[5] Dona Antonia, age seventy, is widowed and poor; Dona Iacoma, poor. Zohanna, age 100, is "poor"; Bevegnuda, age fifty, is "widowed and poor." Iacopa, of no stated age, is "widowed, poor and begging"; Donella is a "widow, a wretched little woman, begging"; Dona Iohanna, is also a "widow, poor and begging."

This survey of 1395 is rare in registering another type of woman: the prostitute. Dona Iacoba, who lives with her widowed mother, Taliola, earns the admiration of the census takers; she is described as "best in the superlative."[6] Apparently, her charms earned her some prosperity, as she employs a servant. Her neighbor is Paulus de Regio, "poor and a beggar"; his German wife, Agnesina, is "a prostitute or nearly."[7] Georgius from Venice works in the wool trade, and his wife, Lucia, is "a declared prostitute."[8] But Dona Caterina of Parma, who seems to live alone, is *maxima meretrix* (the biggest prostitute). Dona Iacoba, also from Parma, is "a tacit prostitute." Dona Paula of Florence is called a "public prostitute"; she lives with her husband, Iacobus, who is identified as her *concubitus,* presumably her pimp.[9]

A Dona Margherita is described somewhat ambiguously as

"a not-perfect slave"; she lives with her husband, Guilielmus of Verona, and Bartolomeus, their son.[10] The entire group is characterized as "poor." The prostitute wife and mother is listed first among the household members; presumably, she earned what few resources the family possessed.

Prostitutes form the largest feminine profession at Bologna in 1395. It is surely significant that many of them are immigrants—from Germany, Venice, Parma, and Florence. Either prostitutes were prone to travel or women who traveled were prone to prostitution.

Probably the presence of the university created a strong market for prostitution. Apart from this, the university had no visible impact on the women's occupations—except in fiction. The Italo-French poet Christine de Pisan (ca. 1363–ca. 1431) tells a curious anecdote about a law professor named Giovanni Andrea, a professor at Bologna who lived some sixty years before she wrote.[11] Presumably, he is the same person as Giovanni d'Andrea, professor of canon law, who died in 1348 and whose tomb, by Iacopo Lanfranci of Venice, is now exhibited at Bologna's Museo Civico. When other tasks called Giovanni away from teaching, his daughter Novella would lecture from his chair to his students. "And to prevent her beauty from distracting the concentration of the audience, she had a little curtain drawn in front of her." Giovanni loved and appreciated her so much that he named a collection of lectures after her, the *Novella super Decretalium*. Christine's point was that women were entirely capable of reading law but were arbitrarily prevented from doing so. So it was at Bologna.

Florence

The biggest of all the late medieval surveys is the Florentine Catasto, redacted between 1427 and 1430; it included not only the city of Florence but all the regions—cities and countrysides—subject to its authority at that time.[12] In the entire catasto, almost 7000 women appear as household heads. As the number of occupations they show is so small, we shall consider all these Tuscan women, not only Florentines and not only city dwellers. Table 7.1 lists the occupations of women in 1427. These are occupations that women actually fulfilled; those of

Table 7.1   Occupations of Female Household Heads in Florentine Tuscany, 1427

Occupation*	Number	Average Assessment[†]
Servant (*fante*)	103	54.57
Uncloistered religious (*pinzochera*)	59	128.73
Dependent of a religious house (*commessa*)	41	160.90
Beggar, pauper (*mendicante*)	22	39.18
Weaver (of wool?)	13	43.08
Weaver of silk	12	33.42
Spinner (*stamaiola*)	10	49.9
Servant of state officials	8	44.25
Seller of dishes (*scodellaie*)	8	109.88
Seller of fruits, vegetables (*treccona*)	7	112.29
Laundress (*lava panni*)	6	8.50
Servant of church	5	36.60
Food dealer (*pizzicagnola*)	3	43.33
Innkeeper (*tavernaria*)	3	266.67
Carders (*carditrice*)	3	21.99
Seamstress (*ricamatrice*)	2	58.50
"Worker" (*manovale*)	2	53.50
Mercer (*merciaia*)	2	38.00
Hose maker (*galigaia*)	2	35.0
Wool merchant	2	1695.5
Furrier (*vaiae*)	2	141.00

*Only nonagricultural occupations with two or more appearances are counted.
†Values are in florins.
SOURCE: Florentine Catasto of 1427; based on machine-readable edition. See Herlihy and Klapisch-Zuber, 1978, 1985, for locations and explanations.

deceased husbands are not counted. Finally and unfortunately, the catasto tells us nothing explicitly about prostitution.

The visible participation of women household heads in the productive life of the Tuscan community was exiguous. Out of nearly 7,000 female household heads, only 270, less than one-half of 1 percent of the total, claim an occupation. To be sure, many other women were doubtless employed in households and farms, but they cannot be identified in these records. Nonetheless, the visible economy was a male bastion.

Few in number, the occupations that Tuscan women had in 1427 are also humble, by reason of the wealth or dignity they generated. The largest feminine occupation was service in the employ of private families, of the churches, or of the govern-

ment. The richest women are engaged in Tuscany's biggest industry, the making of woolens, but there are only two of them.
In this, the central source of Tuscan wealth, women chiefly participated in low-skilled occupations as spinners, carders, and
washers. There are women weavers, but other sources suggest
that they worked chiefly in silk and linen rather than in wool.
And these were still small industries in 1427. One Florentine
carnival song tells of women out in search of weavers, who are
males.[13] Many women beggars are also found in Tuscany, as at
Bologna. Religious women too are numerous; they represent,
after the servants, the biggest group. We shall presently look
more closely at them.

The history of the medical profession at Florence, recently
studied by Katherine Park, may lend these figures some chronological depth.[14] No women were matriculated into the guild
of *medici* before 1353, and none after 1408; but there were four
admitted between those two dates, and two others are mentioned
in early tax rolls, dated 1353 to 1355 and 1359. One woman, Antonia di maestro Daniele (matriculated, 1386), is either the daughter or the widow of a Jew. Park concludes, appropriately, that "the
medical profession was relatively open in the decades immediately
following the first epidemic or plague" but by the early fifteenth
century had become restricted. Boccaccio himself complains that
in the wake of the Black Death, unqualified persons, including
women, took up the cure of bodies.[15] It is not unlikely that the
great losses of 1348 opened many occupations to women, but the
gains were temporary and were quickly erased once stability was
restored.

Verona

Verona in the Veneto has preserved a series of *estimi* from 1423.
My analysis is based on the partially surviving *estimo* of 1423 and
the declarations from the same parishes that appear in the survey of 1502. Again, because the number of women showing occupations is so small, Table 7.2 gives combined figures. Women
at Verona throughout the fifteenth century formed a minuscule
part of the officially recognized labor force. Still, the cluster of
weavers should be noted. These most likely worked in silk
rather than in wool, as probably did the otherwise unspecified

Table 7.2 Women's Occupations in Verona, Combined Surveys, 1423 and 1502

Occupation*	Number	Average Assessment[†]
Weaver	14	5.57
Spinner	8	5.643
"Worker"	2	5.50
Skinner (*scardassiere*)	2	4.50

*Only nonagricultural occupations with two or more appearances are counted.
†Values are in Veronese *solidi.*
SOURCE: See Herlihy, 1973, for a description of the surveys.

"workers." The growth of the silk industry was to confer substantial benefits on women, who worked better at several of its processes (spinning, weaving, embroidering) than did men. But its great age lay in the future.

Women and Guilds

Evidence from the guild statutes confirms the picture that the urban surveys present. Women sold foodstuffs at the markets, often spinning during the duller moments of the day. They were petty retailers. They baked bread and kept inns and taverns.[16] They

Fruit and vegetable market. (*Art Resource*)

were important in the production of silk, linen, and cotton, much less so in the manufacture of woolens, apart from washing and spinning the wool and burling the finished cloths. The small participation of women in the labor force parallels their virtual exclusion from the urban guilds. I have found no guilds in Italy that were exclusively female. Paris and, as we shall see, Cologne possessed several guilds of women workers, chiefly involved in producing silk fabrics or cloth-of-gold. At Florence, matriculation lists of the guild of silk merchants, the Por Santa Maria, begin as early as 1225; the lists over the centuries show not a single feminine name.[17]

Some guilds—such as the guild of the used-clothes peddlers and linen dealers at Florence—regulated the work of women but did not admit them into the mastership. The failure of women to obtain full membership in guilds restricted their participation in many sectors of urban life, for guilds not only dominated the town economies but also, in large part, their governments and even the ritual life of the cities.

Still, the impression remains that the cities of thirteenth-century Italy were more open to women workers than they were 200 years later. At Florence, women weavers, even some training male apprentices, are fairly common in the thirteenth-century chartularies.[18] They are, in contrast, hard to find in the fifteenth-century sources.

Religious Women

Apart from household servants, the largest of all feminine professions listed in the Florentine Catasto are *commesse*, wards or servants of a religious establishment, and *pinzochere*, uncloistered religious women. The *pinzochere* appear to be very similar to the northern beguines, except that the Italian women seem not to have lived together in spontaneously organized communities.

Francesco da Barberino in his poem on feminine behavior devoted its eighth part to "those women who have taken a religious habit at home"—to pinzochere, in sum, though he does not use the term.[19] Francesco is harshly critical of this state of life. Very few women, he claims, adopt it out of purely religious motives. Usually, they want the freedom which, rather oddly, they can exercise as professed religious. Unsupervised by a superior, unwatched by diligent sisters, young girls in particular fall easy prey to sexual temptations and seductions.

Though in his view women should not profess religion outside a cloister, Francesco does relate a kind of contrary anecdote. He tells the story of a young girl named Amabile, "lovable." She is, of course, both beautiful and chaste, so much so that her reputation spreads throughout the land. When she attains thirteen years—clearly the nubile age, in Francesco's view—the king of France petitions for her hand. She refuses, preferring virginity, but she does not enter a convent. Rather, she remains at home, living with her nurse, whom she supports. Every working day, after morning prayers and Mass, she makes purses, presumably out of silk, classically the woman's fabric. Her purses are fine and beautiful, and they bring her all the profit she needs to maintain her household in comfort. She keeps silence as she works, but after vespers in the evening she engages in conversation. On Sundays and holy days,

Margaret of York, Duchess of Burgundy, at prayer with her ladies.
(*Bodleian Library, Oxford, MS Douce 365, fol. cxv*)

when manual labor is forbidden, she reads edifying literature. Thus she passes her days in industry, piety, and plenty. Silk work and prayers—these activities circumscribed the lives of many medieval women in Italy, both inside and outside cloisters.

A song sung by masques of uncloistered religious women, the pinzochere, at the Florentine carnival also helps illuminate their lives.[20] The pinzochere claim to possess "secrets," with which they can accomplish "stupendous things." They cast spells from cards or pieces of parchment. They carry with them little boxes that contain the materials of magic—parts of bats or of hangmen's ropes and other objects even more disgusting. Amulets, talismans, blessed candles, and written charms are further means "by which we influence people."[21]

Not only experts in magic, they are learned in the use of cosmetics. By their ointments, young women can clear their skin, remove wrinkles, firm up their breasts, and preserve or restore beauty. They have the means to pluck eyebrows, clean the teeth, and clear the eyes. Their remedies, they claim, "are properly made in paradise."

Finally, they are experts in childbirth. They claim that they can induce childbirth—or perhaps an abortion. Through their secrets, a girl, pregnant outside marriage, can deliver her baby but don again her maidenly dress, preserving her honor and fooling priests into thinking she is a virgin.[22]

Though experts in magic, these carnival women are not witches; they have made no pact with the devil. But they do practice a kind of magical medicine, they restore beauty and counsel about love, and they have the knowledge of midwifery. Their special knowledge enables them to *ir portante,* to walk with bearing. This is better, they remind their lady listeners, than being "a wretch, a washerwoman or a menial."[23] The pinzochere know well the kinds of occupations that many aging and unskilled Florentine women would have to fill.

Osanna Andreasi of Mantua

Francesco's Amabile the purse maker and the beguines of the Florentine carnival are indisputably fictional figures, the one idealized, the others satirized. The life of Osanna Andreasi of Mantua balances these fictions with a view of a historic personage. She was born at Mantua in 1449 and died there in 1502, at the age of fifty-three. Her close admirer, the renowned Isabella d'Este, marchesa of the city, arranged for her a lavish funeral and commissioned a splendid tomb (designed by Cristoforo Romano but no longer in existence). Also through Isabella's influence, Ossana was beatified in 1515, though never canonized. The *Acta Sanctorum* under the date of June 18 contains two biographies and some forty letters written by the holy woman herself.[24]

The two biographies do not agree about her social background. One affirms that her parents were "citizens of the middle class," the other that she was of noble origins.[25] She may have been related through her mother with the Gonzaga, the reigning family at Mantua.

Her childhood was difficult. Her father refused to permit little Osanna to learn to read, claiming that "it was very dangerous and indecent for women to give attention to letters, as often they have turned this to their own perdition and to the disgrace of their families."[26] Osanna appealed to a statue of the Virgin that was in her room. The Virgin herself became her *magistra*. In daily visits Mary instructed her and brought her books, through which Osanna learned her letters. She even mastered Latin texts, "however convoluted and abstruse." This is a telling picture: the Virgin secretly teaches little Osanna how to read, against her father's wishes, in the seclusion of her room.

Osanna's father also believed that her early ecstasies were symptoms of epilepsy. "Oh," she complained, "how many tribulations I bore from the cruelty of my father."[27] When Osanna reached the nubile years, she defied her parents and refused to marry. The conflict was resolved by the death of both father and mother when she was still only fifteen years old.

Osanna asked God for permission to enter a convent, but He directed her to remain in the world "for the salvation and consolation of many."[28] From age fifteen she assumed primary responsibility for the administration of her household. "She showed herself," her biography relates, "a mother to her brothers and sisters." Even after her brothers grew up and married, she continued to manage the family's temporal affairs and retained charge over the education of her young nieces and nephews, training them in both "the divine law" and "civic manners."

The recognition that she earned soon spread beyond her domestic circle and even beyond Mantua. She provided for the citizens of Mantua a kind of consulting service. The leading citizens, their wives and children, flocked to her house, as if she were a modern-day Delphic oracle or a "most excellent prophet." She advised on the management of property and made predictions about contemporary politics. Those who consulted her believed that "nothing bad could happen if they followed Osanna's opinion." When in 1478 Marchese Federigo I Gonzaga went off to make war in Tuscany, he committed his wife and children to Osanna's care. Her advice was valued even in matters of high politics. She assured the marchese that the looming power of the Borgia family, which threatened to engulf Mantua, would vanish like straw set afire.

Though herself unmarried, Osanna was an expert in the delivery of babies. She was often summoned to be present at births, particularly when doctors or midwives anticipated a difficult delivery.[29] "The wives of the said princes," her biography reports, meaning the Gonzaga women, "wished that she be present at their deliveries, and this she never failed to do, out of the great love she bore them." She aided Isabella d'Este, who wanted desperately to conceive a male heir.[30] One day, during a visit, Osanna perceived in Isabella's womb the future Federigo II, in her own words "as if in a glass tabernacle." Isabella was as yet unaware of her own pregnancy, and Osanna was able to tell her the joyous news. Beatrice d'Este, Isabella's older sister and duchess of Milan, also sought Osanna's aid and company, inviting her to Milan; her visit was a kind of triumph. Even the queen of France, Anne of Brittany, asked for her prayers so that she might bear a son.

The foundation of Osanna's extraordinary career was clearly this: She possessed, or was thought to possess, special knowledge, out of which she administered her household affairs, educated her nieces and nephews, gave counsel to Mantuans and others, supposedly predicted the future, and aided women in childbirth. Italian women had little role in the established professions, but avenues of influence and even power remained open to them.

Italy and the North

In spite of some changes over time and the presence always of some remarkable women, it is striking to observe the low visibility of women in the economic life of medieval Italy. Even in the thirteenth century, Italian women did not participate in the urban economies to the extent that they did, for example, at Paris in 1292. The reasons for this lie deeply embedded in medieval Italian—perhaps we should say Mediterranean—culture. Both law and custom expected women to be passive. Lombard law, as mentioned, prevented women from entering into any kind of binding agreement without the consent of a male tutor. The constant theme of Francesco da Barberino's poem is that women should be modest, passive, deferential, and retiring in all their social contacts—hardly the qualities needed for success in the marketplace.

Even the highly urbanized society of medieval Italy was unfavorable to women. Guilds were precocious in gaining power and, as just seen, restrictive in their policies toward women. The late marriages of males in the cities meant that the urban societies contained numerous sexually frustrated and aggressive young men. As a young girl's virginity was prized and regarded as a major asset in negotiating for her an advantageous marriage, families held their daughters under tight rein.[31] Catherine of Siena (1349–1380) as a child had the run of the city, but when she reached the marital age of twelve, she was kept at home "for at Siena it is exceptional that unmarried girls of that age are allowed to leave home."[32]

Nor did the republican governments of the nearly autonomous Italian cities favor women. In the feudal societies of the north and west, queens, princes, and noble women often assumed positions of leadership, serving as regents or administrators for minor, deceased, or absent males. The chivalric epics and romances of northern society, as we have seen, also gave many examples of women acting independently, even, in their love affairs, in defiance of male authority. The republican regimes of Italian towns, dominated by males exclusively, held forth no such models of feminine rule and power.

Italian travelers in the north noted the boldness of the women they encountered. These women even kissed their lovers in public.

Thus, in 1506, Giovanni Rucellai, a Florentine then at Avignon, wrote to a friend in Venice: "Here, I am allowed kisses as with you glances, and I find them here of much sweeter flavor than elsewhere."[33]

Though the economic role of medieval Italian women did change (and, in my view, lessened) over time, at all times the weight of custom and the shape of society hampered their social—and hence, economic—independence.

IBERIA

The Iberian Christian states were also Mediterranean communities, and Iberian women faced many of the same cultural obstacles to independence as did their Italian counterparts. These were the high value placed on feminine virginity before marriage and the consequent need to supervise young girls and to limit their social connections. But there were also compensating factors that created a more favorable environment for working women in Iberia than in Italy.[34] The Visigothic law prevalent in Iberia was perhaps the most liberal of all the Germanic codes for women; it allowed them to enter contractual agreements without male consent, guaranteed them an equal share with their brothers in the paternal inheritance, and granted them a portion of their husbands' acquisitions during their years of marriage. The *reconquista* took males away from home for frequent periods, conferred important administrative functions on women, and ensured that many women would inherit lands and offices from men who died in the fighting. Iberian history and Iberian literature give many examples of resourceful and vigorous women, ruling states and even directing armies.[35] Finally, the effort to resettle lands recently taken from the Moors led the Christian kings to grant generous terms to new settlers—both men and women.[36]

Barcelona

A big city of approximately 35,000 inhabitants, Barcelona in about 1400 was probably Iberia's most active port. Among the articles it produced for export was soap. About 1440, the soap maker Andreu Dea Brull formed a company with the merchant Bartholomeu Sagarra and his widowed mother, Eulalia.[37] The Sagarras invested, in two payments, 30 florins and 200 florins respectively. They would purchase the needed raw materials, sell the manufactured soap, and keep the accounts; Andreu would make the soap. It is not clear how Bartholomeu and his mother divided up their tasks, but clearly Eulalia was an equal and active partner. As a widow, she may have been continuing the work and investments of her deceased husband.

Women *custureras*, dressmakers or seamstresses, also appear at Barcelona.[38] As with women throughout Europe, the women at Barcelona seem to have been especially active in working linen. On March 2, 1448, the confraternity of linen and cotton weavers required that candidates for the mastership pass an examination and pay a fee. The fee was set at 10 sous for men and 5 for women. Like the men, the women who passed the examination and paid the fee became masters; they could open a shop and, if they wished, become a member of the confraternity, a *confraressa de la dita confraria*. Further regulations in 1456 set the apprenticeship period at three and one-half years, and raised the fee for admission to the mastership to 10 sous for women, 30 for men, and 60 for foreigners. The low fee for women may mean they earned less as masters, but otherwise the statutes were not visibly discriminatory. In linen and cotton manufacture, women were indispensable.

The situation is very different in regard to the wool trades at Barcelona. Although women masters had helped establish the industry at Barcelona in the thirteenth century, by the fifteenth their participation seems limited to the poorly remunerated, low-skilled work of spinning. In weaving, dyeing, fulling, and finishing the cloth, they appear in the statutes and chartularies neither as masters nor as apprenticeships, nor even as workers. "Outside of spinning," Claude Carrère, the historian of Barcelona's economy, concludes, "the textile trades seem to have been almost uniquely male."[39] Even the widows of masters were by then harshly treated. An ordinance of 1402 prohibited the widow of a weaver from taking over his shop unless she had a son of twelve years to succeed him.[40]

Seville and Granada

Seville, the Andalusian port in the southwest corner of the Iberian Peninsula, was in about 1400 a moderate-sized town of some 13,000 inhabitants. A *padròn* (survey) from 1384 names 2457 household heads, more than 100 of them women, and 55 of these show an occupation.[41] Women's occupations trace a now familiar pattern. They are retailers of many kinds of food: barley (*cebadera*), honey (*melera*), milk (*lechera*), bread (*panadera*), fish (*pescadera*), fruit (*frutera*), and spices (*especiera*). They are potters (*ollera*), ribbon or lace makers (*cordonera*), apparently brokers (*corredera?*), and peddlers (*buhonera*). But they are also still actively engaged in cloth making, as drapers (*lencera*), tenters (*tendera*), and weavers (*texedera*—three, as opposed to thirty-eight male *tejedores*). The contemporary guild statutes also refer to weavers as both men and women.[42] Would it be fair to attribute this large participation of women in Seville's labor force in 1384 at least partially to its diminished population, recently wracked by plagues, and to the labor shortage that must have accompanied it?

The urban economy becomes visibly less favorable to women as the fifteenth century progresses. Surveys from late in the century show us women engaged in textile work, but almost all of them are spinners. In 1484 a Guiomar Rodriguez declares "that she has no work except the distaff with which to earn her bread."[43] In the survey of the neighborhood of San Lorenzo in 1500, there are fifty-two women with distaffs and two more with spinning wheels but only two with looms, and these latter may have been weaving linen or wool. A compensating factor was the establishment, from the early fifteenth century, of silk working in the city—an art traditionally open to women. The statutes of the *sederos* or silk merchants excuse from examination the girls and "honest women" who work at the trade at home. On the other hand, the statutes of the other textile trades were following the now common policies of imposing tests and high entrance fees on those who would open a shop.[44] These tough requirements went against the interests of women, who always commanded fewer resources than men.

The life of St. John of God (1495–1550), a former shepherd and soldier, shows women's work in an Iberian city from another perspective.[45] The city is Granada, newly taken from the Moors. John is appalled by the number of impoverished persons in the town, especially "girls and women of slim means," who are too poor to marry and too ashamed to beg. He begs money from rich women, and buys for the poor girls "bread, meat, fish, charcoal and wood, and other daily necessities." But lest the poor women remain idle, he persuades merchants to donate "silk, wool, linen and the like," which the women spin into thread. They thus support themselves, but only by the humble work of spinning. John also tries to convert the prostitutes of the town, "the number of whom was very great," and sees the need of providing them with either honest marriages or honest employment. Even Iberia had its problem of dislocated women.

NORTHERN EUROPE

Entrepreneurs

Women appear as entrepreneurs in northern Europe to an extent that they rarely do in the south—at least not in Italy. The life of St. Lidwina of Schiedam (d. 1433) in modern Holland contains an interesting anecdote about such a woman.[46] One day, a widow comes to Lidwina and asks her whether she should pass her years in pious meditations or whether she should devote herself to labor. Lidwina replies: "I do not recommend idleness, for you know the art of making wool [*lanificium*]." The widow protests that a life of buying and selling tempts to avarice, but Lidwina will have none of it. Espousing what might be considered a Protestant ethic *ante verbum*, she lectures the widow on the value of labor. "The art of making wool," she instructs, "is good and necessary for sustenance." It will feed herself and others, free her from idleness, and allow her to help the poor. God will direct her in her business, but she in turn should consecrate to God—that is, to the poor—the wool of one of her fleeces.

The woman is not a humble artisan. She must be careful never to defraud her workers (*operarios*) of their wages. She also deals with "her" merchants in large sums of money. Her business brings her at first "many profits," but, given "the fluctuating fortunes of merchandising," she also suffers some losses.

One time, her merchant, in settling accounts, errs and gives her one more gold coin than she should receive; although she recognizes the error, she feels justified, after her own losses, in keeping the coin. Her merchant then dies, but comes back in a dream to tell Lidwina of the incident. Lidwina summons the businesswoman, and reprimands her for her dishonesty.

The woman knows the trade, hires workers, commissions merchants, and settles her accounts with gold coins; she is clearly a *drapière*, and for the most part a successful one. Even her slight moral failing is a *felix culpa*, as it won for her story a place in Lidwina's life.

In the realm of imagination, Chaucer's wife of Bath was also an expert in cloth making:

> Of clooth-making she hadde such a haunt
> She passed hem of Ypres and of Gaunt.[47]

But the poet tells us nothing more about her activities.

In England, the life—in fact a spirited autobiography—of the mystic visionary (and eccentric) Margery Kempe, dictated in 1436, records two of her entrepreneurial ventures, both failures but nonetheless illuminating.[48] In the town of King's Lynn she first took up brewing, "for pure covetousness and to maintain her pride." She claims that she was for three or four years "one of the greatest brewers in the town." The workers that she hired were "cunning in brewing." But disaster followed. The barm, or yeast, repeatedly failed, "and all the ale was lost, one brewing after another, so that her servants were ashamed and would not dwell with her." Margery lost much money, "for she had never been used thereto".

Her next venture was a horse-driven grain mill. "She got herself two good horses and a man to grind men's corn." But the enterprise survived only a short time. On the eve of Corpus Christi, one of the horses balked at pulling the mill. The man tried everything to urge the horse forward: "Sometimes he led him by the head, sometimes he beat him, and all availed not, for [the horse] would rather go backward than forward." Nor was the second animal any more willing to work. The frustrated man quit, and Margery's business failed. "Anon," she lamented, "it was noised about the town of [Lynn] that neither man nor beast would serve the said creature [Margery]."

It is very much worth noting that Margery was married (from age twenty), but that her husband played no role in her various businesses. She was an independent businesswoman, even if not a successful one.

In Germany, the Rhine city of Cologne was an important center of silk manufacture; like Paris, it even contained guilds, four as compared with the five in Paris, that were exclusively feminine in membership. These were the yarn makers, the gold spinners, the silk spinners, and the silk weavers.[49] A few women in late medieval Cologne were even functioning as entrepreneurs, hiring workers, importing raw materials, and exporting their finished products. Grietgen van Berchem, for example, was a silk maker who between 1469 and 1476 employed ten girl apprentices. She was married to Jakob van Berchem, from a family of wine importers. Fygen Lutzenkirchen, another prominent silk maker (a *Hauptseidenmacherin*) active between 1474 and 1496 and the wife of an important merchant, took in twenty-five apprentices. Though married, these businesswomen seem to have been no more subordinate to their husbands than was Margery Kempe in England.[50]

In spite of much hostility on the part of male doctors and governments, some women continued to achieve success as physicians.[51] In 1479 a woman surgeon named Guillemecte du Luys did services for King Louis XI of France and was paid the substantial sum of 19 livres 5 sous.[52] Guilds of midwives existed at Paris, Rheims, Orleans, Dijon, and Lille.[53] Fourteen women doctors are mentioned at Frankfurt between 1394 and 1495, seven of them Jewesses.[54] And in northern Europe as in the southern part of the continent, women dominated the ranks of religious mystics. Dukes and professional theologians traipsed through the chamber of the bedridden Lidwina of Schiedam in order to gain the benefit of her political counsel and spiritual insights.[55]

Nonetheless, in spite of individual tales of success (or, in the case of Kempe, of failure), the numbers of employed women in relation to men seem to have fallen all over northern Europe throughout the late Middle Ages; the guilds, moreover, especially in the fifteenth century, were everywhere curtailing in assorted ways women's access to training and employment.[56]

Paris, 1421–1438

Paris in the last years of the Hundred Years' War possesses
three short surveys of its population, which invite comparison
with the great tailles of the reign of Philip the Fair, more than
100 years earlier. In 1421, King Charles VII of France and
Henry V of England (Charles' heir by the treaty of Troyes of
1420) imposed a tax in marcs on the city of Paris; two of three
accounts, comprising nine out of sixteen urban parishes, have
survived, listing 1394 household heads. In 1423, the king imposed a loan, with assessments stated in francs, on the whole
city, but only 502 household heads were registered. In 1438,
Charles VII, who had recently retaken Paris from the English,
collected another *aide* from the city; the full account has survived, though the number of household heads included is again
small, 578. In 1970, Jean Favier edited all three rolls and provided a critical introduction.[57]

Though short, these fifteenth-century surveys are complex
documents, showing numerous emendations. (In the following
analysis, I count only those households to which the editor
Favier assigns a number; many of these same households are
subsequently listed as exempt.) The names of occupations also
show numerous shifts. There were no *boulengiers*, or bakers, in
the taille of 1292; presumably, the names *fourniers, pastaiers,
oublaiers*, and others covered the occupation. *Boulengier* does appear in the taille of 1313 and has become, with thirty-four appearances, the common name for "baker" in the fifteenth century. So also, the generic title *marchant* has become much more
common (133 appearances) in the later than in the earlier surveys. Men bearing the title *maistre* without further specification
of profession or trade proliferate in the late surveys (195 appearances in 1421 to 1438, 197 in the much larger combined
surveys of 1292 and 1313). Nobles and clerics were exempt in
all the surveys, but the small size of the fifteenth-century surveys suggests that the assessors were registering well-to-do citizens only.

Restriction of the late surveys to the wealthier citizens of
Paris should have reduced the number of women who appear
in them but not necessarily the proportion of women who show
an occupation. Women with an occupation were likely to be bet-

ter off than those without a trade, and thus presumably were more likely to appear in a survey that concentrated on assessing the rich. Table 7.3 shows the breakdown by sex of the household heads in the three late surveys.

Women continue to be registered as household heads at Paris throughout the late Middle Ages, but their frequency of appearance falls from 15 percent in 1292 to 12 percent in 1313 to 8.5 percent in 1421 to 1438. In 1421 to 1438 only 20 percent of the women (41 out of 204) show an occupation, as opposed to 41 percent in the combined surveys of 1292 and 1313 (1229 out of 2973 women household heads). The proportion of visibly employed women household heads thus drops by one-half. The number of occupations shown by women falls by 92 percent from those displayed in 1292 and 1313 (from 212 in the earlier combined surveys to only 19 in 1421 to 1438). The proportion of men showing an occupation actually increases from the earlier to the later surveys, from 56 percent in 1292 and 1313 combined to 64 percent in 1421 to 1438 (1416 out of 2206 male household heads). However, many of the men (197) in the later surveys bear only the title *maistre*, without further specification of the art they exercised. The number of occupations displayed by males in these small, later surveys is 124—a decline of 64 percent from the 366 professions that males showed in the earlier two surveys. Still, the drop is far less than the 92 percent registered by women.

Given the few women that show an occupation (only forty-one) in the late surveys, these surveys can at best show those economic sectors in which women retained some representa-

Table 7.3   The Tailles of Paris, 1421–1438

	Men	Percent	Women	Percent
1421 heads	1187	89.2	143	10.8
With occupation	816	97.5	21	2.5
1423 heads	475	94.6	27	5.4
With occupation	408	95.8	18	4.2
1438 heads	544	94.1	34	5.9
With occupation	192	99.5	1	0.5
Total heads	2206	91.5	204	8.5
With occupation	1416	97.2	41	2.8

SOURCE: Favier, 1970.

tion. Table 7.4 lists the occupations of these forty-one Parisian women.

Although these numbers are small, it remains notable that employed women at Paris are more numerous and they show a greater variety of occupations than revealed, for example, in the much bigger Italian surveys. Women in Paris in the early fifteenth century were still important as innkeepers and food preparers. They were retailers, especially of food products and clothing. They worked in wax. Although female weavers, dyers, seamstresses, and goldsmiths have altogether vanished, women retained at least a presence in the silk industry and in making (probably out of silk) purses and gloves. Women doctors have vanished too, but women still played a small role in the related arts as barbers and spice dealers.

It remains hard, however, to avoid the conclusion that women's place in the economic life of Paris had diminished markedly during the period of more than a century that separates our two sets of censuses. In 1313, women showing an occupation accounted for 7.7 percent of all household heads showing an occupation; that figure falls to 2.8 percent in the fifteenth century. While many factors influenced this complex picture, the conclusion seems incontrovertible: Women were economically less active, or at least less visible, in the Parisian

Table 7.4   Women Showing Occupations in the Parisian Tailles, 1421–1438

Occupation*	Total	Women	Occupation*	Total	Women
Merchant	125	8	Maker of amices	2	1
Mercer	42	7	Purse maker	1	1
Draper	46	4	Butcher	33	1
Spice dealer	87	3	Silk worker	1	1
Innkeeper	64	2	Tapestry worker	5	1
Hostel keeper	16	2	*Patinière*†	1	1
Baker	64	2	Hay dealer	1	1
Barber	10	2	Used-clothes dealer	9	1
Maker of hutches	5	1	Glove maker	3	1
Candlemaker	13	1			

*Key: maker of hutches = *huchière,* used-clothes dealer = *fripière,* candlemaker = *chandelière.*

†The one *patinière* who appears may have been a "polisher."

SOURCE: Fautier, 1970.

economy in the fifteenth century than they had been in the Paris and the France of Philip the Fair.

Restrictions

Other records, less comprehensive than the surveys but distributed over a longer span of time, also indicate that feminine participation in economic life was diminishing. In 1351 King Jean of France issued a series of ordinances intended to control the inflation of wages that was coming in the wake of the Black Death. In describing the textile trades, Jean uses masculine forms exclusively to identify weavers, dyers, cloth makers, and fullers.[58] He uses only feminine forms for spinners and burlers. To be sure, the phrases cannot be converted into an estimate of the exact proportions of men and women employed in the cloth industry. Moreover, the labor shortage the king was decrying probably helped to keep women numerous in the work force. Nonetheless, in Jean's perspective, the central operations of cloth making were now done predominantly by men. Women worked in the low-skilled jobs set at the beginning or the end of the manufacturing process: the spinning of thread and the burling, the smoothing and unknotting, of the finished cloth.

At Paris, the statutes of the guild of pastry bakers, dated 1397, forbade women of any sort to bake communion wafers or to go about the city selling any product of the trade.[59] And no woman pastry baker without a husband who was also a baker could take an apprentice.[60] The Parisian statutes occasionally show outright discrimination against women workers. For example, women enjoyed a traditional visibility among the barbers, as they did in all the quasi-medical professions; but the statutes of the barbers, dated 1438, contain the following provision:

> Also, that no male or female barber, of whatever condition he may be, may or ought to allow to be hired in the said trade any woman or girl or to support her in his house or shop, unless that she be the wife or daughter of a master of the said trade, and of good life and reputation.[61]

In sum, at Paris only the wife or daughter of a barber could aspire to become a barber, but males faced no such restriction.

By 1450, the five women's guilds at Paris were reorganized and absorbed into predominantly male corporations.[62]

In 1488, the statutes of weavers and drapers of the small Norman town of Gruchet-le-Valesse seem to exclude women, except the wives and daughters of masters, even from spinning:

> Also, no woman, who is not the wife of a master or their [sic] daughters can do anything of the said art under pain of three sous nine deniers of penalty, except that they may burl [*espincher*] the cloth and that only.[63]

England, Flanders, and Germany

At Bristol in England in 1461, the town government forbade weavers to employ their wives, daughters, or maids at the loom.[64] This is one of the few texts that states a reason for the restriction: "lest the king's people likely to do the king's service should lack employment." Obviously, in the view of the city fathers, the king's people were exclusively males.

At Ghent in Flanders in 1374, the wives of fullers—in fact, women of any sort—were forbidden to wash any type of clothes.[65]

The status of women workers in late medieval German towns has attracted much recent attention. The point of departure for this research is the thesis put forward by Karl Bücher in 1883.[66] Bücher argued that because of wars and plagues women outnumbered men in the German towns and that they were admitted into every kind of work their strength allowed them to perform.

The recent research revises both these conclusions. Women often did outnumber men in commercial towns (at Cologne or Nuremberg, for example, at least in certain years). But men outnumbered women in industrial towns, especially those with many workers in the wool or metal industry. Women's participation in the work force was limited and small. Cologne, with four female guilds, was exceptional; only Nuremberg and Basel in Switzerland had each one guild of women members.[67] Women did not freely enter into every occupation. The occupational names that widows often inherited from their husbands do not prove that they continued to work at their husbands' trades. Concentrated in household service, food sales, and petty retailing, they tended to form the lowest, least trained, and least paid level of the urban work force.

> For girls [concludes Peter Ketsch], at least in the late Middle Ages, it was in no way usual to learn a trade. General government regulations, that admit young men and women in equal measure into training, should not be overvalued, for they derive in part from a time in which girls certainly could not learn a trade.[68]

Finally, guild and government regulations in many towns imposed mounting restrictions upon women, both religious and lay. In 1421 at Cologne, as the result of a dispute between linen weavers and beguines, the government allowed the beguines to operate only six looms; in 1437, the number was reduced to three. By the second half of the fifteenth century, the government forbade all kinds of textile work in religious houses.[69] In 1330, the aldermen of Strasbourg allowed women weavers of linen or of silk to work independently, but if they wove wool or cotton or employed helpers, then they were to be subject to the male weavers.[70] In the biggest of the textile industries—that of wool—women at Strasbourg, as indeed in many towns, were reduced to being helpers and auxiliaries.

The status of the wives, widows, and daughters of the male masters attracted much attention in the regulations. At Lüneburg, the widow of a shoemaker could continue his practice for one year, but if she had no children or only daughters, then she had to sell her franchise.[71] Almost everywhere, however, some privileges were extended to widows and daughters. A man who married a master's daughter could usually enter the guild with a reduced fee and other exemptions. This doubtless served the masters by facilitating the marriages of their daughters and reducing the required dowries. Widows too could usually continue the trade. But almost everywhere, they could not take on apprentices unless they married another master. The regulation allowed widows to support themselves but not to compete with the male masters.

Peter Ketsch sums up the situation in German lands:

> Without doubt with the closing of the guilds in the late Middle Ages the tendency grew stronger to force women completely out of the crafts and to disqualify them.[72]

A Backward Glance

The history of labor in Europe over the last two centuries of the Middle Ages seems to show the following pattern: The earliest efforts to limit access to guild masterships date from even before the great epidemic of 1348. If we can take Florence as an example, the guilds in their matriculation policies had begun to favor the sons or male relatives of masters from the late 1320s.[73] The medieval economy, expanding for an extraordinary three centuries, was by then reaching its limits of possible growth, under prevailing levels of technology. Diminishing or disappearing opportunity frightened the masters, at Florence and doubtless elsewhere, into a defensive posture. They sought to ensure that they and their male descendants would retain first claim on the available jobs.

The great epidemics, beginning in 1348, and the resulting radical decline in human numbers created a shortage of workers, from which women drew immediate benefit. But the plagues, wars, and social disturbances of the late fourteenth and early fifteenth centuries did nothing to instill in those who governed the guilds a sense of confidence and security; rather, a contrary feeling prevailed. By the late fifteenth century, when renewed population growth relieved the labor shortage, the masters reinstituted with enhanced determination their policies of limiting competition.

From Spain to Germany, guilds required that those seeking to enter produce a masterpiece. The masterpiece itself was likely to be judged arbitrarily and unfairly; those seeking entry would also have to pay steep matriculation fees. The established masters exonerated from these prohibitive requirements their own sons, and thus tended to make the crafts at least in part hereditary castes. Women, along with foreigners, outsiders, and marginal workers, found their own access to masterships and to remunerative employment severely restricted. These policies would persist well into the modern age.

NOTES

1. He has been several times edited; a recent and good edition is Francesco da Barberino, 1957. For comment, see Festa, 1910, pp. 155–60, on occupations.

2. *Bologna populazione*, 1966, p. 64.
3. *Ibid.*, p, 98: "pauperes et mentici."
4. *Ibid.*, p. 96: "pauperes, infirmi, qui mendicant et de elemosina vivunt."
5. *Ibid.*, p. 64.
6. *Ibid.*, p. 96: "dona Iacoba eius filia optima in superlativo."
7. *Ibid.*: "dona Agnesina de Alamania putana vel quasi."
8. *Ibid.*: "dona Lucia eius uxor rufana expressa."
9. *Ibid.*, p. 97: "dona Paula de Florencia putana publica, Iacobus eius maritus suus concubitus."
10. *Ibid.*: "dona Margherita sclava non perfecta."
11. Christine de Pisan, 1982, pp. 154–55.
12. On the catasto, see Herlihy and Klapisch-Zuber, 1985.
13. *Canti carnascialeschi*, 1936, p. 107: "Donne, che tessitor cercando andate...."
14. Park, 1985, pp. 71–72.
15. Boccaccio, 1939, p. 7, in the preface to the Decameron, notes that the number of doctors had grown very large because of the influx of incompetent persons, including women.
16. See, for example, *Bologna*, 1939, II, 165: "nullus tabernarius vel tabernaria"; *ibid.*, 168: "nullus tricolus vel tricola emat vel emi faciat caseum vel pullos vel ova vel fructos arborum vel aliquas alias res ad tricolariam pertinentibus"; *ibid.*, 169: "item quod nulla tricola filet super vel iuxta tricolariam suam...."
17. The matriculation lists are preserved in the Manoscritti deposit of the Florentine State Archives. I have prepared a machine-readable edition of the lists from 1225 to 1430.
18. See page 96.
19. Francesco da Barbarino, 1957.
20. "Canzona delle pinzochere andate a Roma." *Canti carnascialeschi*, 1936, pp. 121–23.
21. *Ibid.*: "con che facciam le genti andar costrette."
22. *Ibid.*, p. 123: "Abbiam ancor molti altri bei segreti / da far sgravidare / e ritornare il panno virginale / co' quali a molti preti / abbián fatto gustare / piú volte una per vergine, la quale / era uscita di sale / poco avanti del parto per amore / di salvar col nostr'utile 'l suo onore."
23. *Ibid.*: "...vi ricordiamo ch'egli è meglio ir portante / ch'essere meschina, lavandaia o fante."
24. *ASS*, IV Junii, pp. 552–664. For recent comment on her life, see Redigonda, 1961, pp. 131–32.
25. *ASS*, IV Junii, p. 551: "medio ordine cives"; p. 605: "nobilibus civibus Mantuanis."
26. *ASS*, IV Junii, p. 578.
27. "O quantas tribulationes sustinui a duritia mei patris." *ASS*, IV Junii, p. 607.
28. She did not take solemn religious vows until she was fifty years old, three years before her death.
29. For a rather lurid picture of a breech birth, see *ASS*, IV Junii, p. 598.

30. Cartwright, 1923, I, 255, on Osanna's relationship with the marchesa.
31. At Florence in 1427, the estimated age of first marriage for males was a full thirty years, though it was slightly lower in smaller cities. For a full discussion, see Herlihy and Klapisch-Zuber, 1985, p. 210.
32. According to Raymond of Capua, *ASS*, III Aprilis, p. 863.
33. "Et maxime che qui mi sono leciti e baci come costí li squardi; ma li trovo qui d'uno sapore molto più suave che nelli altri luoghi." Rucellai, 1887, p. 243. For other examples of the seeming boldness of French women, from the Italian viewpoint, see Del Lungo, 1926, p. 85.
34. For a collection of studies of women and work, largely concerned with the late Middle Ages in Spain, see *Trabajo*, 1988.
35. See page 60.
36. Dillard, 1984.
37. Carrère, 1967, p. 380.
38. *Ibid.*, pp. 371–74. The textile trades at Barcelona are also discussed by the "Equip Broida" in *Trabajo*, 1988, pp. 260–73; it discerns "una marginación femenina a principios del siglo XV," most pronounced in the wool industry.
39. Carrère, 1967, p. 484, n. 1: "...en dehors de la filature, les métiers du textile semblent avoir été presque uniquement masculins."
40. *Ibid.*, p. 476.
41. The occupations of 1384 are discussed in Gonzalez, 1975.
42. The following discussion is based upon Collantes de Teran Sanchez, 1977, pp. 311–30.
43. *Ibid.*, p. 323: "que no tyene fasienda saluo la rueca con que gana de comer."
44. *Ibid.*
45. *ASS*, I March, pp. 809–33.
46. *ASS*, II Aprilis, pp. 302–64.
47. Chaucer, 1963, p. 248 (Prologue, lines 447–48).
48. Kempe, 1934, p. 3. On women brewers in late medieval England, see Bennett, 1986; Labarge, 1986, pp. 163–64; and Ide, 1983, p. 58. On women and work in England in the early modern period, see Duffin and Lindsey, 1985.
49. The fundamental study of women workers in medieval Cologne is Wensky, 1980. She largely agrees with the classic statement by Karl Bücher, published in 1882, that German women in the late medieval towns participated in all the trades that their strength allowed them to engage in. For a review of Wensky's data but with differing interpretations, see Howell, 1986, pp. 124–58. For further discussion of women's work and its restricted range in early modern Germany, see Wiesner, 1986; and the studies in Pohl (ed.), 1985.
50. Howell, 1986, argues that Grietgen and other prominent businesswomen at Cologne owed their status to their husbands, but the

documents do not show that they were any more dependent upon their husbands (who were usually involved in a different trade) than was Margery Kempe in England. The fact that many came from prominent families shows only that they emerged out of a mercantile tradition, not that they were subordinate to male relatives. That tradition may have been supported by their female as much as by their male relatives.

51. On women empirics in England, see Gottfried, 1986.
52. Cited in *Histoire de Paris*, 1886–97, I, 623: "A Guillemecte du Luys, sirurgienne, en faveur d'aucuns services qu'ell lui a fair, 19 liv. 5 s. t."
53. According to Jacquart, 1981, p. 49.
54. Ketsch, 1983–84, I, 278.
55. *ASS,* II Aprilis, p. 276.
56. For a recent general survey of guild policy, see Mackenney, 1987. On women and work in the late medieval period, see the collection of studies in Hanawalt, 1986. And on guild policy in Languedoc, see Gouron, 1958.
57. Favier, 1970.
58. *Histoire de Paris*, 1886–97, I, 41. The professions named are *tixarrens de draps, tainturiers, faiseurs de toilles, foulons, filleresses,* and *pigneresses.*
59. *Ibid.,* II, 371: "Item, que feme quelle qu'elle soit ny puisse faire pain a chanter ne a celebrer en eglise: aussi ne puisse porter aval la ville vendre aucune chose dudit mestier."
60. *Ibid.:* "Item, que feme oubloyere senz mary oubloyer ne put prendre apprentiz audit mestier de l'oubloyere."
61. *Ibid.:* III, 654: "Item, que nul barbier ou barbiere, de quelque condition qu'il soit, ne pourra ne devra souffrir besongner dudit mestier aucune femme ou fille, ne tenir en son hostel ou ouvrouer, sinon qu' elle soit femme ou fille de mastre dudit mestier et de bonne vie et renommee."
62. Ennen, 1986, p. 162.
63. Chaumet, 1975, p. 110.
64. Cited in Green, 1895, II, 96, n. 1.
65. *Recueil,* 1906, I, 171: "20. Item, que nulle femme de foulon ne autre quelle que soit, puis hores en avant, ne puist laver piece ne drap quelconque, sous 5 s. d'amende."
66. There are good introductions to the literature in Howell, 1986, pp. 1–6, and Ennen, 1986, pp. 134–63. See also Pohl (ed.), 1985.
67. Ennen, 1986, p. 162.
68. Ketsch, 1983–84, I, 117.
69. Wensky, 1979, pp. 38–40.
70. Ketsch, 1983–84, I, 179. If they weave "wollenes Tuch oder Baumwolltuch oder Stuhltuch oder Knechte beschäftigen, si solen mit der Webern dienen."
71. Ennen, 1986, p. 137.

72. Ketsch, 1983–84, I, 117: "Ohne Zweifel verstärkt sich jedoch mit dem Abschliessen der Zünfte im ausgehenden Mittelalter die Tendenz die Frauen gänzlich aus der Handwerken zu verdrängen und sie zu dequalificieren."

73. For example, in Florence in the guild of Por Santa Maria, made up of merchants, the earliest citation of a *beneficium Patris* (the "favor of a father") dates from 1328.

Conclusion: Toward the Modern World

L'esprit de monopole, qui a présidé à la confection de ces statuts, a été poussé jusqu' à exclure les femmes des métiers les plus convenables à leur sexe, tels que la broderie, qu' elles ne peuvent exercer pour leur propre comte....

The spirit of monopoly, which presided over the redaction of these [guild] statutes, has gone so far as to exclude women from the employments most suited to their sex, such as embroidery, which they cannot exercise on their own account....

—Turgot, on the ancient guild
statutes of France (1776)

Women's participation in productive enterprise changed dramatically during the Middle Ages. The best measure of that participation is the cloth industry; it is well illuminated, and developments within it seem to have been paralleled in other occupations and professions. In the manufacture of quality woolens, specifically, women lost the central role they had long held in both Mediterranean and barbarian antiquity.

THE EVOLUTION OF WOMEN'S WORK

It is possible, I believe, to distinguish three phases within this lengthy evolution. From the start of the Middle Ages (and even from ancient times) until the twelfth century, women fully retained their traditional importance as cloth producers. Between the twelfth and the fourteenth centuries, men in large and growing numbers found employment in making cloth, but their entry did not immediately bring a corresponding exclusion of women. Thus, in the central Middle Ages, women and men worked side by side in a great variety of jobs. The closing period

185

of the Middle Ages, the fourteenth and fifteenth centuries, was a violent age of deep crises and difficult recovery; it saw the end of this easy partnership of the sexes. Guilds and governments, especially in the fifteenth century, imposed severe restrictions on women's work. These restrictions amounted at times to the complete exclusion of women from prestigious and well-paying jobs.

At the close of the Middle Ages, a domestic mode of production had come to dominate the industrial economy. As the word "domestic" implies, the unit of production became family-based. Under this system the household members worked under the supervision and for the benefit of the usually male household head. Thus, in the manufacture of woolens, women and children would clean, comb, or card the wool; women would spin it into thread; and males would weave it into cloth. The family units obtained their raw materials from a merchant entrepreneur, to whom they also delivered the woven cloth. Because the entrepreneur "put out" work to the separate domestic units, this arrangement of production is traditionally called the "putting-out system."

In early modern times and perhaps even before, agricultural families also took in work, particularly during the slack periods of the agricultural calendar. They worked in their cottages, hence the term, "cottage industry," another common expression describing the early modern industrial economy.

The point I emphasize is that these arrangements—most notably, the domestic mode of production—are late in appearing. While a putting-out system of some sort surely functioned at Paris under Philip the Fair, the many employed women showing hundreds of occupations were working independently (and were taxed independently); they could not have been working under the supervision and for the benefit of the male heads of their households. The assessors regarded them as personally responsible for and able to pay their own taxes, and tax collectors are close observers.

The Paris evidence suggests further that households were not alike in their economic functions; not all of them were self-contained units of production. Rather, some (surely the larger and wealthier) took in journeymen, apprentices, and servants, whom other households (surely the smaller and poorer) supplied. Not all and perhaps not most Parisians worked in their own homes.

FACTORS BEHIND THE EVOLUTION

The total subordination of women's work—the change to household work under the supervision of the male household chief—awaited the late Middle Ages; it was directly linked to the establishment of guild monopolies and the exclusion of women from the masterships. Women's work thus is quite different at the end of the Middle Ages than it was at the beginning. Women no longer possessed, in Ambrose's phrase, the wisdom of weaving.

The factors that drove this long evolution are hard to isolate and still harder to weigh; and their respective weights surely varied from period to period. But five factors merit thought: domestication, urbanization, specialization, capitalization, and monopolization.

Domestication

By "domestication," I mean the disintegration and disappearance of the gynaecea on the great estates of the early Middle Ages and the dispersal of the work of producing quality cloth among small units, households, and shops. The early medieval elites, churchmen included, needed elegant fabrics to decorate their persons, rites, and rituals; they could not rely on peasants to produce them. Unable to purchase them either, they had little choice but to organize workshops and to recruit, train, and maintain skilled workers, chiefly women. But we ought not to think that these laborers worked in isolated units, within closed manorial communities. Rather, in this early medieval economy of gift and tribute, fine cloths circulated widely, and skilled workers too.

From roughly 900, even perhaps from an earlier date, the great estates seem to have encountered difficulties in enlisting large numbers of workers, women in particular, and in getting them to make quality cloth. Numerous factors contributed to this: the waning of slavery; the erosion of manorial authority;

the slow loosening of the bonds of serfdom; the religious value given to emancipation; and perhaps even the sense, on the part of ecclesiastical lords, that it was inappropriate for monks and clerics to live in close proximity to young women workers who were not their relatives. Liutbirg in the ninth century trained girls in cloth making, and she entertained requests for their services from neighboring lords. But she also emancipated some and allowed them to go wherever they wished. Presumably, these girls would have preferred marriage over life service in the gynaeceum. The decline of cloth manufacture in the gynaeceum was the critical first step in the transformation of fabric manufacture in the Middle Ages. It touches on issues of manorial organization and its unraveling that are still not completely understood.

Urbanization

The disintegration of the gynaecea, rapid by the twelfth century, allowed the making of quality cloth to move to the towns. Of course, many other factors that we cannot consider here contributed to the revival of towns; crucial among them were the growth of trade and markets. For cloth workers, there were clear advantages in this urbanization of cloth production. The reliance on small domestic units raised problems of supply, of coordination with related trades, and of sales of the product. Settlement in cities, where workers were close to each other and to markets, was thus more attractive for the small production units than it had been for the large workshops. But urbanization in turn transformed the nature of the industry.

Specialization

In the rural economy of the early Middle Ages, the sexual division of labor assigned the heavy tasks of plow agriculture to the males and left domestic chores chiefly to the women. The making of cloth and clothing was a principal domestic chore, and women dominated it almost totally. The growth of population in the central Middle Ages induced many persons to leave the old, crowded regions and to seek out new lands—or new occupations in the towns. But in the growing towns, men needed to ply a trade in order to earn a living, and understandably they entered many professions which were formerly the preserves of women. Poverty and hunger prompted Severus of Ravenna to take up the "women's work" of cloth making and to labor alongside his wife and daughter.

Urbanization also brought with it the specialization and professionalization of productive activities. Artisans had to sell their products in order to live, and markets were becoming intensely competitive. The artisans had to satisfy a discriminating demand for quality products at affordable prices, and men could develop the necessary specialized skills more easily than could women. In coming from the countryside, women were not entirely freed, as were the men, from their former duties. Even in the countryside, most women had been "life-cycle" fabric workers, going to the gynaeceum at very young ages and leaving it at sexual and social maturity, usually to marry; as adults, they assumed other tasks without altogether abandoning their fabric work. In the towns, women still delivered and nursed the children; took care of the sick in the household; cooked and cleaned. Although they could combine these domestic tasks with some market-oriented work such as spinning, they had neither the time nor the freedom to develop real expertise in most crafts. The men in the urban households became the professional artisans, and the women served as their helpers and assistants.

The salient exceptions to this pattern were the manufacture of linens and the production of silks. The preparation of linen from flax was still carried on largely in the suburbs or in the countryside, and this may have ensured the continuing and significant participation of women. The prominence of women in silk production may reflect their superior dexterity over men in unraveling the cocoons and in spinning, weaving, and sewing the fine silk threads. But in comparison with the manufacture of woolens, the making of silks remained a comparatively minor industry throughout the Middle Ages.

A further, subtle change was occurring in the central Middle Ages. In both the ancient world and early medieval society, cloth work was considered honorable for women but demeaning for men. This cultural interpretation of gender roles changed in the central Middle Ages. In rural Flanders, the weavers involved with the wheeled ship claim dignity, in that they earn their living by honest labor, even though they are weaving woolens.

Capitalization

Still another factor is the difficulty experienced by women in marshaling capital. Women, as shown in the Paris tailles, consistently appear poorer than men in the same occupation by a substantial margin—about one-third. The growth of the cloth industry was significantly stimulated by technological changes— the development of large and complex horizontal looms, the application of water power in fulling, and the use of a larger range of dyes and mordants. Technological change in turn required capital infusions. Women, part-time workers in an urban context, neither accumulated nor attracted nor controlled capital to the same extent as did men. Their comparative deprivation also undermined the influence they could exert within occupations and professions.

Monopolization

Monopolization, the effort on the part of established masters to limit entry into their ranks to their own sons, is a development of the late Middle Ages. Europe's depopulation in the immediate wake of the fourteenth-century epidemics for a while sustained a heightened demand for workers, but stabilized numbers and then renewed growth in the fifteenth century seem to have threatened the status of the established masters. The exclusionist policies adopted by guilds all over Europe were primarily aimed against outsiders and marginal workers in the crafts. Women, already pushed to the margins, had to bear the onus of these further restrictions.

In the eighteenth century, Turgot, the great French physiocrat and statesman, gave this perceptive account of the origins of guild monopolies:

> It seems that, when the towns began to free themselves from feudal servitude and to form themselves into communes, the ease of classifying the citizens by means of their occupations introduced this usage, unknown up until then. The different occupations thus be-

came like particular communities, out of which the general community was composed....

The communities, once formed, redacted statutes, and, under various pretexts regarding the public good, had them validated by the authorities. The basis of these statutes is to exclude from the right of exercising the craft whoever is not a member of the community; their general spirit is to restrict as much as possible the number of masters, to render the attainment of the mastership of nearly insurmountable difficulty for everyone except the children of present masters. This is the purpose for the multiplicity of charges and of formalities of admission, the difficulties of the masterpiece (always judged arbitrarily) and, above all, the useless expense and delay of the apprenticeship and the prolonged servitude of the *compagnage* (status of journeyman)—institutions designed to permit the masters to enjoy for nothing the labor of the novices for many years.[1]

Turgot specifically adds, in the passage cited at the opening of this chapter, that this "spirit of monopoly" has excluded women from the trades, such as embroidery, that he considers "most suitable to their sex."

Turgot's chronology may be vague and his knowledge of the early Middle Ages faulty, but his analysis is striking. His final, eloquent words are also worth citing:

God, in imparting needs to man, in making the resource of labor indispensable for him, has made the right to work the property of every man, and this property is the first, the most sacred, and most imprescriptible right of all.[2]

Work for all people is at once a duty and a dignity. Women fulfilled many jobs throughout the long medieval centuries. It is instructive, perhaps even inspiring, to survey the work that medieval women performed and the dignity that they earned.

NOTES

1. *Histoire de Paris,* 1886–97, I, 164. Turgot's words are embedded in an ordinance issued in February 1776 in the name of Louis XVI abolishing guild monopolies.
2. *Ibid.,* 165.

REFERENCES

SOURCES

Abelard, Peter. 1849. *Petri Abaelardi Opera*, ed. V. Cousin. Paris: Durand.

Adenet le Roi. 1946. *Adenet le Roi's Berte aus grans piés*, ed Urban T. Holmes, Jr. University of North Carolina: Studies in the Romance Languages and Literatures, 6. Chapel Hill, N.C.

Aelfric. 1659, 1970. "Glossarium." In: William Somner, *Dictionarium Saxonico-Latino-Anglicum.* Menston: Scolar Press.

———. 1880. *Aelfrics Grammatik und Glossar*, ed. Julius Zupitza. 1 abt: Text und Varianten. Berlin: Weidmann.

Antoninus. 1898. Antonini placentini itinerarium. In: *Itinera hierosolymitana saeculi III–VIII*, ed. P. Geyer. Vienna: F. Tennsky.

Arnobius Afer. 1934. *Arnobii adversus nationes libri vii*, ed. C. Marchesi. Corpus Scriptorum Latinorum Paravianum. Turin.

Arte dei fornai. 1945. *Statuti delle arti dei fornai e dei vinattieri di Firenze (1237–1339)*, ed. Francesca Morandino. Fonti e studi sulle corporazioni artigiane del Medio Evo, Fonti, 5. Florence.

Arte dei rigattieri. 1940. *Statuti dell' arte dei rigattieri e linaioli di Firenze (1296–1340)*, ed. Ferdinando Sartini. Fonti e studi sulle corporazioni artigiane del Medio Evo, Fonti, 2. Florence.

Arte della lana. 1940. *Statuto dell' arte della lana di Firenze (1317–1319)*, ed. Anna Maria Agnoletti. Fonti e studi sulle corporazioni artigiane del Medio Evo, Fonti, 1. Florence.

ASS. 1863–1931. *Acta sanctorum quotquot toto orbe coluntur.* Paris: V. Palmé.

ASS O.S.B. 1935–40. *Acta sanctorum ordinis S. Benedicti*, ed. J. Mabillon. 3 vols. Mâcon: Fratres Protat.

Bethada. 1922, 1968. *Bethada Náem nÉrenn. Lives of Irish Saints*, ed. and trans. Charles Plummer. 2 vols. Oxford: Clarendon Press.

Boccaccio, Giovanni. 1939. *Il Decameron*, ed. Luigi Russo. Florence: Sansoni.

Boileau. 1879. *Le livre des métiers d'Etienne Boileau*, ed. René de Lespinasse and François Bonnardot. Paris: Imprimerie Nationale.

Bologna popolazione. 1966. *Documenti sulla popolazione di Bologna alla fine di trecento*, ed. Paolo Montanari. Fonti per la storia di Bologna, 1. Bologna: Istituto per la Storia di Bologna.

Bologna statuti. 1939. *Statuti di Bologna dell' anno 1288*, ed. Gina Fasoli and Pietro Sella. Studi e testi, 85. Città del Vaticano.

Cáin Adamnáin. 1905. *Cáin Adamnáin: An Old Irish Treatise on the Law of Adamnan*, ed. and trans. Kuno Meyer. In: *Analecta Oxoniensia.* Medieval and Modern Series, 12. Oxford: Oxford University Press.

Canti carnascialeschi. 1936. *Canti carnascialeschi del Rinascimento*, ed. Charles S. Singleton. Scrittori d'Italia, 159. Bari: Laterza.

Chartularium. 1889–97. *Chartularium universitatis parisiensis*, ed. H. Denifle and A. Chatelain. Paris: Delalain.

Chaucer. 1963. *Chaucer*, ed. Louis O. Coxe. New York: Dell.

Chrétien de Troyes. 1987. *Yvain. The Knight of the Lion*, trans. Burton Raffel; afterword by Joseph J. Duggan. New Haven and London: Yale University Press.

Christina of Markyate. 1959. *The Life of Christina of Markyate*, ed. and trans. C. H. Talbot. Oxford: Clarendon Press.

Christine de Pisan. 1982. *The Book of the City of Ladies*, trans. Earl Jeffrey Richards; foreword by Marina Warner. New York: Persea Book.

CIL. 1862–. *Corpus Inscriptionum Latinarum.* Berlin: Akademie der Wissenschaften.

Collectio salernitana. 1852, 1967. *Collectio salernitana; ossia documenti inediti e trattati di medicina appartenenti alla scuola medica salernitala*, ed. G.E.T. Henschel, C. Daremberg, and S. de Renzi, pubblicati a cura di Salvatore de Renzi. Naples; reprinted, Bologna: Forni.

Columella. 1956. *On Agriculture and Trees*, trans. E. S. Forster and Edward H. Heffner. 3 vols. Loeb Classical Library. Cambridge, Mass., and London: Harvard University Press.

Conflictu. 1843. De conflictu ovis et lini. In: *Poésies populaires latines antérieurs au douzième siècle*, ed. Edelstand Duméril. Paris: Brockhaus et Avenarius. Pp. 379–99.

CS. 1966. *Vitae sanctorum Hiberniae ex codice olim salmanticensi nunc brusellensi*, ed. W. W. Heist. Subsidia Hagiographica, 28. Brussels: Société des Bollandistes.

CT. 1952. *The Theodosian Code and Novels and the Sirmondian Commentary*, ed. and trans. with commentary, glossary, and bibliography by C. Pharr, with T. S. Davidson and M. B. Pharr; introduction by C. D. Williams. Princeton: Princeton University Press.

Dubois, Pierre. 1891. *De recuperatione Terre Sancte. Traité de politique générale*, ed. Ch.-V. Langlois. Collection de textes pour servir à l'étude et à l'enseignement de histoire. Paris: Alphonse Picard.

Eadmer. 1962. *The Life of St. Anselm Archbishop of Canterbury*, ed. and trans. R. W. Southern. London and New York: T. Nelson.

Etienne de Bourbon. 1877. *Anecdotes historiques, légendes et apologues tirés du recueill inédit d'Etienne de Bourbon*, ed. A. Lecoy de la Marche. Paris: Librairie Renouard.

Eudes of Rouen. 1964. *The Register of Eudes of Rouen*, ed. Jeremiah F. O'Sullivan and trans. Sydney M. Brown. Records of Civilization, Sources and Studies, 64. New York: Columbia University Press.

Eusebius. 1890. *Church History, Life of Constantine the Great and Oration in Praise of Constantine*, trans. Arthur C. McGiffert and Ernest Cushing Richardson. A Select Library of Nicene and Post Nicene Fathers of the Christian Church, Second Series. New York, Oxford, and London: Christian Literature Company.

Farfa. 1879–92. *Il regesto di Farfa compilato da Gregorio da Catino*, ed. I. Giorgi and U. Balzani. 5 vols. Rome: Biblioteca della Società Romana di Storia Patria.

Favier, Jean (ed.). 1970. *Les contribuables parisiens à la fin de la guerre de cent ans: les rôles d'impôt de 1421, 1423 et 1438*. Hautes études médiévales et modernes, 11. Geneva: Droz.

Fleta. 1955–72. *Fleta*, ed. H. G. Richardson and G. O. Sayles. Publications of the Seldon Society, 72 and 89. London: B. Quaritch.

Francesco da Barbarino. 1957. *Del reggimento e costume di donne*, ed. G. F. Sansone. Collection di "Filologia Romanza." Turin.

Freising. 1905–09. *Die Traditionen des Hochstifts Freising*, ed. Theodor Bitterauf. 2 vols. Quellen und Eröterung zur bayerischen und deutschen Geschichte, Neue Folge, 4–5. Munich.

Greek Drama. 1938. *The Complete Greek Drama*, ed. Whitney J. Oatis. 2 vols. New York: Random House.

Gregory of Tours. 1884–1969. *Gregorii Turonensis Opera*, ed. W. Arndt and Br. Krusch. 2 vols. MGH Ss rerum merovingicarum. Hannover: Hahn.

———. 1927. *The History of the Franks*, trans. O. M. Dalton. 2 vols. Oxford: Clarendon Press.

———. 1951. *Historiarum libri X, Editio Altera*. Ed. B. Krusch and W. Levison. MGH Ss rerum merovingicarum. Hannover: Hahn.

Guy de Chauliac. 1890. *La grande chirurgie...composé en l'an 1363*, ed Edouart Nicaise. Paris: G. Baillière.

Heinrich von dem Türlin. 1989. *The Crown. A Tale of Sir Gawein and King Arthur's Court*, trans. J. W. Thomas. Lincoln and London: University of Nebraska Press.

Herodotus. 1971–82. *History*. Trans. A. D. Godley. 4 vols. Loeb Classical Library. Cambridge Mass., and London: Harvard University Press.

Hesiod. 1982. *The Homeric Hymns and Homerica*. Trans. Hugh E. Evelyn-White. Loeb Classical Library. Cambridge, Mass., and London: Harvard University Press.

Hincmar. 1980. *Hincmar von Reims, De ordine palatii*, ed. and trans. Thomas Gross and Rudolf Schieffer. MGH. Fontes iuris antiqui in usum scholarum separatim editi. Hannover: Hahn.

Histoire de Paris. 1886–97. *Histoire générale de Paris. Les métiers*, ed. René de Lespinasse. 3 vols. Paris: Imprimerie Nationale.

Huillard-Bréholles, J.-L.-A. 1859. *Historia diplomatica Friderici secundi*. Paris: H. Plon.

ILCV. 1961. *Inscriptiones latinae christianae veteres*, ed. Ernst Diehl. 4 vols. Berlin: Weidmann.

IS. 1717–22. *Italia sacra sive de episcopis Italiae,* ed. Ferdinando Ughelli. Venice: S. Coleti.

Isidore of Seville. 1911, 1985. *Etymologiarum sive originum libri XX,* ed. W. M. Lindsay. Oxford: Clarendon Press.

Jaffe, Philip (ed.). 1885–88. *Regesta pontificum romanorum ab condita ecclesia ad annum post Christum natum mcxcviii,* 2d ed. by G. Wattenbach. 2 vols. Leipzig: Veit.

Jean de Jandun. 1867. "De laudibus Parisius." In: *Paris et ses historiens aux 14. et 15. siècles,* ed. Le Roux de Lincy and L. M. Tisserand. Paris: Imprimerie Impériale.

John of Garland. 1837. Magistri Johannis de Garlandia dictionarius. In: Géraud, 1837, pp. 585 ff.

Kempe, Margery. 1944. *The Book of Margery Kempe (1436). A Modern Translation,* trans. W. Butler Bowdon; introduction by R. W. Chambers. New York: Devane Adair.

Lactantius. 1890–97. *L. Caeli Firmiani Opera Omnia.* Ed. S. Brandt and G. Laubmann. 3 vols. Vienna: Temsky.

Lattimore, Richmond. 1962. *Themes in Greek and Latin Epitaphs.* Urbana: University of Illinois Press.

Laudatio Turiae. 1950. *Eloge funèbre d'une matrone romaine (éloge dit de Turia),* ed. and trans. Marcel Durry. Paris: Belles Lettres.

Laws of the Alamans. 1977. *Laws of the Alamans and Bavarians,* trans. with an introduction by Theodore John Rivers. Philadelphia: University of Pennsylvania Press.

Leges Alamannorum. 1966. *Leges Alamannorum,* ed. K. Lehmann. Editio altera K. A. Eckhardt. MGH, Legum Sectio I, 5, 1. Hannover.

Leges longobardorum. 1868. *Leges longobardorum,* ed. F. Bluhme. MGH, Legum Sectio I, 4. Hannover.

Lex Salica. 1949. *Lex Salica,* ed. Karl August Eckhardt. MGH, Legum Sectio 1, 4, 2. Hannover.

Liber feudorum. 1945. *Liber feudorum major,* ed. F. Miguel Rosell. 2 vols. Madrid: Casa Provincial de Caridad.

Lombard Laws. 1973. *The Lombard Laws,* trans. with an introduction by Katherine Fischer Drew; foreward by Edward Peters. Philadelphia: University of Pennsylvania Press.

Mansi, J. D. 1759–98, 1901–27. *Sacrorum conciliorum nova et amplissima collectio.* Florence and Venice; Paris: H. Welter.

Marie de France. 1959. *Les lais de Marie de France,* ed. Jeanne Lods. Les classiques français du Moyen Age. Paris: Honoré Champion.

Martial. 1903, 1929. *M. Val. Martialis epigrammata,* ed. W. M. Lindsay. Oxford: Clarendon Press.

Martin of Braga. 1950. *Martini episcopi bracarensis opera omnia,* ed. C. W. Barlow. New Haven: Yale University Press for the American Academy in Rome.

MB. 1763–1829. *Monumenta Boica.* Munich: Academia Scientiarum Boica.

MGH. 1825–. *Monumenta Germaniae Historica.* Leipzig and Hannover: Societas aperiendis fontibus rerum Germanicarum Medii Aevi.

MGH Capit. 1893–97. *Capitularia regum Francorum,* ed. A. Boretius and V. Krause. 2 vols. MGH Legum Sectio II, 1. Hannover.

MGH Conc. 1906, 1979. *Concilia, II: Concilia aevi karolinorum,* ed. Albertus Werminghoff. MGH Legum Sectio III. Hannover and Leipzig.

———. 1984. *Concilia, III: Die Konzilien der karolingischen Teilreiche, 843–859,* ed. Wilfred Hartmann. MGH Legum Sectio III. Hannover.

MGH Ss. 1826–1934. *Monumenta Germaniae Historica. Scriptores rerum Germanicarum.* Hannover and Leipzig.

Michaelsson, K. (ed). 1951. *Le livre de la taille de Paris, l'an de grace 1313.* Acta Universitatis Gotoburgensis, 57. Göteborg.

———. 1958. *Le livre de la taille de Paris, l'an 1296.* Acta Universitatis Gotoburgensis, 64, 2. Göteborg.

———. 1962. *Le livre de la taille de Paris, l'an 1297,* Acta Universitatis Gotoburgensis, 67, 3. Göteborg.

Neckham, Alexander. 1863. *De naturis rerum et de laudibus divinae sapientiae,* ed. Thomas Wright. Rerum britannicarum medii aevi scriptores, 34. London: Longman, Green.

Nepos. 1984. *Cornelius Nepos.* trans. John C. Rolfe. Loeb Classical Library. Cambridge, Mass., and London: Harvard University Press.

Notitia. 1876. *Notitia dignitatum accedunt Notitia urbis Constantinopolitanae et laterculi prouinciarum,* ed. Otto Seeck. Berlin: Weidmann.

Notker. 1962. Notker der Stammler, *Taten Kaiser Karls des Grossen,* ed. Hans F. Haefele. MGH Ss. Nova series, 12. Berlin: Weidmann.

Ordericus Vitalis. 1969–80. *The Ecclesiastical History of Ordericus Vitalis,* ed. Marjorie Chibnell. Oxford: Clarendon Press.

Ordonnances générales. 1886. *Ordonnances générales, Métiers de l'alimentation,* ed. René de Lespinasse. Histoire générale de Paris, 1; XIVe–XVIIIe siècle. Paris: Imprimerie Nationale.

Origen. 1953, 1980. *Contra Celsum,* trans. with an introduction and notes by Henry Chadwick. London, New York, New Rochelle, Melbourne, Sydney: Cambridge University Press.

Padua. 1872. *Statuti del comune di Padova dal secolo XII al anno 1285,* ed. Andrea Gloria. Padua: F. Sacchetto.

Passio Perpetuae. 1972. Passio Perpetuae et Felicitatis, in *The Acts of the Christian Martyrs,* ed. Herbert Musurillo. Oxford: Clarendon Press. Pp. 106–31.

Passio S. Romani. 1932. In: Hippolyte Delehaye, "S. Romain martyr de Antioch," *Analecta Bollandiana,* L: 241–83.

Pausanias. 1954. *Description of Greece,* trans. W. H. S. Jones. Loeb Classical Library. Cambridge, Mass., and London: Harvard University Press.

PG. 1857–86. *Patrologiae cursus completus. Series Graeca.* Ed. J. P. Migne. 165 vols. Paris: Garnier.

Philippe de Navarre. 1888. *Les quatre âges de l'homme,* ed. M. de Fréville. Société des Anciens Textes Français, 27. Paris.

PL. 1844–64. *Patrologiae Cursus Completus Series Latina.* Ed. J. P. Migne. 221 vols. Paris: Garnier.

Recueil. 1906–. *Recueil de documents relatifs à l'histoire de l'industrie drapière en Flandre,* ed. G. Espinas and H. Pirenne. 7 vols. Brussels: Kiessling.

Renart, Jean. 1925. *Galéran de Bretagne. Roman du XIIIe siècle,* ed. Lucien Foulet. Les classiques français au Moyen Age, 37. Paris: E. Champion.

Rucellai, Giovanni. 1887. *Opere,* ed. Guido Mazzoni. Bologna: Anichelli.

St. Germain. 1844, 1886–95. *Polyptych de l'abbé Irminon,* ed. B. Guérard. Paris: Imprimerie Royale. Reprinted with some revisions as *Polyptych de l'abbaye de Saint Germain des-Prés,* ed. A. Longnon. Paris: H. Champion.

St. Pierre. 1868–71. *Chartes et documents de l'abbaye de Saint Pierre au Mont Blandin à Gand depuis sa fondation jusqu'à sa suppression,* ed. Auguste von Vokeren. 2 vols. Ghent: H. Hoste.

Ste. Elisabet. 1883. *Cartulaire du Béguinage de Sainte-Elisabet à Gand,* ed. le Baron Jean Béthune. Bruges: A. de Zuttere.

Salzburg. 1910. *Salzburger Urkundenbuch,* I: *Traditionen,* ed. Willibald Hauthaler, O.S.B. Salzburg: Gesellschaft für Salzburger Landeskunde.

Sidonius. 1980. *Sidonius. Poems and Letters,* trans. W. B. Anderson. 2 vols. Loeb Classical Library. Cambridge, Mass., and London: Harvard University Press.

Suetonius. 1914. *Suetonius. The Lives of the Caesars,* trans. J. C. Rolfe. Loeb Classical Library. London and New York: Macmillan.

Tacitus. 1983. *De origine et situ Germanorum,* ed. Alf Önnerfors. Taciti libri qui supersunt, II, 2. Stuttgart: Teubner.

Thomas Becket. 1875–85. *Materials for the History of Thomas Becket, Archbishop of Canterbury,* ed. J. C. Robertson and J. B. Sheppard. 7 vols. Rerum Britannicarum Scriptores, 67. London.

Tibullus. 1982. *Elegies. Introduction, Text, Translation and Notes,* ed. Guy Lee. 2d ed. Liverpool: F. Cairns.

Toulouse. 1941. *Early Guild Records of Toulouse,* ed. Sister Mary Ambrose Mulholland, B.V.M. New York: Columbia University Press.

————. 1956. *Les "estimes" toulousaines des XIVe et XVe siècles,* ed. Philippe Wolff. Toulouse: Association Marc Bloch.

Trotula. 1940. *The Diseases of Women by Trotula of Salerno,* trans. Elizabeth Mason-Hohl. Los Angeles: Ward Ritchie Press.

————. 1981. *The Medieval Woman's Guide to Health: The First English Gynecological Handbook,* ed. and trans. Beryl Rowland. Kent, Ohio: Kent University Press.

Vegetius. 1885. *Flavi Vegeti Renati epitoma rei militaris.* Leipzig: Teubner.

Vita Gerardi. 1841. *Vita s. Gerardi episopi Tullensis et miracula auctore Widrico abbate S. Pari Tullensis monasterii. MGH Ss.,* IV. Hannover.

Vita Liutbirgis. 1937. *Das Leben der Liutbirg*, ed. Ottokar Menzel. Deutsches Mittelalter. Kritische Studientexte des Reichsinstituts für ältere deutsche Geschichtskunde. Monumenta Germaniae Historica, 3. Leipzig: Karl W. Hiersemann.

Vita Melaniae. 1889. "Vita S. Melaniae iunioris," *Analecta Bollandia,* 8: 16–63.

Vitae sanctorum. 1910. *Vitae sanctorum Hiberniae,* ed. C. Plummer. 2 vols. Oxford: Clarendon Press.

Westfalia. 1847–51. *Regesta Historiae Westfaliae accedit Codex diplomaticus,* ed. Heinrich-August Erhard. Münster: F. Regensberg.

Zink, Michel. 1978. *Belle: essai sur les chansons de toile, suivi d'une édition et d'une traduction.* Paris: Champion.

STUDIES

Astill, Grenville, and Grant, Annie (eds.). 1988. *The Countryside of Medieval England.* Oxford: Blackwell.

Baker, Derek (ed.). 1978. *Medieval Women. Dedicated and Presented to Professor Rosalind M. T. Hill on Occasion of Her Seventieth Birthday.* Oxford: Blackwell.

Bennett, Judith M. 1986. "The Village Ale-Wife: Women and Brewing in Fourteenth-Century England." In: Hanawalt, 1986, pp. 20–26.

––––––. 1987. *Women in the Medieval English Countryside: Gender and Household in Brigstock before the Plague.* Oxford and New York: Oxford University Press.

Benton, John F. 1985. "Trotula, Women's Problems and the Professionalization of Medicine in the Middle Ages," *Bulletin of the History of Medicine,* 59: 30–53.

Botero, Giovanni. 1956. *The Reason of State,* trans. P. J. and D. P. Waley, and *The Greatness of Cities,* trans. Robert Peterson (1606). New Haven: Yale University Press.

Bullough, Vern L. 1966. *The Development of Medicine as a Profession.* Basel and New York: Karger.

Cagnat. R. 1896. "Gynaeceum," *Dictionnaire des antiquités grecques et romaines d'après les textes et les monuments.* Paris: Hachette. II: 1706–13.

Carrère, Claude. 1967. *Barcelone: centre économique à l'époque des difficultés, 1380–1462.* Paris and The Hague: Mouton.

Cartwright, Julia. 1926. *Isabella d'Este Marchioness of Mantua, 1474–1539. A Study of the Renaissance.* 2 vols. New York: E. P. Dutton.

Cazelles, Raymond. 1966. "La population de Paris devant la Peste Noire." In: *Académie des Inscriptions et Belles Lettres: Comptes Rendus.* Paris. Pp. 539–54.

Chadwick, Nora. 1970. *The Celts.* Harmsworth, Eng.: Penguin Books.

Chandler, Tertius, and Fox, Gerald. 1974. *3000 Years of Urban Growth.* New York and London: Academic Press.

Chapelot, Jean, and Fossier, Robert. 1980, 1985. *The Village and House in the Middle Ages*, trans. Henry Cleere. Berkeley and Los Angeles: University of California Press.

Chaumet, Louise. 1975. "La corporation des tisserands." In: *Le textile en Normandie: Etudes diverses.* Rouen: Société libre d'émulation de la Seine-Maritime. Pp. 107–18.

Collantes de Teran Sanchez, Antonio. 1977. *Sevilla en la baja Edad Media: la ciudad y sus hombres.* Seville: Sección de Publicaciones del Exc. imo. Ayuntamiento.

Crane, Thomas. 1890. *The Exempla or Illustrative Stories from the Sermones Vulgares of Jacques de Vitry.* London: D. Nutt.

Del Lungo, Isidoro. 1926. *La donna fiorentina del buon tempo antico.* 2d ed. Florence: Bemporad.

den Boer, W. 1950. "*Gynaeconitis.* A Center of Christian Propaganda," *Vigiliae Christianae. A Review of Early Christian Life and Languages,* IV: 60–64.

De Poerck, G. 1951. *La draperie médiévale en Flandre et en Artois. Technique et terminologie.* 2 vols. Rijksuniv. Gent. Werken uitg. Facult. Wijsb en Lett. fasc 110. Bruges: De Tempel.

De Renzi, Salvatore. 1857, 1967. *Storia documentata della Scuola medica di Salerno.* 2d ed. Naples: G. Nobile.

Dillard, Heath. 1984. *Daughters of the Reconquest: Women in Castilian Town Society, 1100–1300.* Cambridge: Cambridge University Press.

Dollinger, Philippe. 1956. "Le ciffre de population de Paris au XIVe siècle: 210,000 ou 80,000 habitants?" *Revue Historique,* CCXVI: 35–44.

DuCange, Charles du Fresne. 1938. *Glossarium mediae et infimae latinitatis,* ed. G. A. L. Henschel. Paris: Librairie des Sciences et des Arts.

Duffin, Lorna, and Lindsey, Charles. 1985. *Women and Work in Preindustrial England.* Bloomington: Indiana University Press.

Dufrenne, Suzy. 1978. *Les illustrations du Psautier d'Utrecht.* Paris: Ophrys.

Ennen, Edith. 1986. *Frauen im Mittelalter.* Munich: C. H. Beck.

Fagniez, Gustave. 1879. *Etudes sur l'industrie et la classe industrielle à Paris.* Paris: F. Vieweg.

Fell, Christine. 1984. *Women in Anglo-Saxon England and the Impact of 1066.* With Cecily Clark and Elizabeth Williams. London: British Museum Publications.

Festa, G. B. 1910. *Un galateo femminile del Trecento.* Bari: Laterza.

Fort, George F. 1883, 1970. *Medical Economy during the Middle Ages. A Contribution to the History of European Morals from the Time of the Roman Empire to the Close of the Fourteenth Century.* New York: A. M. Kelley.

Fournier, Paul. 1880. *Les officialités au moyen-âge; étude sur l'organisation, la compétence et la procédure des tribuneaux ecclésiastiques ordinaires en France de 1180 à 1328.* Paris: E. Plon.

Frank, Tenney. 1940. *An Economic History of Ancient Rome and Italy.* Baltimore: The Johns Hopkins Press.

Géraud, Hercule. 1837. *Paris sous Philippe le Bel d'après les documents originaux.* Paris: Crapelet.

Geudens, F. M. 1911. "Premonstratensian Canons," *The Catholic Encyclopedia.* New York: Appleton. XII: 387–90.

Ghirardacci, Cherubino. 1596–1657. *Della Storia di Bologna.* 3 vols. Bologna: G. Rossi.

Gies, Frances. 1978, 1980. *Women in the Middle Ages.* New York: Barnes and Noble.

Gonzalez, Julio. 1975. "La poblacion de Sevilla a fines del siglo XIV." *Hispania,* XXVI: 49–74.

Goodman, Peter. 1985. *Poetry of the Carolingian Renaissance.* Norman: University of Oklahoma Press.

Gottfried, Robert S. 1986. *Doctors and Medicine in Medieval England, 1340–1530.* Princeton: Princeton University Press.

Gouron, André. 1958. *La réglementation des métiers en Languedoc au Moyen Age.* Geneva and Paris: Droz.

Green, Alice. 1895. *Town Life in the Fifteenth Century.* 2 vols. New York and London: Macmillan.

Green, Monica. 1989. "Women's Medical Practice and Health Care in Medieval Europe," *Signs,* XIV: 434–73.

Gross, Charles. 1890. *The Guild Merchant.* 2 vols. Oxford: Clarendon Press.

Hanawalt, Barbara (ed.). 1986. *Women and Work in Preindustrial Europe.* Bloomington: Indiana University Press.

Herlihy, David. 1962. "Land, Family and Women in Continental Europe, 701–1200," *Traditio,* 18: 89–120.

_____. 1973. "The Population of Verona in the First Century of Venetian Rule." In: *Renaissance Venice,* ed. J. R. Hale. Totowa, N.J.: Rowman and Littlefield. Pp. 91–120.

_____. 1975. "Life Expectancies for Women in Medieval Society." In: *The Role of Women in the Middle Ages,* ed. Rosmarie Thee Morewedge. Albany, N.Y.: State University of New York. Pp. 1–22.

_____. 1985a. *Medieval Households.* Cambridge, Mass., and London: Harvard University Press, 1985.

_____. 1985b. "Did Women Have a Renaissance?: A Reconsideration," *Medievalia et Humanistica. Studies in Medieval and Renaissance Culture,* new series, 13: 1–22.

_____. 1988. "Tuscan Names, 1200–1530," *Renaissance Quarterly,* XLI: 561–82.

_____, and Klapisch-Zuber, Christiane. 1978. *Les Toscans et leurs familles. Une étude du catasto florentin de 1427.* Paris: Fondation nationale des sciences politiques.

_____ and _____. 1985. *Tuscans and their Families.* New Haven and London: Yale University Press.

Howell, Martha C. 1986 *Women, Production, and Patriarchy in Late Medieval Cities.* Chicago and London: University of Chicago Press, 1986.

Hughes, Muriel Joy. 1943. *Women Healers in Medieval Life and Literature.* New York: King's Crown Press.

Ide, Arthur Frederick. 1983. *Special Sisters: Women in the European Middle Ages.* Mesquite, Tex.: Ide House Inc.

Jacquart, Danielle. 1981. *Le milieu médicale en France du XIIe au XVe siècle.* Geneva: Droz, and Paris: Champion.

Jones, A. H. M. 1960, 1974. "The Cloth Industry under the Roman Empire," *Economic History Review,* XII: 183–92, reprinted in *The Roman Economy: Studies in Ancient Economy and Administration,* ed. P. A. Brunt. Oxford: Blackwell. Pp. 350–64.

Kantorowicz, Ernst. 1931, 1963, 1964. *Kaiser Friedrich der Zweite. Ergänzungsband.* Düsseldorf and Munich: Georg Bondi.

———. 1957. *Frederick II,* ed. E. O. Lorimer. New York: Unger.

Ketsch, Peter. 1983–84. *Frauen im Mittelalter. Quellen und Materialen,* ed. Annette Kuhn. I: *Frauenarbeit im Mittelalter.* II: *Frauenbild und Frauenrechte in Kirche und Gesellschaft.* Düsseldorf: Schwann.

Kirbe, Pearl. 1953. "The Faculty of Medicine at Paris, Charlatanism and Unlicensed Medical Practice in the Later Middle Ages," *Bulletin of the History of Medicine,* XXVII: 1–20.

Klapisch-Zuber, Christiane. 1985. *Women, Family, and Ritual in Renaissance Italy.* Chicago: University of Chicago Press.

Kristeller, Paul Oscar. 1945. "The School of Salerno: Its Development and Its Contribution to the History of Learning," *Bulletin of the History of Medicine,* 17: 138–94.

Labarge, Margaret W. 1986. *A Small Sound of the Trumpet: Women in Medieval Life.* Boston: Beacon Press.

Lebalme, Patricia H. (ed.). 1982. *Beyond Their Sex: Learned Women of the European Past.* New York: New York University Press.

Leclercq, H. 1925. "Gynecée," *Dictionnaire d'archéologie chrétienne et de liturgie.* Paris: Letouzey et Ané. VI: 1923–27.

Lesko (ed.), Barbara S. 1989. *Women's Earliest Records from Ancient Egypt and Western Asia.* Brown Judaic Studies, 166. Atlanta, Ga.: Scholars Press.

Levison, Wilhelm. 1901. "Die Urkunden des Elsässischen Grafen Eberhard (d. 747) und die Vita Desiderii Alsegaudensis," *Neues Archiv der Gesellschaft für ältere deutsche Geschichtskunde,* 27, 1: 368–99.

Levy, Edmond (ed.). 1983. *La femme dans les sociétés antiques.* Strasbourg: Institut d'histoire romaine.

Lopez, R. S. 1945. "The Silk Industry in the Byzantine Empire," *Speculum,* 20: 1–43.

McDonnell, Ernest W. 1954, 1969. *The Beguines and Beghards in Medieval Culture with Special Emphasis on the Belgium Scene.* New Brunswick, N.J.: Rutgers University Press.

Mackenney, Richard. 1987. *Tradesmen and Traders. The World of Guilds in Venice and Europe, c. 1250–c. 1650.* Totowa, N.J.: Barnes and Noble.

MacMullen, Ramsay. 1980. "Women in Public in the Roman Empire," *Historia*, 29: 208–18.

Maurin, J. 1983. *"Labor matronalis*; aspects du travail féminine à Rome." In: Levy, 1983, pp. 139 ff.

Melania, 1985. *The Life of Melania the Younger*, trans. with an introduction by Elizabeth Clark. Lewiston, N.Y.: Edwin Mellen.

Michaelsson, Karl. 1950. "Les noms d'origine dans le rôle de la taille parisienne de 1313," *Acta Universitatis Gotoburgensis*, LVI, 3: 355–400.

Mols, Roger. 1954–56. *Introduction à la démographie historique des villes d'Europe du 14e au 18e siècle*. 3 vols. Gembloux: J. Duculot.

Nicholas. David. 1985. *The Domestic Life of a Medieval City: Women, Children and the Family*. Lincoln: University of Nebraska Press.

———. 1987. *The Metamorphosis of a Medieval City. Ghent in the Age of the Arteveldes, 1302–1390*. Lincoln: University of Nebraska Press.

Origo, Iris. 1957, 1986. *The Merchant of Prato. Francesco di Marco Datini, 1335–1410*. Foreward by Barbara Tuchman Boston: David R. Godine.

Otis, Leah Lydia. 1985. *Prostitution in Medieval Society: The History of an Urban Institution in Languedoc*. Chicago: University of Chicago Press.

Park, Katharine. 1985. *Doctors and Medicine in Early Renaissance Florence*. Princeton: Princeton University Press.

Pernoud, Régine. 1980. *La femme au temps des cathédrales*. Paris: Stock.

Persson, A. W. 1923. *Staat und Manufactur im römischen Reiche. Eine wirtschaftsgeschichtliche Studie nebst einem Exkurse über angezügene Götterstatuen*. Lund: C. Blons.

Pohl, Hans (ed.). 1985. *Die Frau in der deutschen Wirtschaft*. Zeitschrift für Unternehmensgeschichte, Beiheft 35. Stuttgart.

Power, Eileen. 1965. *Medieval Women*, ed. M. M. Postan. New York: Cambridge University Press.

Redigonda. A. L. 1961. "Andreasi, Osanna." *Dizionario biografico degli Italiani*. Rome: Istituto della Enciclopedia Italiana. III: 131–32.

Reilly, Bernard F. 1982. *The Kingdom of Léon-Castilla under Queen Urraca, 1109–1126*. Princeton, N.J.: Princeton University Press.

Robertson, A. J. (ed.) 1925. *The Laws of the Kings of England from Edmund to Henry I*. Cambridge: Cambridge University Press.

Rostovtzeff, Michael, 1922, 1979. *A Large Estate in Egypt in the Third Century B.C.* Madison; reprinted New York: Arno Press.

———. 1957. *The Social and Economic History of the Roman Empire*. 2d ed. Oxford: Clarendon Press.

Ruether, Rosemary, and McLaughlin, Eleanor. 1979. *Women of Spirit: Female Leadership in the Jewish and Christian Traditions*. New York: Simon and Schuster.

Thompson, Sally. 1978. "The Problem of Cistercian Nuns in the Twelfth and Early Thirteenth Centuries." In: Baker, 1978, pp. 227–52.

Tillemont, Le Nain de. 1847–51. *Vie de Saint Louis roi de France*. 6 vols. Paris: Jules Renouard.

TLL. 1900–. *Thesaurus linguae latinae editus auctoritate et consilio academiarum quinque Germanicarum.* Leipzig: Teubner.

Trabajo. 1988. *El trabajo de las mujeres en la Edad Media Hispaña,* ed. Angela Muñoz Fernández and Cristina Segura Graiño. Madrid: Asociación Cultural Al-Mudayna.

Van de Vyver, A., and Verlinden, Charles. 1933. "L'auteur et la portée du Conflictus ovis et lini," *Revue belge de philologie et d'histoire,* XII: 59–81.

Weinbaum, Martin. 1924–26. "Beiträge zur älteren englischen Gewerbe- und Handelsgeschichte," *Vierteljahrschrift für Sozial- und Wirtschaftsgeschichte,* XVIII: 276–311.

Wensky, Margret. 1980. *Die Stellung der Frau in der stadtkölnischen Wirtschaft im Spätmittelalter.* Quellen und Darstellungen zur Hansischen Geschichte, NF 26. Cologne and Vienna: Böhlau.

Wesoly, Kurt. 1980. "Der weibliche Bevölkerungsanteil im spätmittelalterlichen und frühneuzeitlichen Städten und die betätigung von Frauen in zünftigen Handwerk (insbesondere am Mittle- und Oberrhein)," *Zeitschrift für die Geschichte des Oberrheins,* new series, 89.

Wiesner, Merry E. 1986. *Working Women in Reformation Germany.* New Brunswick, N.J.: Rutgers University Press.

Wipszycka, Ewa. 1965. *L'industrie textile dans l'Egypte romaine.* Wroclaw: Zaktad Narodowy im. Ossolińskich.

Wolff, Philippe, and Mauro, F. 1959. *L'age de l'artisanat (Ve–XVIIIe siècle.* Histoire générale du travail, ed. Louis Henri Parias. Paris: Nouvelle Librairie de France.

INDEX

Aachen, 92, 93
Abelard (philosopher), 117–118, 141
Acre (Palestine), 140
Adamnan (Irish abbot), 29, 30, 31
Adelhard of Corvey (abbot), 79
Aedan (Irish saint), 27, 28, 30
Aelfric of Eynsham, 77–80
Agatha (Christian martyr), 12
Agnes (countess of Goseck), 55, 71
Alamanni (German tribe), 37
Albero of Bremen, 115
Albigensian (heretics), 61, 67, 121
Alexander II (pope), 91
Alexandria (see Catherine of, Clement of)
Alpaix (French saint), 51, 52, 53
Alsace, 33, 82, 84
Ambrose of Milan (Latin Christian Father), 0, 1, 12, 187
Amiens, 137
Andreasi, Osanna (Mantua), 164–166
Anglo-Saxon England, 33, 77, 78, 97
Anne of Brittany (queen of France), 166
Anselm of Canterbury (saint), 50, 51
Ansger (bishop of Bremen), 89
Antioch (Syria), 8, 22
Antonius of Piacenza, 18, 24, 30
Apprentices, 4, 21 n. 9, 95, 96, 133, 144, 145, 147, 148, 153 n. 49, 156, 162 n. 49, 163, 169, 173, 177, 179, 186, 191
Apulia (Italian province), 120
Aquila (Roman province), 10
Aragon (Iberia), 59, 95, 115, 140, 152
Arnobius Afer (Christian apologist), 12, 23
Augustine (Latin Christian father), 15, 120
Augustus (Roman emperor), 6, 15
Ausonius (Gallo-Roman author), 14
Autun (France), 10
Avicenna (Arab physician), 104
Avranches (Normandy), 62

Barcelona (Catalonia), 95, 102, 168; guilds of, 182; population of, 168; women workers at, 95, 169
Basel, guilds of women at, 178
Batavia (Roman province), 7
Bavaria, 85, 91, 92, 112, 116
Bayeux (Normandy), 62
Beatrice d'Este (duchess of Milan), 166
Beauvais (town of Paris basin), 137
Beghards, 67

Beguines, 60, 66–70, 73, 75, 118, 132, 146, 163, 164; at Cologne, 179
Belgicae (Roman provinces), 7, 10
Belgium, 41, 92
Bellencombre (Normandy), 64
Benedict (saint), 33, 99
Benedictine monasticism, 107
Benton, John F. (American historian), 106–107, 123 n. 2, 124 n. 9
Bernard (saint and abbot), 120
Bertin (Flemish saint and abbot), 90
Boccaccio, Giovanni, 140, 161
Boecius (Irish saint), 29, 30
Bologna (city), 96, 102, 110, 116, 125, 160, 162, 181; women workers at, 157–159; school of law, 159
Bondeville (Normandy), 65
Bordeaux, 140, 141
Botero, Giovanni (Italian savant), 130–131
Bourges (France), 131
Bourgny (Normandy), 64
Braga (Portugal), 25, 30, 34, 35, 39, 46
Bremen (see Albero of; Ansger of)
Bretons at Paris, 133, 136, 138, 139, 141
Brigid (Irish saint), 30, 31, 44
Bristol (England), 178
Britain, medieval, 30, 110; Roman, 7
Brittany, 55, 76, 131, 141, 142, 166
Bruges (Flanders), 137
Brussels (city), 137
Burgundians at Paris, 138, 139
Burgundy (French province), 131
Bücher, Karl (German historian), 178
Byzantine empire, 18, 24, 30

Caen (Normandy), 64
Caesarius of Nuremberg, 103, 112
Cahors (France), 140
Cambrai (France), 137
Canosa (Italy), 85
Canterbury (see Anselm of)
Carcassonne (France), 140, 141
Carolingian age, 33, 75, 76, 79, 94, 98, 107; government, 88; rulers, 32, 36, 43, 59 (See also manors, scholars)
Castellonzio (Tuscany), 96
Castle of Infinite Misfortune, 80–81, 84, 87–88
Catalonia (Iberia), 95
Catasto (Florentine survey), 159–160, 163

205